homesick

Why Housing Is Unaffordable
and How We Can Change It

Brendan O'Brien

Published by Chicago Review Press Incorporated
814 North Franklin Street
Chicago, Illinois 60610
ISBN 978-1-64160-969-2

Library of Congress Control Number: 2023940181

Cover design and typesetting: Preston Pisellini
Front cover photo: Eric Brehm/Unsplash

Some names have been changed to protect the identity of interviewees.

Printed in the United States of America

To my family and to all the neighbors throughout my life,
especially Jim (1930–2021) and Karen Dexter (1945–2021),
who taught me that home is more than brick and mortar.

And finding only the same old stupid plan
Of dog eat dog, of mighty crush the weak.

—Langston Hughes, "Let America Be America Again," 1936

Contents

List of Keywords

affordable housing

Housing which costs 30 percent or less of household income. This includes utilities. There is dispute about the usefulness of this measurement, with many commentators claiming it is too high and fails to consider differences in income and circumstances. But it remains the value used by the Department of Housing and Urban Development and in nearly all affordable housing efforts.

buy-to-rent housing

An ongoing trend in which housing is bought with the primary intention of renting it out or using it to turn a profit. This trend also speaks to an increasingly common mindset in which housing is viewed as a real estate investment, not a human right.

nonprimary home

A housing unit which nobody actively lives in full-time, instead being rented on a short-term basis or held as a second, third, fourth, etc. home.

public lands

Land owned and maintained by the federal government and accessible, by law, to all people within the United States. "Public" land in the United States can be owned and operated by the municipal, district, county, and state governments as well. This book focuses exclusively on federal land for the sake of its national tax base and access.

short-term rental

A housing unit rented for less than thirty days.

the West

The eleven western-most states in the continental United States: Washington, Oregon, California, Nevada, Idaho, Utah, Arizona, New Mexico, Colorado, Wyoming, and Montana.

preface

The Sign

THIS BOOK WAS BORN from a sign in a stranger's yard. It was February of 2017. I'd fled the Minnesota winter for a much-needed vacation with three friends in New Orleans. We stayed in an Airbnb because it was cheaper and offered more space. In a way, it also felt more authentic. We spent our days seeking out jazz music, touring famous sites, and eating phenomenal food. At night, we felt almost like residents, going home to a regular house on a regular block.

Up the street, one house had a sign which read simply: NEIGHBORS, NOT AIRBNBS. I noticed it, but it didn't interrupt my weekend. After all, though we never met our Airbnb host, the listing had emphasized that she was a resident of the city. And we were far quieter than the guests in the house next door, also an Airbnb. Still, that sign made an impression.

It made an impression because Airbnb operated under the slogan "Belong Anywhere," and the question of what it meant to belong was already a familiar one for me, living in Minneapolis. The city was gentrifying fast. Through tax breaks, zoning changes, and extensive marketing, pockets of the city that had been affordable to longtime residents were being transformed. The price of housing was going up, higher-income individuals were moving in, and existing residents were being forced out. One 2015 study by data analysis firm Governing found that gentrification was happening in 50.6 percent of all eligible areas of Minneapolis, placing the city behind only Washington, DC, and Portland, Oregon, for the highest rate in the country.[1]

In many ways, being White, college-educated, and not native to the city, I knew I was part of this influx of gentrifiers. Through city branding and efforts to build more housing, more commercial properties, more bike lanes, more roads, more art installations, Minneapolis had laid out a welcome mat for anyone seeking to make a home in the city. Like a lot of new residents, I'd seen it and shown up.

But, like Airbnb's slogan, this invitation had a caveat. Everyone was welcome and anyone could belong—just as long as they had the money. For three years, I worked full-time, lived with multiple roommates, and went without a car. Still, I struggled to make rent. When I finally left, I hadn't been evicted or forced out. I'd just scraped by for long enough to take the hint: I didn't belong.

Had all my experiences with housing been just like this one, it's possible that I would have been jaded into accepting that this was just the reality. The question of who got to belong would be as simple as who had the bigger bank account. Home would be nothing more than filling empty space.

But this wasn't my only experience with housing. Instead, my family moved to the house that I grew up in a few months after my younger brother was born, when I was just two years old. It was in that house that I sped around on a plastic horse on wheels, moving so fast and getting so close to furniture that my mom still finds it amazing that I never broke anything. My brothers and I built forts, raced toy cars, and invented games which usually involved throwing a ball and sometimes, yes, did involve breaking a few things.

When my sisters went off to college, my brothers and I all got our own rooms. I was allowed to paint my room a bright blue-green that remains to this day. I covered the walls with pictures cut from *Sports Illustrated* magazines to make the room mine. Still, I spent most of my time outside. In the summer, my brothers and I routinely spent just about every hour of daylight playing with other neighborhood kids in the street or on the hill behind our house.

On Halloween, some neighbors would have special treats set aside for us. On St. Patrick's Day, they all gathered at my family's house for our annual party. My siblings and I went to high school a stone's throw from our house and cut through our neighbors' yard when we were running late, which was most days for me. My neighbors never minded, because they knew us. And we knew them.

My parents are still in that house. They spent their lives working as a civil servant and a teacher, careers that allowed them to help the five of us get through college, hoping we would use our degrees to do something meaningful on this earth. To make the world a little brighter. And, no matter how far we roamed from that house in Davenport, Iowa, we've always had a place that we could call home.

· · · · · · ·

I roamed quite a bit. I left Minneapolis just two months after my trip to New Orleans, heading west to work for the US Forest Service. For the next two and a half years, I worked seasonal jobs on public lands. I lived in a forest service bunkhouse in California, a tent deep in the woods of Montana, and the back of my car. I slept on a friend's couch, in a hostel, in a trailer, and a long, varied list of places that makes the standard background check prompt—*List your addresses for the last seven years*—one of the most stressful tasks anyone can give me.

I had at least a degree of choice in living all these places, a freedom of movement that often seemed preferable to the anxiety that had become my constant companion as I sought to make rent in Minneapolis. It also seemed preferable to the dread with which people spoke of their mortgage, like an alarm tearing them from their dreams.

On some level, I knew that my desire to roam was partially rooted in the stability I'd felt growing up. Though it seemed far away, I knew that this stability would likely be more appealing someday. But I'd also begun to wonder if I would ever be able to afford such a life anyway. Like a lot of people in my generation who'd been lucky to grow up in households that didn't face hunger or violence or prejudice, who'd been raised to believe that hard work and integrity would guarantee some degree of security, I'd begun to feel uneasy about the future.

This feeling only grew in the years after I left Iowa. In Minneapolis and in every place that I worked across the West, I saw the possibility of some more stable life shrinking. As rental rates and property prices rose, outsiders with money were encouraged to feel that they belonged just about anywhere. Tourists and new residents moved in even if that meant existing residents were forced to leave.

I worked hard to avoid thinking about this. After all, I was in my twenties, healthy, childless, and rudderless. I didn't need to contemplate whether I wanted to be someone pushed out or someone who pushed others out.

And then, suddenly, I did. In 2018, while clearing trails for the forest service in Montana, I hurt my lower back. By the end of the season, the pain was so bad that I was gritting my teeth to simply tie my shoes. It slowed me down and woke me up at night, but the biggest impact of this pain was that it caused me to think about doing something less physically taxing. Something that allowed me to call a place home beyond the season.

I spent that winter studying for the GRE and applying to master's programs that would allow me to fuse my past work in social sciences with my desire to be connected to the natural world. When another applicant deferred, I was offered and accepted a teaching assistantship at Northern Arizona University. I moved to Flagstaff, Arizona, to pursue a master's degree in geography in August of 2019.

· · · · · · ·

My attention was quickly drawn back to housing. Driving around the mountain town, I was struck by the sheer number of people living on the streets. Reading the local paper, I was inundated with articles about the exorbitant cost of Flagstaff's housing. And, within a few weeks of arriving, I saw another sign in a stranger's yard, this time calling for HOMES, NOT HOTELS.

At that time in 2019, existing research about short-term rentals focused almost exclusively on large cities. While visitors were drawn to these by conferences, events, and spectacles only a large city can routinely support, they were also drawn to much smaller cities with populations of under one hundred thousand, the places where the vast majority of people in the country actually live. And one of the main features drawing people to these small cities was their proximity to nearby national parks and forests. In short, a place like Flagstaff, surrounded by the Coconino National Forest and just ninety miles from the Grand Canyon, could easily be inundated with tourists. What happened to local housing markets when these tourists stayed in houses instead of hotels?

This question formed the basis for my master's thesis. My advisor approved, suggesting that I compare Flagstaff with similar cities. I would look at St. George, Utah, the gateway to Zion National Park, and Bozeman, Montana, the launchpad into Yellowstone. Each was home to the adjacent park's nearest commercial airport and situated along major highways, making them common points of departure for the more than four million annual visitors each park received. If short-term rentals had a major impact on housing, it would be visible in these three cities.

I hypothesized that the study would yield modest results, showing that short-term rentals do have an impact on the housing market in these cities. My study would end up being fairly straightforward, even boring. I was told to keep this narrow scope in mind. Test my hypothesis, get my degree, and move on to something else. Maybe afford stable housing somewhere myself.

But I've never been very good at moving on. So, as I pitched this project in February of 2020, I had a hunch that the answer to my simple question about short-term rentals in mountain towns actually said quite a lot about housing throughout the country. What I did not know—what nobody knew—was that the economy was about to crumble for the second time in my relatively short adult life. The tourism industry was about to be upended. The housing market about to explode. By the time the summer ended, my original question would be warped into something much larger: a quest to figure out why housing was so unaffordable for so many across the country.

The problem with asking uncomfortable questions is that it leads to uncomfortable answers. As I questioned the state of housing in the United States, I also questioned what it meant to belong. Before long, I was left grappling with the pattern of violent displacement and broken promises that characterizes this country's history.

The United States is a contradiction. It is bursting with evangelists for equality of opportunity who are proud to acknowledge "life, liberty, and the pursuit of happiness" as "inalienable rights" for all who call this country home. These evangelists run every level of government and the major banks. They are landlords and sometimes tenants, employers and sometimes employees. They are overwhelmingly White, almost invariably property owners, and typically male. In other words, the first to proclaim the country's benevolence are from the same demographic that wrote the Constitution and the only one granted any express power to shape the country's early history.

Perhaps this is why, despite their soaring rhetoric and self-proclaimed patriotism, these are not evangelists for the country's best but for the country's status quo. They jealously guard any advantage for themselves, their kin, their side, no matter how clearly linked to the theft of those who came before and no matter how difficult it makes life for others. For the sake of maintaining their advantage, they are willing to distort arguments, silence critics, and exploit the grievances of anyone easily swayed. Their bitter cries drown out any attempt to change—or even discuss— the inequality and injustice that still informs every aspect of the United States, particularly when it comes to where people live.

Throughout the country's history, settlers have easily invoked a song of freedom while traveling unimpeded from "sea to shining sea." But when would-be settlers have bumped into existing residents—when their rapacious desire to accumulate has been thwarted—their song of freedom has quickly become their battle cry.

This mindset spreads quickly. Survival becomes linked with accumulation and the gap between more and enough grows wider. Those of us who had previously refused this call to arms now enter the fray. The spirit of mutual aid which once existed between coworkers, friends, and neighbors is suppressed and replaced by a tacit agreement: "You get yours; I'll get mine." Asked to square this with the freedom, the equality of opportunity, the democracy, the promise of this country, we shrug.

Dog eat dog is all we've ever known.

introduction

The Birth of a Unicorn

THE SKY WAS FALLING. It was 2007 and the US housing and stock markets had started to spiral. Their crash would send shockwaves through the entire global economy. In the immediate aftermath, nearly nine million people in the United States would lose their jobs. Millions would lose their homes while millions more would watch the value of their homes crater, leaving them burdened with hundreds of thousands of dollars in debt. Within a few years, an estimated $19.2 trillion in US household wealth would be wiped out.[1]

I don't remember where I was when I realized the extent of the damage. I don't remember watching tears stream down newscasters' faces. I don't remember my parents hugging me a little tighter that night or feeling uniquely proud to be an American. In this way, the housing crash was decidedly different than 9/11, the memory of which became a defining feature in separating my generation from Gen Z.

What I remember most about the housing crash that triggered the Great Recession was not a declaration of war or the certainty that stems from having someone to blame. Rather, it was a pervasive sense that things were unraveling. Retirement accounts were being reduced to pennies. Credit was becoming nearly inaccessible. And nobody seemed to have the slightest idea how this had happened or how to fix it.

As politicians huddled in Washington to prop up the banks that had caused the crash, people were hurting. Individuals who'd worked salaried jobs for decades took on contract work and side hustles. A few of them worked beside me for minimum wage at a fast-food restaurant. Others stayed in miserable jobs and moved back in with family. Would-be home-buyers now cut off from loans remained at the mercy of landlords. In this context, I finished high school and legally entered adulthood.

· · · · · · · ·

But the sky did not fall for everyone. In the fall of 2007, just as the stage was being set for the worst economic recession since the Great Depression, two roommates in San Francisco "thought of a way to make a few bucks" by renting out a room in their apartment during a major design conference.[2] When the idea worked, the roommates used their own design background to create a website with a publicly visible mutual ratings system that allowed hosts to rent out space to guests. The site soon took off. By 2011, just four years later, the numbers spoke for themselves: Airbnb, deriving its name from the air mattresses used by the first visitors, was present in 89 countries and had facilitated more than a million stays.[3]

Valued at more than $1 billion, Airbnb became known as a Silicon Valley "unicorn." It was held up as a prime example of how the right idea at the right moment can take off. That right moment was millions out of work and struggling to afford housing payments, making hosts more willing to welcome strangers into their homes as a supplement or alternative to traditional income. For the sake of cheaper lodging, guests were willing to forgo professional cleaning, hotel brand accountability, and the security of private rooms. At the same time, smartphones were becoming commonplace among US adults, opening a space for digital platforms to quickly supplant better-known commercial brands.[4] Short-term rental sites like Airbnb, Vrbo, and FlipKey were primed to go viral.

· · · · · · ·

Meanwhile, recovery from the Great Recession was uneven, to put it mildly. Even going into 2019, a report by Harvard's Joint Center for Housing Studies found that three in every ten US households, including one in every five owner-occupied households, spent at least 30 percent of their income toward housing, leaving less money to put toward food, clothing, education, healthcare, retirement, or a host of other possibilities.[5] They met the Department of Housing and Urban Development's definition of being burdened by housing costs. Many others, unable to cut nonhousing costs, dealt with exhausting commutes, cramped spaces, and incessant repair needs.

The possibility of owning a home was getting further out of reach. A ratio of 2.6:1 is commonly used to denote an affordable price-to-income ratio in buying a home. In other words, a couple earning $100,000 a year should cap their search at homes listed around $260,000. Analyzing census data, one study found that the median price-to-income ratio across the country in 2017 was 3.6:1. It had not come close to 2.6:1 in almost twenty years.

A March 2019 analysis by real estate firm Zillow showed that there were still affordable places to buy, but many of these—places like Toledo, Ohio (2.14), and Rochester, New York (2.43), and Harrisburg, Pennsylvania (2.57)—were in areas that were bleeding jobs and services. The median price-to-income ratio of others—Boise, Idaho (4.93), and Seattle, Washington (5.69), and San Jose, California (9.69)—made homeownership a fairy tale. The ever-growing number of properties owned by nonprimary residents and investors was not confined to these areas.

Leilani Farha noticed these patterns as the United Nations special rapporteur on adequate housing. In a 2017 report, she wrote that the spate of foreclosures and evictions following the Great Recession made clear that housing was a commodity in the United States, not a right. The same report placed the value of global real estate at $217 trillion, 60 percent of all global assets, with residential housing making up the vast majority.[6] Manuel Aalbers, a geographer, sociologist, and urban planner, referred to this commodification of housing as the "financialization of home."[7] Anyone looking for housing was now competing on a national—even global—scale.

They also searched for housing in the context of growing inequality. In 2019, the top 10 percent of families owned 76 percent of all the wealth in the United States, according to the Federal Reserve Board's Survey of Consumer Finances. The bottom 50 percent owned just 1 percent of all wealth, with 13.4 million families, or approximately one in every ten, having negative wealth. When comparing White and non-White families, older and younger families, or college-educated and non-college-educated families, this gap was even more pronounced.[8] Nearly a decade after the Great Recession, these measures suggested that the United States was more economically unequal than any time since the Gilded Age of the early 1900s.

· · · · · · ·

By this time in 2019, as I started a master's in geography at Northern Arizona University, the country was in rough shape. The stock market was having another phenomenal year, and those with money to burn were making a fortune. But wages had barely budged. The vast majority of people, those whose days consisted of driving trucks and managing accounts and scheduling appointments, saw no relief from the ballooning costs of healthcare and student loans and natural disasters.

Looking for relief from government seemed naive at best and masochistic at worst. The wars and terrorism threats that characterized the early part of the 2000s were replaced with financial distress and uncertainty in the latter half. In the 2008 presidential election, the country traded former-president's son George W. Bush for a young candidate named Barack Obama touting hope and change. With huge majorities in both the House and Senate, President Obama signed a major healthcare bill into law in 2009, but nothing more to fundamentally change the prevailing economic system that had directly caused the crash.

When Obama lost his congressional majorities in 2010, the remainder of his first term and much of his second term became characterized by political gridlock and obstructionism. Voters from both parties lost faith in traditional government. When businessman and reality TV host Donald Trump asserted that he was the only one who could fix the country at the 2016 Republican National Convention, many people believed him.

Three years later, when Trump was impeached for allegedly withholding funding to Ukraine until their government granted a political favor, it sounded conspicuously similar to the billionaire-turned-politician's self-admitted style of running a business: utilizing any available leverage, putting pressure on people in vulnerable positions, and acting with impunity. Civil servants with knowledge of the phone call in question delivered damning testimony at great risk to their careers. But the result of the trial in the Senate, with the vote breaking almost entirely along party lines, was never in question. As David Roberts wrote for Vox, "We are split in two, living in different worlds, with different stories and facts shaping our lives. We no longer learn or know things together, as a country, so we can no longer act together, as a country."[9]

The world kept spinning. In this environment, inequality reached astonishing heights. A generalized anxiety seemed to settle in that rivaled what I saw when the economy crashed at the end of high school. Perhaps, though, this anxiety had never truly gone away. As friends and family members spoke more frankly about long-standing mental health concerns, I realized this was a far bigger trend. The national suicide rate had been rising since the early 2000s, with the male suicide rate particularly troubling. The increase coincided with the economic downturn in 2007 and peaked in 2018, 26 percent above 2006 totals.[10]

Something was fundamentally wrong. I started to hear family, friends, and strangers of all political stripes ask stark questions about where we were going as a country. Journalists, politicians, and professionals in every industry announced the death of the city, the death of the small town, the death of community, civility, and even democracy itself.

But what's not dead—what's instead flailing and potentially dying—requires more than an elegy; it requires an investigation. So, when I heard locals in my new home of Flagstaff, Arizona, complain about how short-term rentals were killing the small city, I decided to investigate it myself.

I focused on Flagstaff, St. George, and Bozeman, but it wasn't long before I was seeing a much larger phenomenon. Yes, short-term rentals made it harder for locals in these places to afford housing, but short-term rentals were only part of the issue. The more people I interviewed and the deeper I delved into housing trends, the more dire I understood the situation to be, especially for people who weren't White and who weren't in the highest income brackets.

These were the same trends that had led Leilani Farha to declare that housing was "at the centre of an historic structural transformation in global investment."[11] This transformation—from investment in the stock market to investment in real estate—had put stable and affordable housing out of reach for millions and undermined the vibrancy of towns and cities across the country.

A 2018 Federal Reserve study found that 39 percent of people in the United States could not personally pay for an unexpected $400 expense.[12] In this context, the dire state of housing has far-reaching consequences that are hard on individuals and downright crushing for families. When housing is unaffordable, people start making difficult decisions about how they spend their money. They begin making impossible choices between nutritious food and housing, reliable transportation and housing, having children and housing, and the list continues. They do not save, start businesses, or think to the future; they seek to make it through the month.

In this context, they start allocating their time differently, which changes their relationship to their community. It's hard to justify keeping a garden just to move in the middle of the season. It's hard to justify keeping a pet when this will limit future housing options. It's hard to justify forming relationships with neighbors when they likely won't be your neighbors for long. In short, when every decision is driven by the anxiety of affording the roof overhead, it becomes difficult to justify forming relationships or engaging in community events.

This leads to a cruel irony. Having stable housing is personal. Having to settle for expensive or substandard housing—or being forced to move—is personal. But as people focus more on their personal struggle to afford housing, they become less connected to others facing similar issues, less aware of the structural transformation Farha speaks of. The housing market feels personal and localized, but it isn't. Households struggling to afford their apartment in the suburbs of Minneapolis or their single-family home in rural West Virginia or their trailer in Carbondale, Colorado, face pressures from the same sources. Whether renting or owning, they have perhaps more in common with each other than ever before. But they increasingly face their problems alone.

In talking with government officials and poring over research, I began to connect the dots. Government officials throughout the country repeated the same talking point: housing's unaffordable because there's not enough supply; we just need more housing. In other words, the market will solve it; we just need to incentivize the market.

But there was the contradiction. Cities across the country have an insatiable demand for more housing because they've induced this demand. They don't have any intention of creating the supply of affordable housing needed to give locals a chance, because they are always actively inviting greater demand. If affordable housing was as big of an issue as they said it was—as all the evidence said it was—why did they seem so unwilling to do something about it?

● ● ● ● ● ● ●

Short-term rentals are often depicted as a new "disruptive innovation," but there's nothing new about outsiders looking to make a fortune at the expense of existing communities. Centuries ago, this same unchecked greed was used to justify the genocide of Native peoples in the Americas and give birth to the transatlantic slave trade in Africa. Short-term rentals—and government officials' reticence to regulate them—are not the same. But the logic is the same. And the effects—fusing Whiteness and affluence, turning homes into commodities for sale to the highest bidder—are part of the same continuum.

In coming to terms with the dire housing situation in which we find ourselves and where this situation originated, patterns emerge. The growing number of short-term rentals in Flagstaff is not so different than the abundance of second homes owned by foreign millionaires in New York. This is not so different than the sudden arrival of Silicon Valley employees to Santa Fe, New Mexico. In every situation, local housing markets are transformed into one global fire sale.

The specifics of these trends are possible only in our hyperconnected modern world, but they are part of a long history of expensive and unstable housing for at least part of the population. There is perhaps nowhere that this history is more salient than western mountain towns. The covered wagons that once moved west across the country have been replaced by minivans and SUVs. Pioneers who once fled the noise and pressures of society for a home in forested outposts like Flagstaff have been replaced by hikers and bikers and climbers and boaters who chase the remaining wild. But the real similarity emerges only upon closer inspection: both the settlers of the eighteenth century and the tourists of today occupy former homes that have been emptied of their past residents.

Frontiers demand these empty spaces and the frontiers of the past were easy to track. They followed ships across the Atlantic Ocean and covered wagons across the Appalachian Mountains. They followed settlers pulling plows across the plains and soldiers chasing Native peoples across the Rockies. In short, the frontiers of the past followed the path of the gun west. Always the West.

Today's frontiers—the next empty spaces—are not restricted to the West. They are being created in cities of all sizes across the country. This starts casually, with construction increasing to match the growing population. As housing prices start to rise, city officials focus even more attention on growth. Buildings get taller, development sprawls. Still, the price of housing swells. Existing residents start to move to cheaper areas of the city, replaced by an influx of new residents who can afford these higher prices. City officials encourage growth at all costs, convinced that the city can boom forever, or at least until they leave office.

Over time, the pockets of affordability become increasingly scarce. Existing residents begin to feel chased out and many leave the city entirely. As housing prices continue surging throughout the city, even high-income residents start to feel the squeeze. They supplement their income by renting out rooms as short-term rentals but soon find they cannot compete with the slate of short-term rentals offering up entire houses. Mom-and-pop landlords soon find they cannot compete with private equity firms buying up entire blocks.

When a house comes up for sale, longtime locals who've saved for a decade nervously waive the inspection and put in an offer. But they are relics of a quaint and foolish past in which housing was not a commodity. They soon find themselves outbid by a cast of nonresidents who made cash offers 20 percent over the asking price.

These outsiders are buying a second or third or fourth home, but mostly they are buying to rent. For the bulk of the year when they're not around, they'll list it as a short-term rental. In this way, they are claiming a piece of the meteoric rise in housing prices. When they finally sell the property to an investor, the neighborhood will be a shell of itself, the charred landscape of a once-thriving community. But they won't see this. They'll be off chasing the next frontier.

In the past, frontiers were places of open violence signaling the construction of new worlds on top of the old. They moved westward across the United States, forever chasing the arc of the sun. Though the sun has set on these frontiers, they've been replaced by a new frontier that hides its violence in dollar signs and evictions. The biggest difference, however, is that there's no line to mark this new frontier. This new frontier is your home.

where we are

Zombie Town, USA

JEROME WASN'T ALWAYS A GHOST TOWN. At one time in the early 1900s, the Arizona town boasted a population of nearly fifteen thousand, making it the fourth-largest in the state. It got that way by following the familiar Old West script of centering an entire economy on one extractive industry, in this case copper.

Prospectors staked the first mining claim in 1875 at a spot that came to be called Cleopatra Hill. Mining expert Dr. James A. Douglas Sr. validated the quality of the find but advised against investment; the land was just too steep.

People invested anyway. One investor named William A. Clark was so enamored by a copper specimen featured at the 1884 New Orleans World's Fair that he bought $60 million worth of stock in the United Verde Copper Company. Word spread quickly and immigrants flocked to the booming town.

This mine made Clark fantastically rich, one of three "copper kings" of Butte, Montana. He had a town built in the valley below Jerome, which he modestly named Clarkdale, and hired laborers to assemble what would be called "the crookedest [rail] line in the world" to connect the two towns. Jerome became an ethnically diverse place, with people from as many as thirty nationalities laboring side by side to extract the impossibly green ore. The town boomed and boomed, making the county one of the largest producers of copper in the country by 1930.[1] And when the copper industry was no longer profitable to build a town around, the story of Jerome, Arizona, became the story of a bust.

The Old West is full of Jeromes, boom towns whose economies collapsed like the walls of a mine, leaving ghost towns in their wake. The story of Bannack, Montana, is not so different, just with different lives bound up in the place. The same goes for Bodie, California, and Independence, Colorado. Few people, if any, now live in these places, but the lives of those who came before are palpable. These towns are virtually all soul, no body.

Just twenty-eight miles from Jerome, nobody who sits in traffic on Sedona's main stretch or stands shoulder-to-shoulder in its many souvenir stores would call it a ghost town. Unlike Jerome, Sedona grew by preserving, not extracting, nearby nature in order to attract tourism. By the time the red rock community was formally incorporated as a town in 1988, tourism was its biggest industry, by far.

No, Sedona is not a ghost town. In fact, its annual visitation continues to grow. So, too, do the number of homes selling for over a half-million dollars and the number of monthly rents surpassing $2,000. And yet, the town's population has shrunk in recent years. Its former residents and current workforce have been pushed to Cottonwood and the farther-flung towns of Camp Verde and Clarkdale.

Sedona is not a ghost town, but there's still something eerily familiar about it, something familiar about a place that balanced its tourism industry so well with a strong civic and social life . . . and then flipped. Big attractions—the Pink Jeep tours, the crystal sales, the New Age tourism retreats marketing energy vortexes, the entire constellation of shops, restaurants, and bars—eventually eclipsed the everyday life of the people who lived there. Gradually, then all at once, the people who built the town and made it a community woke up to find that it wasn't theirs anymore.

. . . .

Many Sedona residents woke up to this sometime after 2016. That was when Senate Bill 1350 passed the Arizona state legislature. With broad, bipartisan support, the bill prevented all city-level regulation of short-term rentals. Additionally, the bill dictated that all state lodging taxes be collected directly by short-term rental companies rather than municipalities. It became outright illegal to pass local short-term rental laws.

Sedona, which had banned rentals of less than thirty days since 1995, suddenly found thousands of outside visitors within former neighborhood homes.[2] According to AirDNA, a vacation rental management and analysis site often used in housing studies, the city of ten thousand people was host to 1,819 distinct short-term rentals as of April 2022. Approximately 87 percent of these offered entire homes.[3] In other words, nearly one in every three housing units was being used as a short-term rental.

All of this has produced a hollowness to Sedona, a sense of loss that's hard to describe. Just an hour's drive from Flagstaff, I find myself in Sedona for a hike or work or the promise of warmer weather in the winter months. I see this loss not in the line of tourists' cars entering town on a Friday, but rather in the line of workers' cars leaving town on a Tuesday or Wednesday. I wonder how many of these tourists are staying in the former homes of these workers. I hear this loss not in the whine of ATV excursions or helicopter tours, but rather in the unanswered questions of locals I talk to: *At what point does the cost of living around Sedona cease to be worth it? At what point does the boom come for me?*

For many, it already has. Even before the pandemic, a 2019 article on AZ Central stated that more than 40 percent of Sedona's nongovernmental workforce lived outside the city. The then city manager Justin Clifton estimated that the figure doubled for city employees, many of whom had families to support and had to afford housing without the assistance of roommates. Normally sought-after jobs were not immune: candidates for both police chief and assistant city attorney turned down the jobs after failing to find affordable housing.

This is not merely an economic issue. According to Clifton, less than 2 percent of all residents in Sedona were born and raised there. As he explained, "'When you walk down the street and you're not seeing neighbors [with whom] you can establish some kind of relationship and a sense of place, that's a threat. It comes across as kind of a fluffy idea, until you're living it.'"[4]

The New West is full of these places, small towns like Jackson, Wyoming, and Aspen, Colorado, as well as larger ones like Boulder, Colorado; Bend, Oregon; and Bellingham, Washington. They look busy and even beautiful, but upon closer inspection, all of it starts to seem like a façade or some type of shell. They are not ghost towns but zombie towns. By measures like home value and annual visitation, they are booming, but the workforce has been priced out.

· · · · · · · ·

This phenomenon, though perhaps more pronounced in these small western towns, is happening across the country. In large cities, suburbs, so-called micropolitan areas, and rural towns spanning from coast to coast and every area between, more and more people are struggling to afford the cost of housing, with one Harvard University study listing as many as 30 percent of all households as housing-cost burdened.[5] These people are elderly, middle aged, and young. They reside in single-family homes, apartments, condos, trailers, cars, tents, and any place that offers some shelter from the elements. At the same time, there have never been so many short-term rentals.

At first glance, these two facts may not appear related. Short-term rentals—as seen on sites like Airbnb, Vacasa, Vrbo, FlipKey, and so many more—don't immediately appear to pose a threat to long-term residents. When Airbnb was founded in 2007, short-term rental platforms were seen as a novel challenge to the established hotel industry. "Disruptive innovation[s]" definitely, but not yet to the housing market.[6] In fact, amid the dim economic prospects that followed the Great Recession, short-term rentals offered the promise of extra income to hosts and cheaper lodging to guests. Airbnb became the poster child of the sharing economy.

The problem was that, within a few years, there wasn't much sharing happening. Rather, as short-term rental platforms turned individuals into entrepreneurs, travelers into critics, and empty spaces into financial windfalls, they increasingly turned toward offering entire homes to a steady stream of tourists throughout the year. Across the country and the world, they began facing enormous backlash from residents and city officials who claimed that short-term rentals were making housing less affordable. It wasn't long before evidence emerged to back all this up.[7]

· · · · · · ·

Short-term rentals primarily raise housing prices in two ways. First, entire-home short-term rentals remove properties from the long-term residence market, whether homeownership or rental. This is fairly straightforward. If there are one hundred houses available for year-long leases and ten are suddenly put up for short-term rent instead, the remaining ninety can be listed for higher prices. The demand has not changed, but the supply is smaller.

The second method is a little less straightforward but still easy to grasp. If a home can—or is expected to—directly generate income, that potential will likely be reflected at the point of sale, thereby forcing long-term residents to compete directly with tourists. If landlords can make more money by renting out nightly or developers can make more money by selling to a short-term rental host, many will do so. A 2020 study led by David Wyman, a professor of management and marketing, showed this effect in action. As they put it, "Using home sales data from the City of Isle of Palms, SC, we find short-term rental properties sell at a price premium relative to long-term rentals and owner-occupied properties."[8]

This result also holds up to general market logic. Someone seeking to buy a commercial space and choosing between two identical buildings, with one in a highly trafficked area and another in a lightly trafficked area, could expect more income from the space in the highly trafficked area. As a result, they would likely be willing to pay a higher price for that space. They could be confident that the initial difference in price would be offset by the larger market of potential customers, and therefore the potential for higher revenue.

In the same way, the potential profits of renting nightly drive the price of residential housing higher. The demand for long-term housing has not changed. The demand for short-term lodging has. If someone is buying a property that costs more initially, they will likely want a higher return on their investment and be more likely to rent it out to short-term visitors who will pay nightly than long-term ones who must be able to afford it consistently.

All this matters because digital short-term rental platforms eliminate what geographer Bill Travis referred to as the "friction of distance," further opening the housing market to investors who can then identify new markets and pursue profit in the short-term rental industry without necessarily requiring them to actually step foot inside a place.[9] In this way, short-term rental owners can easily call themselves hosts without ever making contact with their guests. The shared-space or room-rental model often promoted as the norm has instead become the outlier. In many places, it is almost nonexistent.

For these reasons, short-term rental platforms have been highly contested within large cities in the United States and across the globe. Many cities are entrenched in legal battles over how to regulate the platforms. But while short-term rental critics have grown louder in their claims that platforms are disrupting their neighborhoods and pricing residents out, the short-term rental platforms themselves have been unwilling to give up the data that would either support or discredit these concerns. Instead, much of the data has come from academic studies and vacation rental management and analysis sites that scrape data from short-term rental platforms.

The best way to determine the true impact of short-term rentals on housing supply is to determine their number in relation to the total number of housing units. Researchers at FiveThirtyEight, a data-focused news outlet, undertook an analysis of this type between June 2015 and May 2016. Using AirDNA data to study Airbnb's twenty-five largest markets, the study found 9.7 percent of all active Airbnb listings were commercial, defined as whole units rented out more than half the year. This commercial share varied greatly across cities. At one extreme, one in every five short-term rentals in Honolulu was considered commercial. At the other, one in every twenty could be described as such in Philadelphia. But across all cities, the report estimated that "well below 1 percent" of housing units were being used as commercial short-term rentals.

At first glance, FiveThirtyEight's headline seemed accurate: "Airbnb probably isn't driving rents up much, at least not yet." But the devil was in the details. While fewer than one in every ten short-term rental listings was labeled commercial, nearly $3 of every $10 earned by hosts went to commercial short-term rentals. The highest commercial revenue percentage for any city was Los Angeles, with 46.4 percent.

With Airbnb earning a percentage of every booking, this meant that the company stood to gain a lot from keeping these commercial properties available. As the report states, "Dependence on commercial operators complicates Airbnb's claims that it represents homeowners and renters making extra money 'sharing' their living spaces, and strengthens the hand of critics who say that cities should treat the services more like traditional hotels, which are generally far more tightly regulated."[10]

The study also appeared to show that Airbnb has broken one of the few initial rules articulated by its founders, that "rooms can't be a commodity, which excludes most hotels."[11]

A major study in New York published in 2016 came to similar conclusions about the role of commercial operations. Murray Cox, founder of the website Inside Airbnb, and Tom Slee, author of a book critiquing the sharing economy entitled *What's Yours Is Mine*, summarized their analysis of Airbnb's New York City data by saying, "Airbnb's New York City 2014–2015 data set, which runs to November 1, shows that multiple-lister hosts earned 41% of the complete Entire Home revenue during the 2014–2015 year."[12] Commercial listings, many of them illegal according to New York state law, had become the norm.

Everywhere I looked, I found similar evidence. A 2019 study published in the *Harvard Business Review* found that increases in Airbnbs across a zip code translated to higher rent and housing prices. The researchers even developed an estimate for what proportion of annual housing price increases can be tied back to the short-term rental site: "in aggregate, the growth in home-sharing through Airbnb contributes to about one-fifth of the average annual increase in US rents and about one-seventh of the average annual increase in US housing prices."[13]

But perhaps the best evidence that short-term rentals are negatively impacting housing doesn't come from housing advocates or academic studies but the largest short-term rental company itself. Although platforms have fought cities' attempts to regulate them, Airbnb cofounder Brian Chesky recently admitted the company's negative impact on cities. In an August 2020 interview, Chesky said, "We grew so fast, we made mistakes. We drifted. We really need to think through our impact on cities and communities."[14]

In the months following this interview, Airbnb became a publicly traded company legally bound to act in the best interest of shareholders. Cities are not shareholders.

* * * * * * *

Following its public listing on the stock market, Airbnb's valuation grew to somewhere in the range of $100 billion, far beyond the $1 billion valuation by which Silicon Valley start-ups are termed "unicorns." Airbnb and other short-term rental platforms would say there are many different types of hosts, that many people own a piece of this unicorn. But it's become harder and harder to ignore the fact that investors and nonprimary homeowners dominate short-term rental markets. Cities across the country are seeing tens of thousands of long-term residential options taken off the market in order to serve the lodging desires of visitors.

Vacation rental–related sites are now everywhere, creating entirely new industries to promote, manage, and internally regulate this market.

Industries have exploded in vacation rental management, cleaning services, noise monitoring, and many more to complement the short-term rental platforms themselves. None of these are needed if hosts are on site. In fact, for most short-term rental properties, the "host" is nothing more than a property manager.

Some short-term rental companies like Vrbo make no claim to be offering shared space, instead priding themselves on offering separation from other people. As the company stated in a July 2022 ad, "The thing that's different about a Vrbo vacation home: you always have the whole place to yourself. No stranger at the dinner table making things awkward. Or in another room taking up space."[15] What the ad doesn't say is that this "stranger" would be the host and a wealth of information about the local area. While this person is operating the business that provides temporary lodging for tourists, he or she is first and foremost a resident. Or was a resident until houses became nothing more than investments, with permanent occupants viewed as taking up too much space.

Vacation rental management sites reiterate this message, continually highlighting stories like Scott Shatford's. Shatford wrote of finding freedom by leaving a "lucrative" business job to "explore the world" in 2012. But a story that would have once involved selling his possessions or relying on savings instead became one in which he became wealthier by being gone. As Shatford put it, he "snapped a few photos with [his] iPhone, created a[n Airbnb] listing, recruited a friend to manage the apartment in exchange for free use of [his] car," and was soon gone on a one-way ticket.

Shatford did not just break even. In his self-published ebook, *The Airbnb Expert's Playbook: Secrets to Making Six-Figures as a Rentalpreneur*, he describes how he streamlined his process and soon had a monthly income of $6,500 with less than four hours of weekly work.[16] When he did the same with four other properties to create an annual profit around $200,000, he maintains that this was a small operation. Other so-called rentalpreneurs he spoke to had between twenty and fifty Airbnb rentals with a few having more than one hundred.[17] The rest of the narrative is a how-to guide for real-estate investors looking to maximize profit in the short-term rental business.

This, of course, is not true for everyone. Some short-term rental hosts do not rent out an entire place and, of the majority who do, many rent out one and only one. Many of these property owners take home quite modest profits, with some losing money entirely. But while governments and short-term rental proponents often balk at restricting short-term rentals under the argument that they allow hosts to supplement their income, the prevalence of stories like Shatford's poke holes in their argument.

Even if short-term rental hosts are renting out a spare room or their entire home when they leave town, not all neighborhoods are equal. Just as more desirable areas command higher prices when it comes to housing and hotels, the same is true for short-term rentals. This means that short-term rental hosts able to afford housing in these more financially rewarding areas stand to make more money than hosts elsewhere. And while hosts may benefit from living there initially, vacation rental management sites are continually identifying new areas—new frontiers—for investment. The market is always ready to move on if another area proves more profitable.

While every location is different in terms of regulations, tourist preferences, and alternative lodging options, trends can emerge by looking at individual cities as case studies. In research led by Brian Fabo in 2017, for example, scientists analyzed the income of short-term rental hosts in Vancouver, Canada. They concluded that "Airbnb is not a viable option for replacement income in Vancouver. Yet, it can certainly be considered an added source of income, especially for the most sought-after neighbourhoods. In these cases, roughly 10% of the costs of living can be covered by renting or sharing rooms, which is not a negligible amount."[18]

Just as not all neighborhoods are created equal for potential short-term rental profit, neither are all short-term rentals. Widespread availability of entire-home rentals drives down the amount that can be charged by individuals offering only a private room. This means that most short-term rental revenue is captured by individuals and companies with multiple properties to begin with.

Finally, not everyone can operate a short-term rental. Leasing agreements or homeowner associations (HOAs) frequently restrict residents' ability to operate short-term rentals on the property. The important caveats in who can make a large income from short-term rentals greatly diminish the potential for it being used widely by long-term residents struggling to afford increasing housing costs.

While many can—and do—earn supplemental income from short-term rentals, those able to offer entire-home rentals for more of the year and those who already live in the most desirable areas stand to gain the most. Many, like the bulk of the population under prohibitory leases or HOA covenants, conditions, and restrictions commonly known as CC&Rs, cannot directly benefit at all.

This inequality of earning potential ripples across the community. In some neighborhoods, not a single house becomes a short-term rental. In others, nearly all do. Some people are displaced. A few make a fortune. Short-term rentals create a blank space next to an occupied one, an unregulated space alongside a regulated one. In other words, they create a frontier.

· · · · · · ·

The market has blurred the line between homes and hotels, with regulations failing to keep pace.[19] That's why large cities from New York to Barcelona to Detroit have fought back, often banning them in some residential areas.[20] That includes San Francisco, the site of Airbnb's founding and headquarters, which didn't have a legal framework for short-term rentals at all until 2014.[21] In these cities, if illegal listings were found by government officials or complaints were reported by neighbors experiencing noise or trash violations, property owners faced steep fines.

Cities across the country have entered protracted legal battles over the impacts of short-term rental platforms. Citizens have organized for ballot initiatives. People have taken to the streets. And where they've won, they've had an effect. Changes in New York's law are part of the reason that, of the short-term rentals listed in the country's five largest cities, New York has the lowest percentage of entire homes.

Conflicts between short-term rentals and residents will not go away on their own. A 2016 study conducted by Goldman Sachs showed that those who had stayed in Airbnbs did not desire to return to hotels.[22] Meanwhile, the Miles Partnership, a firm that analyzes tourism trends, stated in a 2018 report that "tourism around the world has been growing fast with total visitor spending now in excess of $7 trillion USD and 11% of global GDP."[23] And as the number of short-term rentals increases, so does the cost of housing.

These trends are often taking place in tight, low-vacancy markets. In these places, even slight changes have a critically outsized effect. When the cost of housing goes up or a unit is taken off the market, it is not just a change in that unit. It fundamentally changes the neighborhood and entire community. When a person leaves an area, someone else loses a babysitter, another loses a passing conversation, another loses a ride to work. Every individual's exit touches off a web of changes that are difficult to articulate and impossible to replicate.

These effects compound, resulting in the closure of stores, offices, and schools. Such is the case in Sedona. Between 2009 and the end of 2018, total enrollment in the Sedona-Oak Creek Unified School District had plunged from 1,300 students to just 766. Earlier in 2018, the district shuttered one of its two elementary schools for good. Then city manager Justin Clifton saw this as a "downward spiral." He stated flatly, "Point out to me a vibrant community that has no school."[24]

Sedona may end up facing that challenge. In 2021, sixth grade was added to Sedona's only junior high, which had already been attached to the only high school. With housing prices showing no sign of slowing, it's possible more consolidation awaits.

Regardless, Clifton won't be around to see it. He accepted the job of city manager in Palm Springs, California.[25] He'll be well-suited for the role. In recent years, Palm Springs has emerged as a favorite site for short-term rental investment.[26] All the while, its population has flatlined. Of special note is the percentage of its population under eighteen. Hovering around just 10 percent of the total population, this is a slightly higher proportion than Sedona but less than half of that seen throughout the country.

• • • • • • •

Events like a school closing come about slowly, nightmare scenarios creeping closer in full view of anyone directly affected. But while kids notice friends moving away and teachers notice dwindling class sizes, the closure comes as a shock to residents who lack direct connections. This is a symptom of communities coming apart: individuals come to see themselves as independent of each other. At least, they do until they are forced to see otherwise. Homeowners don't notice rising rents until the house next door becomes the short-term rental party house next door. Residents with job security don't notice the worker shortage until their favorite coffee shop reduces its hours.

Buried behind a screen, just a click away from any product imaginable showing up at their doors, it becomes easy for residents to forget just how complex and fragile society really is. How interconnected their lives truly are. As Jane Jacobs argued in The Death and Life of Great American Cities, "Most of it is ostensibly utterly trivial but the sum is not trivial at all."[27] It takes something that cuts across all of society, something that disrupts the flow of everyday life and forces everything to come to a grinding halt, to be reminded how important something as simple as a roof overhead is.

It takes something like a virus.

2

Going Viral: Short-Term Rentals in Flagstaff

GREY TAMPA AND HIS FRIENDS had a difficult decision to make. They'd planned for months. They'd hired a company to supply their meals and gear. Out of tens of thousands of applicants, their group had been awarded a coveted permit to raft the Grand Canyon section of the Colorado River. But as growing uncertainty about the transmission and lethality of the COVID-19 virus brought most travel to a screeching halt, Tampa's group was left debating whether to go at all.

In the end, the pull of the canyon was too strong. The group converged from across the Western United States, with Tampa, who spends his winters working ski patrol and the rest of his year running his own tree care business, driving down to Arizona from Washington. The group began their trip downriver on March 18, just hours before Grand Canyon National Park revoked all outstanding permits. They'd won the lottery once again.

River trips through the Grand Canyon typically run the 280-mile stretch of the Colorado River between Lees Ferry and Pearce Ferry and can last as long as thirty days. Traversing a raging ribbon of water at the base of mile-high canyon walls, crews are cut off from most news of the outside world. The combination of isolation and intensity tends to foster incredibly strong bonds between people, something only magnified in the spring of 2020.

"It was like we were brought tighter by kind of the fatalism of it all," Tampa explained. "Everything's on fire. Everything's exploding and we don't know what's going on in the world. . . . It was a little heavier, or maybe it was a little more all-consuming, because it was like we didn't know what we were going to be coming back to. And so, I think we really just kind of threw ourselves into the community experience all the more."

Outside of an occasional message on their satellite communication device, Tampa's group was entirely fixed on the next meal and the next rapid. But these scant messages, relaying headlines like *number of COVID cases surging on East Coast and millions applying for unemployment*, were signs of the changed world they would face when their trip concluded. Many wondered if they'd have a job to go back to themselves.

The group grew even closer in the following days, bound by uncertainty. Tampa described the final two days as producing some of his favorite memories from the entire trip. "We all felt so close to each other right then and it was just like this last kind of desperate and endearing—you know, just trying to clutch on to this really special thing. . . . We knew it was all going to be gone and it was all going to be different when we took out."

When they arrived at Pearce Ferry on their final day, an employee from the company who'd provided the gear and rafts explained this new world. People were wearing masks and being encouraged to keep their distance from each other. States were considering closing their borders. The love and camaraderie of what Tampa referred to as their "little floating society" had been replaced by the anxiety of a much larger one.[1]

But the loss of this little society and the disruption of the annual procession of millions of tourists would be felt across the world. This went far beyond the inconvenience of shuttered hotels and restaurants shifting to takeout only. It reached far beyond the spectacle of airlines struggling to find places to park all their grounded planes and the eerie sensation felt by adventurers returning to their respective homes across the country. For cities dependent on tourism, the effect on their economies and the livelihoods of their residents was utterly devastating.

Just ninety miles from the Grand Canyon, Flagstaff was one such place. In the spring of 2020, officials in Flagstaff relied on hotel bookings and Grand Canyon visitation numbers to estimate the number of tourists coming to town. Other tourism towns used this same approach as a means of gauging the health of the overall economy. It wasn't good. William Brune, a leading official for a Flagstaff tourism organization, explained that hotels' typical summer average of 5–10 percent vacancy had been flipped to 5–10 percent occupancy.[2]

Most Flagstaff hotels, restaurants, and tourism outlets make the bulk of their income in late spring and summer, which sustains them through lulls later in the year, a phenomenon seen in high-tourism spots across the country. In 2020, this tourism was almost nonexistent. Even for places like St. George, with tourism spaced more evenly throughout the year, the pandemic impacted travel far beyond the initial spring stoppages.

Brune cited a report by Arizona State University estimating that tourism and business would not return to their prior state for three years.[3] Cities across the world that had built themselves around tourism were floundering.

· · · · · · ·

Flagstaff is an example of what happens when short-term rentals go almost entirely unregulated in an amenity-rich, tourism-heavy city. And local officials know it. When Senate Bill 1350, the bill which so severely impacted Sedona, took effect, cities lost all power to regulate short-term rentals.

Some cities such as Sedona and Phoenix suburb Scottsdale , which had previously outlawed or severely limited short-term rentals, were suddenly forced online. And, very quickly, they were inundated. As of the spring of 2022, approximately three in every ten housing units in Sedona were operating as short-term rentals. The vast majority of these were entire homes.

Short-term rental companies like Airbnb that had lobbied for the bill were ecstatic. Some residents and large companies reveled in the sudden windfall. Many residents were irate. Signs and citizen groups sprung up protesting what residents referred to as hotels on their street.

The new law's impact was especially felt by those who lived next door to so-called nuisance properties. Trash piled up on well-manicured streets. Noise punctured quiet neighborhoods. A steady stream of strangers not tethered by social norms and existing relationships entered the space.

One government official from an affected area spoke repeatedly about a property near their house, referring to it as "a blight on the neighborhood." As they saw it, "When there's no owner, there's like no adult supervision. People can come . . . and party and act—completely ignore the fact that they're having an impact on the people around them."

The situation was so bad that the government official, who requested anonymity, said their family would not have moved in if they'd known. Explaining that other neighbors have had a major issue with the house as well, they said that they may still move away. "If you're not comfortable in your own house or you're not comfortable in your backyard, like what's the point, right? Like, why live there if you can't be comfortable there?"

• • • • • • •

Relief has not come for residents like this. The resistance to regulating short-term rentals in Arizona was so strong among state legislators that even a so-called party house bill passed by the Arizona Legislature in 2019 was severely limited. Similar to a law in Utah, an advertisement, public rating, or even a guest at the house saying they'd booked the short-term rental was not sufficient to show that the house was operating as a short-term rental.

When signing this bill into law, Governor Doug Ducey issued a statement saying, "In Arizona, we respect the right to do what we want with our property without undue government interference. I am open to corrective action if this bill is applied too broadly."[4]

There has been little corrective action. Short-term rentals continue to have almost free reign in Arizona. For cities like Scottsdale, Sedona, and Flagstaff, the law has done little to address their biggest impacts, especially those related to housing affordability. Scottsdale itself has more short-term rentals than its neighbor Phoenix, despite being less than one-sixth its size.[5]

Despite its major impact, the original ban on city-level regulation of short-term rentals sailed through the Arizona State Legislature. One of the most powerful proponents was neither a legislator nor a constituent. It wasn't even a short-term rental company. It was a think tank.

The Goldwater Institute is part of a nationwide network of think tanks known as the State Policy Network, a 501(c)(3) nonprofit which assists state think tanks in researching and advocating for new laws. Recognized by the IRS as a 501(c)(3) itself, the Goldwater Institute is "absolutely prohibited from directly or indirectly participating in, or intervening in, any political campaign on behalf of (or in opposition to) any candidate for elective public office."[6] For this reason, the group is careful not to name a party affiliation.

It doesn't have to. The group describes itself as an advocate for "limited government, economic freedom, and individual liberty." Grover Norquist, described on the Goldwater website as "one of five top leaders of the conservative movement today" and coauthor of the book Contract with America with former Republican Speaker of the House Newt Gingrich, sits on the board of directors. The group also named itself after former Republican senator Barry Goldwater and has the senator's son, also a former Republican politician, on the board of directors.[7]

The Goldwater Institute is not the only think tank fighting against short-term rental regulation. Utah's Libertas Institute was instrumental in limiting enforcement of statewide short-term regulations. A representative of Michigan's Mackinac Center for Public Policy wrote several articles criticizing Detroit's regulations.[8] A representative of the Grassroot Institute of Hawaii followed suit when Honolulu passed regulations.[9]

In every instance, the think tank was affiliated with the State Policy Network.[10]

In the case of the Utah law, the success of Libertas is not surprising. Since its founding in 2011, the organization claims an 85 percent success rate in its proposals becoming law.[11] One way to interpret this statistic is that Libertas is ruthlessly effective at advocating for its interests. Another is that policymakers are mere rubber stamps for the organization.

The impact of these think tanks and the Republican majorities in the Arizona and Utah legislatures would seem to suggest that preventing short-term rental regulation is strictly a Republican priority, but that is not the case. The political landscape cannot be adequately understood in a map of red and blue but rather one of dollars and cents. This is particularly true on issues like short-term rentals, which so fluidly cut across political boundaries. Arizona's bill giving short-term rentals free reign was strongly bipartisan.

Among the bill's detractors were the League of Arizona Cities and Towns and elected officials representing cities across the state that felt that their city would be negatively affected.[12] But nobody in the Arizona State Legislature has been more vocal about rescinding the law preventing city regulations of short-term rentals than Republican John Kavanagh.

Kavanagh discussed the bill at length with media outlets of all kinds and even put together a video explanation of why the bill is flawed and should be scrapped. He repeatedly brought repeal bills up for votes in legislative sessions. So far, the party house bill, though pared down, is the only major dent he's been able to make in the law.

Kavanagh understands why it's been an uphill battle. "It appealed to the conservative deregulation instinct and it appealed to the Democrats" who argued that their "financially struggling constituents can make extra cash renting a room." He added, "It was very, very popular. And it still is popular to a degree. One of the frustrations is the only legislators that have pressure to change this are those that live in areas that people want to go to."[13]

Flagstaff city councilmember Adam Shimoni agreed. When asked if there were specific policies or cities which Flagstaff would use as models for its own short-term rental policies, he laughed.

It's a funny question because, you know, it's so frustrating. Because here in Arizona, . . . our hands are tied as local municipalities when it comes to zoning and regulation of private property, and there's a lot of consequences if you overstep as a government entity. . . . Our housing staff will go to their conference, like national conferences, and a lot of great things discussed and presented our staff laugh about and just kind of chuckle because they're like, "Yep, can't do any of that."[14]

On the surface, state governments overruling local governments would seem to fly in the face of conservative thinking. For his part, Kavanagh was quick to point out distinctions between the Goldwater Institute's worldview and his own, emphasizing that the group was not conservative but libertarian. But there are ideologies inherent to US discourse that political identifications and philosophies barely touch. Short-term rentals bring these hidden beliefs to the surface, forcing everyone to consider what people should be allowed to do and how places should change. Most of all, short-term rentals force communities to reckon with their beliefs about who belongs.

For Kavanagh, giving short-term rentals free reign violated zoning rules, essentially creating hotels in residential spaces. He explained, "I believe that when people make the biggest investment of their life, which is their home, they have a right to certain guarantees about the character of the area it's in. And we . . . instill, or we set, those beliefs in zoning laws."[15]

For Shimoni, the proliferation of short-term rentals undermined a sense of community. "I think a lot of communities have seen many of their neighbors' houses go up for Airbnb, and we all know which houses in our communities are those Airbnbs, because they don't—those aren't neighbors. You know that they're not," he said. "They used to be neighbors, but they're not [anymore]."[16]

As he spoke, Shimoni seemed to be calling to mind the people he'd known before who weren't there anymore. Short-term rentals, known as part of the "sharing economy," were initially understood to be about residents sharing space with visitors. But the term was always a misnomer.[17] Lodging options offered on platforms like Airbnb are not shared; they are rented. And these spaces, particularly entire-home rentals, are almost indistinguishable from hotels.

The goal of Arizona opening its doors to unlimited short-term rentals was never about making better use of space or better balancing housing and tourism. Instead, the law was passed just months after Governor Ducey's 2016 State of the State Address, in which he called for Arizona to "become to the sharing economy what 'Texas is to oil and what Silicon Valley used to be to the tech industry.'"[18]

Ducey followed up his address with the creation of a Governor's Council on the Sharing Economy. The first justification listed for the council's formation was the economic impact of the sharing economy, with mention of a PricewaterhouseCoopers report estimating global revenues in sharing sectors would increase from $15 billion to $335 billion by 2025.[19] The goal of the law was bringing money into the state.

William Brune, the Flagstaff tourism organization official, and Chris Pasterz, the economic development manager for Coconino County, dispute whether this has actually happened. In their view, much of the revenue from short-term rentals is simply cutting into hotels' revenue, the result of an uneven playing field in which short-term rentals do not have to follow the same rules.

Pasterz challenges how far the profit from short-term rentals actually extends. With specific mention of the lack of job creation and lack of commercial property tax, he argues that most of the economic benefit of short-term rentals is confined to "individual homeowners who have these properties and a few select property investors."[20] In other words, the benefits are highly concentrated and the negative impacts are widely felt.

These negative impacts are most visible at the neighborhood level. Daniel Guttentag, a professor of hospitality and tourism, has observed this fact in tourism-heavy cities around the world. Writing for the BBC in 2018, he referenced a 2015 study that "indicated 9.6% of all homes [in Barcelona's Old Town] were listed on Airbnb—and in the Gothic Quarter section of the Old Town this proportion jumped to 16.8%." Guttentag pointed to studies on Barcelona as well as Boston, Los Angeles, and the entire United States that have "suggested a link between the concentration of Airbnb properties in a neighbourhood and rising rents."[21]

Someone may feel pressure to leave New York or Palm Beach or Flagstaff when the price of housing increases across the city, but it's when that price jump hits their block that they begin packing. This was evident as I asked government, housing, compliance, tourism, and real estate representatives for their professional opinion on housing in their community. Inevitably, once they'd listed common data and talking points, they answered as residents. For many, their personal experience with short-term rentals was intertwined with their professional opinion.

Elected officials in both Flagstaff and St. George spoke of staying in short-term rentals themselves while traveling. A planner for the state of Utah and a researcher in Bozeman spoke of being short-term rental hosts as a way of better affording housing costs that have shown no signs of abating. But individuals especially spoke of how they experienced short-term rentals as neighbors.

Pasterz knew from personal experience that short-term rentals affected housing. As he put it, "Nine out of ten of the houses on the street I live in are Airbnbs."[22] Living in a town just outside Flagstaff, his situation makes clear that this problem doesn't stop at the city's boundaries. Brian Guyer, at that time a planner for the Human Resource Development Council (HRDC) in Bozeman, spoke about this impact at length:

> I've seen the conversion of long-term rentals to overnight rentals. And I've seen how that has impacted not only our workforce, but . . . the vibrancy of a lot of the neighborhoods. You know, you have new people walking around the neighborhood every evening and people that you've never seen before. You have houses that go vacant for long periods of time, because the owners can afford to leave them vacant because the Airbnb income is so good that they don't have to have it occupied all the time.

And so that has really decreased the number of long-term rent-
ers and year-round tenants in the neighborhood where I live. . . .
When I got here, you know, it was very common on dog walks to
run into half a dozen people that you know, have a chat, continue
your walk. That's not as . . . frequent of an occurrence here, and it's
because a lot of the houses . . . have been converted to Airbnb or
short-term rentals.[23]

McKenna Marchant, a planner for the state of Utah's community development office who has worked on issues relating to St. George, described planning to host a short-term rental of her own. She did not live in St. George but drew a link between her tourism-dependent area of Utah and St. George: "The only reason we're going to be able to afford moving up there is because we're going to build a house on some family property and because we're going to have our own Airbnb. When we build, we're going to build an Airbnb over the garage. That's almost the only way that you can afford to live in these areas now."[24]

. . . .

Of all the nuanced social impacts of short-term rentals, the economic one is straightforward: they make housing both less available and less affordable to local residents. This is especially the case in places with limited room to grow. People are drawn to Flagstaff by the surrounding Coconino National Forest, home to a portion of the largest ponderosa pine forest anywhere. The San Francisco Peaks tower to the north, rising to an elevation of 12,633 feet. But, as Kendra Strahan, a planner for the city of Flagstaff stated, this also means that "any small change in our market is going to affect our housing supply."[25]

This fact directly implicates the high number of short-term rentals. The country's largest cities all have less than 1 percent of their housing units devoted to entire-home short-term rentals. Still, their impact on housing has spurred major protests, legal challenges, and ballot initiatives. In Flagstaff, between 3.5 and 5 percent of all houses are set aside as entire-home short-term rentals. In a place like Sedona, that number's as high as 30 percent.

If housing was eminently affordable in these places, perhaps this would not be a major issue, but that is far from the case. In Flagstaff, every interviewee cited housing affordability as the biggest issue faced by the city. The same was true in St. George and Bozeman. This makes sense, as a high percentage of residents in each city are housing-cost burdened:

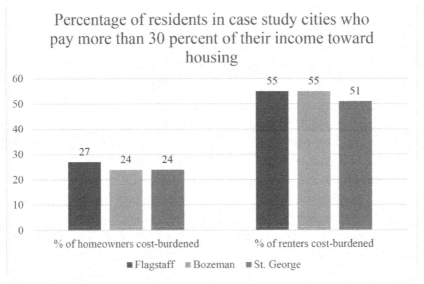

Percentage of residents in case study cities who pay more than 30 percent of their income toward housing

Table 1 [26]

Around one in four homeowners and more than one in two renters in each city puts at least 30 percent of their income toward housing. These residents have less money for nonhousing expenses and feel increases in housing prices faster than other residents. Often, they have extremely limited housing options. This was true for the government official who lived next to a short-term rental frequently used for parties. Their family had originally moved to the house with relatively few choices. If the short-term rental forced them away, the only affordable option might be away from the area entirely.

In this context, Flagstaff officials expressed hope that the economic downturn from the pandemic would mean more short-term rentals were converted to long-term housing. But these hopes would prove unmerited.

· · · · · · ·

A March 2020 Brookings Institute study estimated which communities would be hit hardest by a COVID recession, highlighting tourism-dependent jobs as a sector facing the greatest risks. Flagstaff was number twelve.[27] Other places may have been better able to endure a prolonged shutdown to prevent the spread of COVID, but the predicted economic losses in Flagstaff and similar communities would be devastating. Flagstaff's economy is dependent on tourism and cannot last in its current form without it.

This led to competing goals. Although shutting down or restricting opening may have been the logical decision for the health of community members and visitors alike, the tourism focus of New West economies is an enormous incentive for these places to remain fully open for business. After all, as several officials in St. George explained, nearby closures in states such as California and Nevada had led to more tourism in Utah. So, with places nearby shutting down, Flagstaff saw more visitation and its downtown—like many other places retaining an open posture—seemed as busy as ever in the summer of 2020. This may have allowed some businesses to survive the pandemic that otherwise wouldn't have.

But it came at a cost. As John Feely, a tourism official for the St. George area, put it, "We may be doing well health-wise here, but visitors that are coming from somewhere else may not be."[28] Flagstaff—in fact, all of Arizona—was hit hard. On July 2, 2020, Newsweek reported that intensive care unit beds in Arizona hospitals had reached 89 percent capacity. Arizona's seven-day rolling average of total positive COVID cases was on par with that of the entire European Union's, with a population sixty-three times its size. All the while, cases in Arizona continued rising.[29]

Fewer people stayed in hotels in Flagstaff during this time, but they found a home in short-term rentals. Flagstaff wasn't alone. With travel especially diminished between late March and May of 2020, the country's largest cities saw a severe drop-off in properties rented through Airbnb and Vrbo from quarter one (January through March) to quarter two (April through June). Meanwhile, although they didn't see the gains of 2019, Flagstaff, St. George, and Bozeman fared far better than their metropolitan counterparts. Like other mountain towns, they remained stable or even gained visitors.

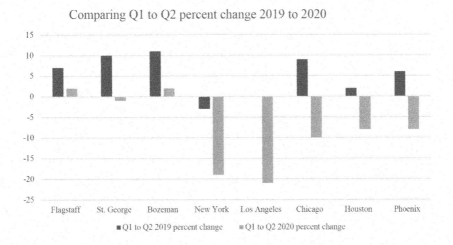

Comparing Q1 to Q2 percent change 2019 to 2020

Table 2

On August 19, 2020, Flagstaff, St. George, and Bozeman had a cumulative 2,769 properties listed on Airbnb or Vrbo. Of these, 92 percent were entire-home rentals while 56 percent were available more than half the year. At the same time, 66 percent of the 50,190 short-term rentals listed on Airbnb and Vrbo in the five largest cities offered entire homes while 29 percent were available more than half the year.[30] Although a portion of these are listed on both sites, the numbers remain staggering. They display both the widespread trend toward short-term rentals being commercial properties and the outsized effect they have in small cities. Flagstaff, despite having a population of nearly fifteen thousand less than St. George, had by far the most short-term rentals.

Breakdown of short-term rentals in the three case study cities (individual)				
City	Population	Current number active	% entire home	% available full-time
Flagstaff	75,038	1,361	91	55
St. George	89,587	855	97	62
Bozeman	49,831	553	88	47
Total	**214,456**	**2,769**	**92%**	**56%**

Table 3

The true test of how much short-term rentals diminish the housing stock is what percentage of the total units—which could presumably be used for long-term residents—are instead being used as short-term rentals.

Of the 86,619 units across the three case study cities, 2,769 total Airbnb and Vrbo units is 3.20 percent, with the 2,555 entire-home rentals representing 2.95 percent of all units. Those listed as available at least 180 days represent 1.78 percent of all units. In comparison, calculations for the five largest cities in the country, which have endured long legal battles with short-term rental companies and provoked vociferous protests, show that Airbnb and Vrbo units were a mere 0.68 percent of total units when estimating based on the national average household size. In these larger cities, entire-home rentals represented just 0.45 percent and those listed as available half the year represented 0.20 percent of all units.[31]

These numbers are jarring. These three smaller cities all have high rental cost and officials consistently cite low supply as an issue, with Bozeman planner Robin Le Page referring to the city's sub 1 percent vacancy rate as "frankly, an unhealthy condition."[32] Each city also has little stock of homes for sale.[33]

If short-term rentals remove even the low end of these numbers—1.78 percent—of possible long-term lodging from these cities, this has a very direct impact on prices. Furthermore, with various areas of these cities—such as college campuses and many HOAs—restricting short-term rentals altogether, those available are concentrated in an even smaller area, and thus compete more directly with long-term residential options there.

But this trend was not limited to these first months of the pandemic. An AirDNA report stated, "Markets in coastal and mountain destinations generated 64% of all booking value in January [2021], or the total revenue for all reservations made during the month of January for future trips, compared to just 52% in 2017–2020."[34] Short-term rental offerings in the United States were down overall in 2020 from years prior, but markets in amenity-rich, relatively low-density cities like Flagstaff, St. George, and Bozeman rebounded more quickly than either hotels or larger city markets.

Saying short-term rentals have rebounded, however, is a major understatement. Short-term rentals increasingly offer entire homes, generally allowing guests more space than hotels. This has been a particularly powerful selling point during a public health crisis, with tourists opting for destinations and lodging that maximize their personal space. But even when COVID vaccines became prevalent and the public perception of crisis seemed to wane in the spring of 2021, the number of properties being rented out as short-term rentals in these three cities continued to grow dramatically. Quarter two active rentals in 2021 were up 18.71 percent in Flagstaff, 51.51 percent in St. George, and 15.53 percent in Bozeman compared to prepandemic totals. By quarter four of 2021, the numbers had risen 9.62 percent, 7.90 percent, and 12.89 percent, respectively, from just six months prior. There had never been more short-term rentals in each city.[35]

This trend wasn't limited to these three cities. In its February 2022 report about changes in the vacation rental market, AirDNA stated, "Our 2022 list is dominated by small and mid-sized cities, as it was in 2021. In fact, the revenue potential of small city/rural areas in the US has risen 55% since the start of the pandemic, followed closely by mountain/lake destinations and mid-sized cities." The report states that towns near public lands had especially been seeing a lot of short-term rental activity since

COVID, but the list was by no means restricted to these gateway communities. Towns and cities ranging from Maui, Hawaii, to Charleston, South Carolina, to Galena, Illinois, were named among the twenty-five "best short-term rental markets in 2022."[36]

• • • • • • •

Government and housing and tourism officials alike consistently cited short-term rentals as having a negative impact on housing affordability in Flagstaff. Without regulation, Flagstaff's short-term rental totals nearly rivaled Boston's, a city ten times its size. Yet, while every elected official agreed that short-term rentals lead to a rise in housing costs, several also emphasized that short-term rentals could help some to afford their mortgages.

There is a peculiar logic at work here. For starters, homeownership is already unaffordable to many in Flagstaff, the most-populous and most-expensive place in what Pasterz, the county's economic development manager, called the "most expensive county" in Arizona.[37] At the time we talked in the summer of 2020, Flagstaff's median household income was $58,685. An individual or family with this income could not afford what was then a $362,700 median home value.[38] In fact, Flagstaff's price-to-income ratio was more than 6:1 and still rising, making it less affordable than all but a handful of large cities. The ratio for median home value to median household income typically cited as the standard of affordability is 2.6:1.

Despite this price-to-income gap, officials in Flagstaff cited residents' ability to earn supplemental income and afford the increasingly high local cost-of-living as a reason to maintain an open posture to short-term rentals. St. George and Bozeman officials said the same. On one hand, officials acknowledged that the prevalence of short-term rentals led to far higher housing costs for all year-round residents. On the other, they justified this increase because a very small number of year-round residents could potentially supplement their income through short-term rentals to afford these far higher costs. This income will do very little to stave off rising home prices, especially when there are so many entire-home rentals devoted exclusively to housing visitors.

This logic was part of a pattern. The Great Recession helped give birth to short-term rentals in part because nine million people had lost their jobs and needed extra income. And as side gigs and hustles became essential to get by, the precarity of work became normalized. In a world where the federal government can employ so-called quantitative easing, essentially printing and distributing nearly interest-free, taxpayer-backed money—accepting IOUs—to bail out Wall Street for the havoc it wreaked on the housing market and entire economy, should it be any wonder that more and more people are feeling the need to supplement their income with short-term rental properties or other real estate investments?

Inflation is hitting hard, competition has gone global, and workers are increasingly at the mercy of macroeconomic changes. As CEOs are rewarded for outsourcing jobs, workers are laid off en masse. As entire industries are propped up by investors hungry for a big payout, they disintegrate when these investors get a hunch that there's a bigger pay-out elsewhere. As cryptocurrencies and the metaverse and nonfungible tokens and amateur stock investment come to dominate discussions of the economy, money has never felt so fake. At the same time, the risk of not having enough of it has never felt so tangible.

In this context, a friend of mine half-joked, "I kind of feel like wage labor is for suckers." She had just finished her master's degree at Northern Arizona University and would presumably be eligible for a higher-paying job that would make any macroeconomic uncertainty more manageable. But she wasn't betting on this. She'd recently seen millions of people lose their jobs in a matter of weeks, including more than one hundred professors at NAU, many with terminal degrees in their field. Instead, she'd just bought stock in video game retailer GameStop.

When government officials embraced the logic that residents should find other ways of paying for housing beyond working traditional jobs, they seemed to express a powerlessness against the forces of the market. Either that, or an apathy to residents' plight that bordered on cruelty. Whichever it was, Flagstaff officials tended to focus on the ways that state law limited the city's ability to regulate short-term rentals or other private development.[39] They repeatedly pointed the finger elsewhere, explaining that short-term rentals—and general housing affordability—were out of their hands. They didn't talk as much about how their policies had increased the city's dependence on tourism or the rapid growth of Northern Arizona University.

More to the point, for the city to have thousands of entire-home short-term rentals, there had to be thousands of empty homes in the first place. As Brumby McLeod, a College of Charleston professor specializing in hospitality and tourism trends put it, this was "a hunger problem when you have big piles of food nearby."[40] When I started looking at other cities, I realized this didn't happen by accident.

Latchkey Town: Second Homes in St. George

THERE'S STILL A FAINTLY VISIBLE TRAIL at the base of Arizona's Vermillion Cliffs. In the late 1800s and early 1900s, Mormon couples living in what was then the Arizona Territory would cross the Colorado River at Lees Ferry and take this wagon road west. They'd pass north of the Grand Canyon, climb the plateau graced by tangled piñon pine and juniper trees and upward through the rust orange ponderosa pine forest. Eventually, they'd begin their descent to the north, arriving in St. George, Utah, in order to seal their marriage before God in the area's only Mormon temple.

The "Honeymoon Trail," as this route to St. George became known, is now paralleled by a paved road, but this route doesn't attract as many young people seeking to start a new life. They can't afford it. With St. George's median household income of $59,989, a home would have to cost approximately $156,000 to be considered affordable.[1] Instead, the median home value in St. George between 2016 and 2020 was $302,300. If the town of ninety-five thousand was larger, this 5:1 ratio would have made it one of the fifteen least affordable cities in the country at that time, rivaling Boise or Miami.[2]

The effects of this are apparent. Homelessness has risen in St. George in recent years and St. George housing official Eric Gallagher said the wait list for the Section 8 housing voucher program that assists a small number of low-income renters is between one and three years. Two large afford-able housing projects have recently been built, but Gallagher explained that this is not enough.[3]

More than half of all renters in St. George are housing-cost burdened. And the 65.6 percent of St. George's population living in owner-occupied homes is not immune. While homeownership is traditionally seen as more stable housing in the United States, nearly a quarter of St. George's homeowners are housing-cost burdened.

Even for those making considerable amounts of money, residents in St. George can't keep pace with the price of housing. In this way, St. George is strikingly similar to Flagstaff and Bozeman. But, as in Flag-staff, I started to realize that short-term rentals were merely a symptom of a far more systemic problem.

· · · · · · ·

It's not surprising that people are attracted to St. George. The relatively small but ever-growing city lies at the heart of southern Utah's red rock country just off I-15, the primary north-south highway connecting the Canadian border with Salt Lake City, Las Vegas, and Los Angeles. Its year-round warm weather has helped spur many retirees to move to the area and aided in the expansion of education, health, professional, and business services. Just forty miles west of Zion National Park, people seem to be applying the translation of *zion*—"paradise"—to the region as a whole. Tourism drives the economy.[4]

And yet, while dependent on tourism, St. George remains embroiled in the debate of how best to maintain its existing community. Gary Lamp-ton, an elected official, said this is "probably why we've taken this kind of hybrid approach to allowing [short-term rentals] but not allowing them anywhere and everywhere."[5] St. George had a fairly restrictive policy in the years after short-term rental platforms took off. Official St. George policy remains more restrictive than surrounding cities, seeking to confine most entire-home short-term rentals to "resort overlay zones" away from neighborhoods of single-family homes.[6] But the Utah state legislature ensured that every neighborhood remained open to short-term rentals.

In 2016, the same year Arizona passed its original ban on short-term rental regulation, the state of Utah made local short-term rental regulations more difficult to enforce. While cities like St. George have sought to monitor the number of entire-home short-term rentals and cite those that operate illegally, the law states that cities cannot use a property being listed on a short-term rental site as evidence that it is operating as a short-term rental, citing this as a breach of an individual's right to free speech.[7]

Even if the rental is booked and even if there are reviews from past individuals who've stayed there, a listing is not enough. In this context, Lampton said, "I couldn't tell you how many we have. But we probably have thousands. Some of them are operating probably without a business license and not per our ordinance."[8]

He's right. Short-term rentals are scattered across St. George, occupying somewhere in the vicinity of eight to nine hundred homes despite the city's law. This is a common theme. While interviewing Jared Greene, a planner for a nearby city, I brought up a website for monitoring short-term rentals. As he scanned the map, Greene noted that many of the ones listed were operating illegally. But all he could do was shake his head and laugh.[9] The state law had stymied any possible enforcement.

The similarity between this law and Arizona's 2019 party house law is likely not a coincidence. The law was championed by Utah's Libertas Institute, which is affiliated with the Goldwater Institute in Arizona through the national network of think tanks that has been openly critical of any short-term rental regulations.

Multiple officials in St. George articulated a divide among residents in their views of short-term rentals. They agreed that individuals had a right to rent out their privately owned property but also that neighbors had a right to safe, quiet, and clean neighborhoods. Elected official Allen

Sanderson argued that it was important to have enforcement and limitation of short-term rentals so that people knew what they were getting into when they bought a house.[10]

The lack of enforcement has prevented this, a fact proven most beneficial to investors and the city's high percentage of second homeowners. In January 2021, 57 percent of all short-term rentals in St. George were listed as full-time and 95 percent offered the entire home.[11] It was this litany of entire-home rentals that attracted residents' complaints, but their concerns quickly collide with the city's other priorities.

In tourism-dependent communities, residents' desires often come second to those of tourists. Most of St. George's overnight visitors stay in hotels but, as Sanderson explained, "There's a different market for hotels and for short-term rentals."[12] Many of these tourists come for outdoor recreation opportunities. Whether that's mountain biking on trails, driving UTVs on sand dunes, or boating on lakes, they opt for short-term rentals for additional privacy and storage space.

This isn't always the case. Data from national studies conducted between 2016 and 2017 suggests overall short-term rental stays may be largely taking the place of hotel stays rather than increasing the number of people traveling.[13] According to another national study published in 2016, many people who have used short-term rental sites claim to be less likely to go back to hotels.[14] Especially during the worst of COVID, with people hesitant to mingle in shared spaces like hotels, short-term rentals came to be preferred. They became safe houses in hostile territory.

For many officials across the country, this short-term rental demand seemed to justify further openness to them. In their eyes, they couldn't afford to lose tourists. And if tourists demanded short-term rentals, they would give them short-term rentals. In this way, government officials were following Winston Churchill's alleged advice at the end of World War II, "Never let a good crisis go to waste." Crises change what's possible, but they also expose priorities. And COVID has exposed a lot of priorities.

· · · · · · ·

Policymakers told me two stories about housing in the summer of 2020. Some officials spoke of a looming "cascading of foreclosures," with people out of work unable to make rent or mortgage demands.[15] Meanwhile, many cited an influx of nonprimary home buyers and remote workers to mountain towns. Interviewees in every city—whether real estate agents, elected officials, housing officials, or planners—claimed home buying had continued unabated and even increased during the summer. All spoke anecdotally, saying they would have to wait and see what the data said more officially.

Seven months later, the data backed all of this up. Driven by a so-called Zoom boom, the housing market was described as hot, erupting, or booming—a seller's market. But for the majority of US residents who weren't selling a home, the housing market was going totally off the rails. Stingy lending and stagnating wages in the decade after the Great Recession had induced pent-up demand. With interest rates hovering near record lows and home suddenly becoming office, school, gym, bar, and so much more, the allure of homeownership seemed to increase tenfold. Anyone who'd been remotely considering buying a home entered the market. This was a fire sale. Everything would go.

A huge portion of these buyers were millennials, who had come to be seen as a generation delayed. For years, everyone from employers to politicians to journalists seemed to be wondering, *What's wrong with millennials?* They weren't buying cars or getting married or having kids. They were killing the napkin industry. And golf. And Applebee's.[16] Worst of all, they weren't buying houses.

In 2019, Deutsche Bank found that the median age of homebuyers in the United States had reached forty-seven. In 1981, it was thirty-one. As with owning a car or playing golf, commentators have pointed to changing values and changing preferences that have slowed the rate of home-buying among millennials. But there's a simpler reason to explain all of it: we couldn't afford it.

Since the 1930s, when the federal government began insuring mortgages and homeownership became accessible to a growing middle class, housing has been the primary way people have built wealth. From the

1930s to 1950s, home prices remained affordable to members of every generation, just as long as they were White men. It was only in the 1960s and 1970s—as more jobs opened to women, as federal subsidies and protections began to include Black, Native, and non-White immigrant populations—that homeownership entered the realm of possibility for most people who weren't White or men. As the country's overall population and the pool of potential homeowners swelled, the price of housing rose and rose. Sometimes, this happened steadily. Sometimes, this rise was astronomical. But it always happened because someone else was willing to pay a higher price.

These populations were willing and able to pay bloated home prices because wages were still rising in lockstep with housing prices. Then they diverged. In recent decades, wages have stagnated, hurt by automation and outsourcing and simple greed. All the while, except for a dip between 2007 to 2012, the price of housing has continued to soar.

This dip in housing prices was the Great Recession, when the US housing market's implosion would crash the stock market and scramble the global economy. When the recession began, the oldest millennials were twenty-six. The youngest were not yet teenagers. As they grew up, they faced inflated mortgage rates and depressed wages. They also faced an obstacle that no generation before them had ever faced: tens of thousands of dollars in student loan debt.

Most had taken on this debt at age eighteen. They hadn't been presented with other options and the ones they had didn't make sense. They could have entered a trade—becoming an electrician or plumber or carpenter—but schools and parents and friends didn't promote these as options. Besides, in 2008, people didn't seem to be interested in many construction projects.

They could have entered the military, but the prospect of fighting a forever war under false pretenses, as the war in Iraq had proven to be, loomed large in their minds.

They could have stayed at home and worked, but their parents and teachers and all the statistics and conventional wisdom said not to worry about the student loan debt, that they could work through school and expect to easily pay off the remaining balance after they graduated.

So, millennials went to school and took on the debt. And, during the long, uneven recovery from the Great Recession, it was this debt—and the high rates of interest attached to it—that prevented them from saving and made them ineligible for mortgage loans. Those without this debt faced limited prospects of earning higher wages. All of them faced steep credit requirements and home prices. Millennials tucked their dreams of home-ownership away until they could afford them.

As Rob Warnock wrote in a March 2020 report for Apartment List, "At 25, the millennial [1981–1996], generation X [1965–1980] and boomer [1946–1964] homeownership rates were all roughly 30 percent. But by 35, after a decade of prime home-buying years, millennial homeownership rose to just 53 percent. . . . 35-year-olds in 1981 (the oldest baby boom-ers) were nearly 20 percent more likely to own their homes than 35-year-olds in 2016 (the oldest millennials)." But this was part of a long-term trend: homeownership had been slowing among people under forty for decades.[17]

Then came the pandemic. Interest rates dropped and the bidding wars began. The price of housing, already high, was growing by the day. Millennials and other buyers anxiously wrote letters to sellers explaining why they wanted the house. They waived inspections. They took on far higher mortgages and property taxes than they'd hoped. But, consumed by fears that prices would climb too high and they would again be left in the cold, they became homeowners.

In doing so, these new buyers achieved what had long been preached, and accepted, as the pinnacle of success in the United States. They gained greater security, more agency, and, most of all, a valuable asset. New homebuyers eased their concerns about high costs with the same refrain used by new homebuyers in the 1940s and 1960s and 1980s: they could always cash out when the market rose. For nearly a century, the right time to buy a home in the United States has always been the previous genera-tion. The system is designed this way, with one generation's wealth built upon the struggles of the next.

To afford these prices, younger generations have frequently required massive subsidies from government programs or parents, but even these measures frequently fail to be enough. This is especially true today.

Millennials and other potential first-time homebuyers aren't just competing against each other. Instead, the market is rife with purchases of nonprimary homes and investment properties. A report by real estate data analysis firm Redfin showed that nonprimary home sales were increasing at twice the rate of primary homes, with an 84 percent year-on-year increase as of January 2021.[18]

Many of these buyers were people from large metropolitan areas who moved to a mountain town to work remotely and ride out the pandemic.[19] But when their job returned to in-person, the question for many of them was not whether to leave their second home or leave their job. Instead, it was how they could keep both.

Randy Carpenter is the project director for Future West, an organization based in Bozeman that helps communities across the West manage growth. He explained the high economic incentive of second homes:

> *There's been a fair bit of speculation that people are going to places like Bozeman and buying a house or condo and [saying], "This is my second home, but when I'm not here, you know, I'll do Airbnb [and] the revenue from Airbnb will pay that mortgage. I'll essentially get a free second home." And then with . . . that comes the appreciation. You know, Bozeman prices are going up 5 to 10 percent a year and it's hard to get that returned anywhere.[20]*

For many people, work has remained remote. They have not needed to return anywhere and so don't need a mountain retreat. They can live extravagantly in a mountain town or beach town or anywhere they'd like, earning a high San Francisco or New York salary while contending with a far cheaper cost of living. But they want it all.

Redfin agent Nisa Sheikh saw this in the Palm Springs, California, market in April 2021:

> *Many of them are tech workers [from San Francisco and Los Angeles] who can do their jobs remotely, and they enjoy the weather and lifestyle here in the desert. People don't want to vacation in a hotel right now, and many of my buyers are planning to turn their*

second homes into Airbnb rentals and earn some extra income when they're not in town.[21]

Dana Anderson, a data journalist at Redfin, explained that this pattern "is indicative of the uneven financial recovery taking place throughout the US. Wealthy Americans are likely to have held onto their jobs—many with the freedom to work remotely—and they're earning money through a robust stock market and rising real-estate values."[22] Increasingly, buying a second home has little to do with the logistics of remote work. Even prior to COVID, nonprimary home buying was surging specifically because of the possibility of short-term rental income.[23]

When these nonresidents buy up what would be homes, they are driving up the cost of housing for local residents. If nonresidents do occasionally come to town, the cruel irony is that the same locals dealing with surging housing prices are the ones to serve the nonresidents in restaurants, bars, grocery stores, and retail shops. These nonresidents may tip well, but a few extra dollars in tips does little to balance housing costs that have risen by thousands and sometimes tens of thousands of dollars. Residents work these jobs for low pay because that is what's available. A town centered around tourism needs few people working in high-earning jobs in law, medicine, or finance. Others in town can't afford these services and tourists don't need them. And it is the tourist's desires that ultimately matter most, even if they desire to stay in what could be someone's home.

Nonresidents who operate these short-term rentals will justify this situation by arguing that they run a legitimate business that supports the worker and the economy. But they are sure to protest if the government calls their short-term rental a legitimate business and taxes them accordingly.

• • • • • • •

The rise of second homes and tension with existing communities is nothing new. COVID just made it all more visible, collapsing what might normally take decades into a couple years and turning what might normally be isolated market events into a national trend. Richard L. Ragatz and Gabriel M. Gelb noted the growth in second homes in 1970, writing, "The quiet boom in vacation housing is about to become much more noisy; the stage has been set for what may become one of the principal contributors to the housing industry." They cited a growing "leisure class," pointing especially to "about 5% of US households" that owned vacation homes around that time.

But their most remarkable insight was predicting that the sheer number of spare rooms would spawn a huge industry in so-called home-sharing. They even thought it might supplant the hotel industry entirely.[24]

Ragatz and Gelb were ahead of their time, seeing this link fifty-two years ago. They did not predict how it would be permitted, encouraged, and even sometimes funded by varying levels of government—but still they saw that short-term rentals and second homes are a revolving door. Cities have a lot of short-term rentals because they have a lot of second homes.

The same is true in reverse: when cities have a lot of short-term rentals, this creates conditions favoring more second homes. In August 2020, Flagstaff had around thirteen hundred homes listed as entire-home short-term rentals. Especially near these homes, those selling or renting the remaining properties feel justified in listing homes at far higher prices than locals can reasonably afford, knowing they can get even higher bids by selling to nonlocals.

In 2021, the city of Flagstaff estimated that approximately 22 percent of all housing units are not functioning as primary homes.[25] That means nearly one in four units are off the market for long-term residents. The result is more nonlocals moving in who then are more likely to set their homes up as short-term rentals. The cycle continues.

Despite the evidence that short-term rental income potential is now driving nonprimary home sales, there are far more nonprimary homes serving as nothing more than secondary spaces for people who don't live or work in town full-time. This is particularly true in even more tourism-heavy resort towns. A 2017 study commissioned for the town of Vail, Colorado, compared the residential occupancy of nine additional ski towns. The findings were alarming. Despite many towns claiming a shortage of affordable workforce housing, eight of the ten had at least 30 percent of their total housing units vacant, presumably being used as second homes. Breckenridge, Colorado, Park City, Utah, and Vail had the most spaces left vacant, with 71.7, 71, and 63.1 percent respectively.[26] This is, as Brumby McLeod refers to it, "a hunger problem with big piles of food nearby."

- - - - - - -

The steady growth of short-term rentals and second home purchases in mountain towns seems to show a unique disregard for local residents. But this isn't new. It was nonprimary homes that helped spur the housing market's rapid growth and price appreciation in the early 2000s.[27] It was also this flourishing market that helped create a housing bubble that popped and caused the worst financial downturn since the Great Depression.

Another way to look at this is as a boom followed by a bust, a concept very familiar in the West with its former reliance on extractive industries. The New West is supposed to be far more resilient to this boom-and-bust cycle. But its primary means of generating new revenue and meeting price increases within cities has been by luring higher-income, higher-spending individuals.

It is not surprising then that there was a significant increase in the percent of nonprimary homes in the West.[28] After the Great Recession, cities across the West and across the country increasingly relied upon these nonprimary home buyers to drive the housing market. In places like Flagstaff, this was justified as necessary to avoid the fate of places like Phoenix, which had been hit hardest by the housing crash. As Ronald Gunderson, an economics professor at NAU, said, "[Flagstaff's] heavily dominated by tourism. We are also heavily dependent on the second-home industry."[29]

As he said this, in 2009, Airbnb was taking off. The wheels were in motion for the purchase of empty homes that could later be converted into short-term rentals. Dependency on tourism and second homes before the crash would only deepen in the aftermath.

- - - - - - -

Utah officials seem aware that they have the tools to address the housing problems that plague places like St. George. Primary and nonprimary homes are taxed differently under Utah law. The assessor's office website shows how taxes for each would be assessed for a home with a $350,000 price tag:

Property tax with residential exemption:

$350,000 market value × .55% taxable portion = $192,500 assessed value

$192,500 assessed value × 1.1% tax rate = $2,117.50 property tax

Property tax without residential exemption:

$350,000 market value = $350,000 assessed value

$350,000 assessed value × 1.1% tax rate = $3,850 property tax

This amounts to a little over $1,700 in annual property taxes being collected on every nonresidential property. With the Washington County Assessor's Office identifying 7,136 nonprimary residential buildings in St. George alone, this appears to be a huge sum of money for addressing housing issues.[30]

But this prompts several major questions. First, if this measure is meant to encourage primary residence, is it working if 7,136 of the 36,182 homes in St. George—19.72 percent—are identified as nonprimary?[31] Especially when these are overwhelmingly single-family homes and may be concentrated to particular neighborhoods, one in five homes subtracted from the pool of available housing is an awful lot.

Second, what happens to the money raised from this tax? Using $302,300 as a standard—the city's median value for owner-occupied homes according to the 2020 Census—this additional tax for nonprimary residences would generate nearly $10.68 million more for the county than the amount that would be taken in if these were primary residences. Every year. If housing affordability is a subject of concern in the area, it seems logical that the first place to look for ways of addressing it would be the money already coming in from the sources contributing to affordability issues. And yet, nearly a quarter of all St. George homeowners and more than half of all renters are housing-cost burdened. These residents are not seeing that money.

Finally, considering the prevalence of second homes across the country, why are policies like this so rare? As second homes dot New York and San Francisco and Bellingham, Washington, and Killington, Vermont, affordable housing options are scarce. In all these places—mountain towns in Colorado and beach towns in South Carolina and metropolitan areas in the Northeast, virtually anywhere that attracts people for an event or vacation or season, long-term residents are being displaced. And yet, as modest as it is, Utah's easily comprehensible tax on nonprimary homes remains one of the only policies of its kind.

Beyond St. George

What happens in one city's housing market doesn't stay there. In part due to St. George's past short-term rental regulations, nearby cities from La Verkin to Hurricane to Washington—especially in the direction of Zion National Park—became frontiers of uneven regulation, havens for outside investors looking to make money in real estate. Jared Greene, the planner for a nearby city, explained that short-term rentals "absolutely have their place" but that the city wanted to limit their negative impacts. He received frequent calls from residents interested in renting out a room or an accessible dwelling unit, also known as an ADU, on their property. This is relatively straightforward, involving an inspection and registration fee.[32]

In addition, the city has designated "resort zones," which allow for high-density short-term rental complexes to operate in specific commercial areas exempt from the per-capita limits. With pools, clubhouses, and on-site management, these resorts are more spacious than hotels and can be rented out through short-term rental platforms. Airbnb cofounder Brian Chesky once said that, unlike hotels, listings on their site would be unique. As he put it, "A Marriott in New York City and a Marriott in Ireland will look exactly the same."[33] Short-term rental companies may have started out trying to be something different than hotels, but they have not put up much of a fight as the market has fused the two together.

Outside of these resort zones, the city places strict limitations on the number of entire-home short-term rentals per capita within residential zones. This has produced an estimated four-to-six-year waiting period, but Greene still identified these as the source of the most calls, with complaints often focused on short-term rentals being party houses and producing excess noise or garbage. Yet, with Utah state law limiting how well cities can enforce their own ordinances, city officials argue that their hands are tied.

Government officials across the country argue that this is the case in all aspects of affordable housing. They listen to residents who are struggling to stay afloat and tell them in earnest how much they wish they could do something, how much they would do if it weren't for state or federal limitations. For most politicians, this is the perfect situation, allowing them to brim with righteous anger that demonstrates to potential voters that they are on their side—but never needing to actually prove that this is the case.

· · · · · · ·

In September 2020, six months after COVID wreaked havoc on the tourism industry, an AirDNA report cited Flagstaff and Sedona in the top twenty-five large markets, those with at least one thousand active short-term rentals, to own vacation rental property. Palm Springs—the California city that Allen Sanderson compared to St. George—led the list.[34] Any hopes voiced by housing officials and elected officials that short-term rentals were going to be converted to long-term housing—or that the outside investment would falter—were dashed.

Several interviewees in St. George mentioned belief that short-term rentals were reaching a point in which supply was exceeding demand and they were beginning to be less lucrative. In other words, *the market is fixing it*. But the market is designed to accomplish one task: to find new frontiers. And, as author Naomi Klein put it, "The reason you build a frontier is always the same: nothing is more profitable."[35]

In this context, the market simply expanded. Though it has since been updated, the same AirDNA report initially identified Munds Park, just twenty miles south of Flagstaff, and Springdale and Orderville, forty and seventy miles east of St. George, as some of the best midsized markets to buy vacation rental property.[36]

The isolation of Flagstaff, St. George, and Bozeman had made them ideal cities to study, but I was starting to realize that they weren't as isolated as I thought. Ever wary of economic busts, armed with examples of formerly thriving towns now reduced to ghost towns, these cities exist in constant competition with each other.

Of course, *cities* do not compete. They do not have goals. They are not motivated by the next sale or the next election and do not advocate or oppose legislation. Cities do not care one way or the other who lives within their boundaries.

But it can start to feel this way. Developers and real estate agents advocate for growth, so that they can build more. Business owners advocate for it, so that they gain new customers. Many property owners advocate for it, just as long as this new growth is restricted to high-income earners so that the value of their house goes up. Those who might say they oppose growth also complain about the lack of advancement opportunities at their company. They call for new roads to ease traffic concerns or more flights to travel throughout the country. They would love Trader Joe's or In-n-Out Burger to add a franchise in their town. And on election day, all these people vote for the most progrowth politicians.

Not everyone buys into the growth project, at least not in the way that it's framed. Many people realize that these efforts toward growth do not simply involve bringing in more people but a certain subset of people. These efforts target the educated, the entrepreneurs, the so-called creatives. In general, these efforts target people perceived as capable of injecting more money into the local economy. With housing as the linchpin of the economy, those wary of unceasing growth predict that the influx of this tranche of people would send the price of housing soaring. But these people—arguing not for growth but for stability, balance, community—are not heard. If they are able to avoid being displaced, they are the loneliest voices in town.

As I turned my attention to Bozeman, a link started to appear between the crowds in Sedona and Airbnbs in New Orleans and gentrification in Minneapolis. All these places were driven by constellations of policymakers, developers, business owners, lobbyists, and many residents who were more than willing to sacrifice the affordability of housing for all in pursuit of economic growth for a few.

Opening the Floodgates: Growth in Bozeman

The Only Question

HIS LAUGH SAID IT ALL. It was the type of laugh that all elected officials give when asked a question they know too well and for which they have no answer.

How does Bozeman balance growth with its existing population?

Bozeman elected official Pat Witton explained, "Before COVID, that was the only question." He was quick to emphasize that the city's growth is not as constrained as other cities. "You know, it's a wide-open valley and it's all private property, so we can fill up."[1] Bozeman seems to be doing everything in its power to fill this space. As city planner Robin Le Page said, "The city is approving new development about as fast as they can get in the door. So, there has—the city has been in a very accommodating development posture for a long time."[2] In cities across the West, and the entire country, variants of this optimism are official policy. Officials argue that filling this space—simply building more housing—will keep the issue of affordable housing in check. The boom could last forever.

Bozeman's room to expand lies in striking contrast to many other cities, particularly in the West, making the vision of a forever boom seem almost plausible. But this underestimates the sheer volume of people flocking to Bozeman.

Between 2010 and 2020, Bozeman's population grew by approximately 43 percent, morphing from a small town to its present-day size of 53,293.[3] In other words, at least two of every five people in Bozeman in 2020 hadn't been there in 2010. The number is higher when factoring in those who left. This is the pre-COVID growth that Witton referred to as "defying gravity."[4]

Visiting in July 2020, I watched a new high school being built. I saw entire subdivisions take shape. The streets and shops of downtown were crowded with visitors. All the while, the price of housing grew higher and higher, which left more than 40 percent of households officially burdened by housing costs. What would happen when gravity kicked back in?

It's not hard to see why people are moving to Bozeman in droves. Summers bring mild temperatures and winters bring heavy snowfall, making everything from fishing and mountain biking to skiing and snowboarding accessible within a relatively short drive of city limits. Between all of these outdoor recreation opportunities and the presence of Yellowstone National Park's north entrance just eighty miles south, interviewees consistently noted that it's a very attractive place to live.

College students at Montana State University, or MSU, realize that, too. Between 2008 and 2017, MSU grew approximately 35 percent, jumping from 12,374 to 16,703.[5] Enrollment has since leveled off in accord with national trends, but an increase of four thousand new students in a decade is no small amount for a city of just fifty thousand. Add to this the fact that the university cannot even house all freshmen, let alone all students looking to rent, and the result is significant tension between the school and town.[6]

Beau Houston, a Bozeman real estate agent, said, "Thirty percent of the deals I'm doing now are working with parents that live somewhere else, their kids are going here, and they want to . . . give them—you know, buy them an investment property where they can live in and then rent out to other college students."[7]

With MSU located just south of downtown and the area nearby more expensive than others, many of these housing deals are spread far beyond the urban core.[8] And it's not just students. This sudden influx has also brought in new staff, faculty, and employees of companies meeting the needs of the increasing population. All these new residents need somewhere to live.

MSU's growth is a major reason Bozeman's housing stock, or total number of homes on the market, rarely extends beyond a few months.[9] It's a major reason why the vacancy rate for long-term rentals hovers around 1 percent, a rate that Le Page, the city planner, acknowledged as problematic. But Le Page also emphasized that the city's "extremely tight" housing market "has been that way for a long time," long before the university's growth in the past decade.[10]

Montana State's growth is only part of Bozeman's growth. Whether for permanent residence, school, or a secondary home, people are moving to Bozeman faster than new housing can be built. The tight housing market underlies most issues in Bozeman, as it does in most rapidly growing cities across the country. But that does not mean newcomers—or especially longtime residents—want to see this door remain wide open forever. As Witton noted, "Most of the residents love Bozeman because of what it is at the moment. They're not wanting to see it grow. So it's a huge political challenge."[11]

Short-Term Rentals in Bozeman

An entire home being continually rented to visitors cannot be rented by a long-term resident. In this way, short-term rentals offer a powerful symbol for residents in determining whether their city values their housing or a visitor's temporary lodging more. It's perhaps not too surprising then that short-term rentals became a contentious issue in Bozeman, finally rising to the level of public debate in 2017. City officials solicited feedback and garnered more than one thousand distinct public comments. Le Page called this "to the best of my knowledge, the single highest amount of public comments we've received on any single subject ever."[12]

Le Page went on to explain that, although people fell into two general camps on short-term rentals—seeing them as a net positive or net negative—the vast majority seemed to agree that "they can have a purpose, but they can be out of control."[13] Bozeman's new short-term rental policy went into effect in December 2017, with the city largely classifying them as businesses and subjecting them to many of the same rules.[14] The policy required annual registration, a state tax license, a county health inspection, and a fire safety inspection.[15]

Besides these requirements, two far-reaching regulations emerged from this period of public comment that shaped the future of short-term rentals in Bozeman. The first was the expansion of accessory dwelling units (ADUs) such as garages or other secondary structures. The idea was to increase in-fill, allowing for occupants in semi-separate spaces without contributing to further sprawl.[16]

The second was breaking down the term short-term rental into three types and identifying zones for each across the city. Type 1 (orange) allowed for short-term rental of bedrooms in an owner-occupied dwelling. Type 2 (yellow) allowed for the short-term rental of a host's primary residence, opposite duplex, or ADU whether or not they're home. Type 3 (green), which was largely centered in commercial areas, allowed for the short-term rental of any housing unit that is not owner-occupied.[17]

· · · · · · ·

Three years after implementation of these regulations, there have been few official complaints related to health.[18] As far as police responses, planner Robin Le Page stated that only two of nearly one hundred thousand total police responses in a given year were listed as related to short-term rentals.[19] The new rules seem to have worked to limit these issues.

When it comes to the law's impact on affordable housing, several officials called the law a success. They emphasized the nuanced policy resulting from public feedback and the city's efforts to continually monitor the prevalence of short-term rentals and enforce its rules. Distinct entire-home short-term rentals in Bozeman hovered around five hundred in an AirDNA snapshot taken in May 2022, a number which translates to a little more than 2 percent of housing units being set aside as short-term rentals.

This is far lower than what's seen in a larger city with extremely limited regulation like Flagstaff. Or in nearby towns functioning as gateway communities to high-visitation national parks. After all, Whitefish, Montana, the 7,751-person gateway to Glacier, has at least 15 percent of its housing devoted to short-term rentals. Or, just eighty miles away, Gardiner, Montana, the gateway town to Yellowstone's North Entrance, has lost more than a quarter of its housing stock to short-term rentals.

But 2 percent of housing units being removed from the long-term housing market is far higher than the percentage typically seen in much larger cities where the issue has been hotly contested. And it's a lot for a city with a 2020 median household income of $59,695 and median home value of $420,000.[20] A 2019 Housing Needs Assessment for the city identified 55 percent of Bozeman residents renting and 24 percent of those owning as housing-cost burdened.[21] As these households put more of their income toward the roof over their head, they have less for groceries, healthcare, education, retirement, or an emergency. To stay in the area, they are often forced to accrue massive debt or become dependent on outside assistance to make ends meet.

To justify this massive cost, I figured short-term rentals must be seen as a massive part of the tourism industry. But city officials consistently said it was a small part, that the vast majority of visitors still stayed in hotels. The data backed this up in Bozeman, as it does in tourist destinations across the country. I knew that tourists are, on average, far wealthier than local populations. In Flagstaff's 2017–2018 "Visitor Study," for instance, the average annual household income for visitors was $100,543, approximately $40,000 more than that of Flagstaff's own citizens.[22] This gap may be even more pronounced among those who stay in entire-home short-term rentals.

Still, would cities really give up hundreds—and in the case of many places, thousands—of long-term housing options and allow housing to become less affordable for a growing percentage of their populations for the sake of appeasing a relatively small number of tourists? I soon realized that they weren't simply catering to tourists; they were recruiting new residents.

· · · · · · ·

If short-term rentals blur the distinction between tourists and residents by allowing tourists to "belong anywhere," as Airbnb's slogan proposes, that separation becomes even less clear when examining where the influx of new residents comes from. In multiple interviews, people pointed to anecdotal evidence that many new residents actually first get the idea of moving to the area after vacationing there.

Randy Carpenter, the project director for Future West, said:

> *Tourism's impact is it brings in dollars for sure. But it also brings people who look around. They come to Bozeman . . . on a trip and they think, "Wow, this is really cool. You know, we should look at if we could live here." And those folks, . . .—some people call them "footloose entrepreneurs"—they can live anywhere. They can create their own jobs when they get here and then they . . . invest in the community. They bring capital with them. And that in turn creates jobs.*[23]

Eric Gallagher, the St. George housing official, described a similar phenomenon. "Many of the people that I talk to and meet that come into St. George, they say, 'Yeah, I just drove through St. George one day. We went and got gas and then we said, "We want to live here!"'" And, you know, they . . . bought a home and they've loved it ever since."[24]

The frequency or breezy nature of this exchange may be overblown, but it raises an important question: if someone can get an idea of moving to a place like St. George while simply passing through, how much stronger is this pull when someone is able to stay in a house and made to feel they "belong" for a couple days? There is plenty of nonanecdotal evidence to support the claim that tourism helps spur residential growth in certain areas of the West. After all, the New West economy does not rely on jobs attracting people; it relies on people attracting jobs.[25]

This side effect of tourism is not simply incidental; it is built into the design of amenity-rich towns in the West and across the country. Megan Lawson has seen this repeatedly as an economist for Headwaters Economics, which describes itself as "an independent, nonprofit research group that works to improve community development and land management decisions." Lawson explained, "You know, the first thing that everyone thinks about is tourism dollars, but I think what's really underappreciated is the impact of thinking about tourism as basically a marketing tool to recruit new residents."[26] She noted a past study she'd been part of in which a similar trend was realized among business owners in an Idaho town. The business owners visited, and then they moved there.

This is why the impact of short-term rentals cannot be measured simply in terms of the number of potential homes which operate as such. It's why researchers for the Harvard Business Review found in 2019 that short-term rentals were linked to "about one-fifth of the average annual increase in U.S. rents and about one-seventh of the average annual increase in U.S. housing prices."[27] And it's why, in a 2021 study, some of these same researchers found the effects went even further. Short-term rentals were so linked with economic growth that regulating short-term rentals often led to less development. In other words, developers would build where they could make the most money. They left communities that passed laws emphasizing affordable housing instead.[28]

The effect is especially insidious for residents struggling to afford housing. The initial impact of short-term rentals is only the beginning, like a hurricane making landfall. As more and more guests stay in each short-term rental, the winds begin to pick up. The property becomes more valuable, spurring more development that emulates this property. Some will bring in new, high-income residents, including those who got the idea to move there while staying at short-term rentals. Some will be short-term rentals themselves. The cycle repeats. This is the storm surge, often deadlier to communities than the initial hurricane.

Especially for a city like Bozeman, with no sales tax, or a city like Flag-staff, with no ability to levy fees on short-term rental bookings, this ability to turn tourists into future residents is a powerful motivator for catering to tourists in the first place. At the same time, it offers nonprimary home-owners and investors an opportunity to make more money more quickly off of housing, opening up another avenue for outside investment. And with it, the price of housing rises, forcing residents to reach deeper into their pockets. Or leave entirely.

• • • • • • •

Bozeman officials continually touted the space to grow west of the city as a means of keeping housing affordable. As Bozeman elected offi-cial Pat Witton said, "We're not Jackson. You know . . . we have an entire valley."[29] Across the Wyoming border, Jackson's ability to grow is strictly limited by surrounding public lands, which is not the case in Bozeman.

But Megan Lawson, who's based in Bozeman, noted how common this line of thinking is. She said, "So many places think like, 'Oh, we're not going to be a Jackson, we're never going to be like that.' And then, you know, the problem gets sort of—it gets out of hand because communities aren't anticipating [the time it takes] to build new housing stock and to expand things."[30]

Jackson—identified by a 2018 report as the most unequal place in the country in terms of the percentage of total income taken home by the wealthiest 1 percent—likely never thought it was going to become a Jack-son.[31] In *New Geographies of the American West*, Bill Travis described this in detail.

One commonality among western places swept up in the resort boom is the surprise and grief that residents express as their towns are "discovered." . . . The swift run-up in real estate prices, the sec-ond homes built by newcomers that dwarf traditional architecture, new businesses displacing locally owned shops, the growth of ser-vice jobs and the service workforce, and a host of other economic changes associated with resort growth . . . [are all hallmarks of sudden outside investment].[32]

In 2007, Travis himself described the purchase and holding of open land by his own place of residence, Boulder, Colorado, as making it "an island of restraint in a sea of unbridled development."[33] As of 2019, Boulder's median home value was $795,000, requiring a median household income of approximately $306,000 to meet the recommended ratio of affordability.[34] "Nature," in this way, is set aside not simply to preserve the natural world or protect area biodiversity. It's set aside because it's profitable.

Public lands are major draws to Flagstaff, St. George, and Bozeman alike, making them representative of the "New West." These also "act as one of the few solid constraints on land use."[35] One of the most striking takeaways from interviewing officials was how much people love where they live. The small-town feel and proximity to public land were often voiced as being central to this attachment. In this regard, each city's path to growth strikes at the heart of why many have chosen to make a home there.

When it comes to growing their populations, cities have three options: growing out, growing up, or growing between. In other words, sprawl, tall buildings, or less open space. But there is a fourth option, obscured by public officials' framing of the question, *How do we accommodate growth?* Steady-state or circular economies are phrases often used solely in reference to reducing environmental impacts, built around the idea of sustaining ecosystems.[36] But the underlying principle of striving for equilibrium also applies to maintaining a community's current population and keeping resources flowing locally. Whenever I broached this topic—the possibility of finding balance, of neither growing nor shrinking—interviewees dismissed it outright. This was particularly true of government officials. In their eyes, equilibrium was failure. Their goals were simple: keep the population and economy growing.

But there is plenty of existing pressure to move away from this mind set. In addition to nearby public lands being a constraint on growth,

Devonna McLaughlin, the CEO of Flagstaff nonprofit Housing Solutions of Northern Arizona, explained that many residents call for growth to slow or stop entirely: "There's also a desire quite honestly from our constituents in our public to not grow even if we could. 'I've got mine. Let's shut the doors. We don't need this to—Don't Phoenix Flagstaff.' We hear that all the time."[37]

In Flagstaff, St. George, and Bozeman, city officials likened opposition to growth as a desire to close the gates, a thought that seemed especially unfair for those not originally from the community in which they now resided. *Nobody closed the gates on us,* the logic goes. *How could we then do this for someone else?*

This ambivalence toward growth was a common theme, but it was a specific type of growth. The growth experienced in different cities was not simply an increase in the population but a preference for outsiders with more money. It was a preference for bigger companies, higher incomes, and higher spending that frequently left locals just trying to hang on. Megan Lawson, the economist from Headwaters Economics, brought up Venice, Italy, as one of the most extreme examples. "It's just a husk of this former community that's really only being propped up by tourists. You know, there's nothing left of the people who actually built it [as] what it is. And so, I think it's—you know, it really is kind of inevitable."[38]

When growth comes to be equated with unaffordability and displacement, it's no wonder that locals typically become resistant to it entirely. Lawson applied this to her home of Bozeman and talked about struggling with the growth in the form of a changing city and higher prices. "But, I don't know, I'm really reluctant to jump on the bandwagon of people who go to a community and want to slam the door behind them. 'Fence it off. This is mine. This is my trailhead. This is my park,'" she said with a laugh.

Lawson wasn't alone. City officials, especially planners and elected officials, cited positives with growth—from more direct airline flights to better healthcare options—but they admitted that it also altered the place. Although increased funding from a larger, more affluent tax base may allow for more options in a city's budget, Pat Witton stated the issue clearly. "The bottom line is that, yeah, nobody either moved here or stayed in Bozeman because of what Bozeman will become. They did it because of what Bozeman was or what Bozeman is now."[39]

Growth was continually identified as the factor putting the greatest pressure on housing costs. In St. George, it was named as the primary reason for rapidly rising land and building costs. As Allen Sanderson, the elected official in St. George, stated, "People know that [the land's] worth money, so they're not letting it go for a lower price."[40] In this way, they were engaging in what Travis referred to as the West's "oldest industry": land speculation.[41]

Much of this speculation comes from outside the city. Bozeman locals looking to buy a house or better afford rent are not competing against each other but against a new resident from Denver or a second homeowner from San Francisco or an investor from China. As scarcity increases value, the market has expanded the world over in order to find a higher bidder, in order to ensure the demand always outpaces the supply. In this situation, locals lose.

Especially in the West, riddled with ghost towns of former extractive industry hubs, warning signs abound of what can happen when revenue streams dry up.[42] This environment, with cities competing to lure money to their door, creates a sort of myopia. Every policy becomes focused on simply maintaining this growth. The booming town itself is the sought-after commodity. As author Naomi Klein stated, "Every frontier is a gold rush," and such a gold rush creates a scramble as long as the commodity lasts.[43] Business booms, existing homeowners receive a boost in prospective home value, and the influx of money makes it easier to govern.

Growth fosters more growth, creating a challenge for small cities like Flagstaff, St. George, and Bozeman to maintain their "ambiance," as Rachel Grant, a Flagstaff city councilmember referred to it.[44] Lawson explained this simply, "If there are a lot of people who live in your town whose main source of income comes from investments, you are very likely to have unaffordable housing. And that's definitely the case of the three communities [of Flagstaff, St. George, and Bozeman]."[45]

• • • • • • •

People in Bozeman continually cited the high cost of living compared to wages, a fact forcing people to leave. Many of them moved to nearby towns, but both Brian Guyer, then a planner and now the housing director for the community action-oriented HRDC, and real estate agent Beau Houston pointed to the rapid rise in housing prices in these towns as well.[46] When asked if there were still options available for small- or medium-income households, Houston discussed this trend in greater depth.

> *"Five years ago, I would have said there are still options, but you know, just as you said, Bozeman's kind of white-collar and blue-collar kind of gets pushed to the edge. That edge is continuing to get pushed. So, Belgrade, seven miles away, and Manhattan, you know, sixteen, seventeen miles away . . . as far as appreciation goes, they're . . . keeping track with Bozeman and it's getting harder and harder for the blue-collar person to be able to afford living in even those towns.*[47]

These towns lie to Bozeman's west. Over the mountain pass to the east, the town of Livingston is growing rapidly as well. And, with this growth, Guyer noted that housing prices were on the rise.[48] Guyer spoke candidly about Bozeman's efforts toward making housing more affordable as well as the limitations of these efforts. He described the many strategies Bozeman has used to tackle the housing gap—smaller lot sizes, incentives to developers who allow for some affordable housing, and minimizing the distance houses are built from the road—in a positive light. He spoke at length about the possibilities arising from the city's increased approval of ADU construction and in-fill projects.

But Guyer also explained that these goals are tempered. While the city and renters saw the housing potential of ADUs, real-estate investors saw the profit potential. He questioned whether these ADUs were primarily used for short-term or long-term rent. He had reason to be concerned. The western part of town where most new housing is being built is mostly zoned for Type 2 short-term rentals, which allow for ADUs to be rented out to visitors. More generally, Guyer questioned whether these measures can truly act as bulwarks against rising real estate prices. The problem, he explained, is not simply an inability to meet demand, but reflective of builders "focusing on a higher-end segment of the market than our workforce can afford."[49]

The question then becomes not whether most local residents will be able to stay but how long they can afford to. And, when they are forced to leave, where will they go? In Gallatin County, Bozeman's surrounding county, the median sales price for a single-family home rose from $420,000 in November 2019 to $615,000 in November 2020.[50] To maintain the recommended median price-to-income ratio, a household would need to earn around $237,000. As of 2019, Gallatin County's median household income was $66,397, putting the median price-to-income ratio at 9.26 for many county residents.

In simpler terms, residents making a median income and paying off the thirty-year mortgage for a median-priced home in the area would already be considered housing-cost burdened before accounting for mortgage interest rates, typical home maintenance costs, utility bills, and property taxes. Nonresidents' visits might support residents' wages, but their purchase of property ensures that the cost of housing will far outpace these wages.

· · · · · · ·

Despite what government officials may say, affordable housing is seldom a top priority. In the rare case when they do speak on behalf of existing residents rather than on behalf of economic growth, they are routinely silenced by other officials. Or by developers.

This is not a coincidence. With housing viewed as simply another commodity, a high price or strict regulation in one town creates a frontier in the next one over. An affordable town remains that way only until people from the unaffordable town next door begin spilling in, seeking out slightly lower prices. This is merely a larger scale of what's been said to happen at the neighborhood level, what geographer Neil Smith identified as the "rent gap."[51] What happens in one neighborhood or city reverberates throughout the whole region. As Guyer put it:

> *There's a standard cast of characters who have implemented policies that have had . . . marginal effects on affordable housing and the affordability of specific cities. What I haven't seen and what I would love to see is regional approaches to affordable housing that account for things like: What is this impact of this rapidly escalating real estate market in this one community? What is the impact on all of the satellite communities . . . and this entire region? . . . As long as you're operating in a silo, all you're really doing when you implement these strategies is passing the buck on to another community to deal with it.*[52]

Everything is connected. In the spring of 2020, there was a lot of talk about a steady stream of outside investment driving up the cost of housing. Now, the evidence is clear: this stream has become a flood. Though the occasional town or neighborhood may opt against growth, building a floodwall in order to stay dry, the flood of development is simply funneled downriver. When one town stays dry, the next is submerged. In our panic to stay afloat, we're holding fast to the same forces that flooded our homes in the first place. This flood is destroying everything we know and love.

5

Money Trees

Jobs bring people. This was the basic tenet guiding the expansion of every population center from the dawn of the industrial age until the late twentieth century. The thinking was straightforward: people need money to live and they need jobs to make money, so bringing jobs would bring people. These people would then pay property, income, and sales taxes to fund all the city services that helped make a place a home and turn a network of streets and buildings into a community.

Corn farmers lived in Iowa because that's where the corn was grown. Car manufacturers lived in Detroit because that's where cars were manufactured. Actors lived in Los Angeles because that's where films were shot. Stockbrokers lived in New York because that's where the stock market operated. Chances are, if you knew what someone did for a living, you knew where they lived. And vice versa.

So, when Lieutenant Joseph Christmas Ives set off in 1857 to explore a vast canyon in what we now know as Northern Arizona, he was looking for something worth mining, something that would bring jobs. Ives, earning his middle name from the day he was born and his rank for his service in the US Army Corps of Topographical Engineers, navigated a fifty-foot sternwheel steamboat up the Colorado River and into what was then called the "great unknown." When the boat wrecked, he and his crew continued on foot, with Ives taking copious notes of what he saw. The crew became the first known European descendants to reach the bottom of the Grand Canyon.

Lieutenant Ives used his words to reconstruct the Canyon's chasms and spires to magnificent effect, but he didn't stray from his primary objectives. Intangibles like beauty or inspiration fell by the wayside as he sought to determine whether the Colorado River could be used as a trade route and whether it held valuable resources like copper and gold. In short, if what he found couldn't be eaten, burned, or sold, it was hardly worth mentioning. He concluded his report by saying,

> *The region is, of course, altogether valueless. It can be approached only from the south, and after entering it there is nothing to do but leave. Ours has been the first, and will doubtless be the last, party of whites to visit this profitless locality. It seems intended by nature that the Colorado river, along the greater portion of its lonely and majestic way, shall be forever unvisited and undisturbed.*[1]

Among the first to prove Ives's prediction wrong was a one-handed Civil War veteran by the name of John Wesley Powell. In 1869 and from 1871 to 1872, he led two separate expeditions, navigating the Colorado River from the north. Powell did not merely find the area to be economically useless; he found it to be deadly. Only six of the nine men who accompanied him on the 1869 journey would complete the trip, the river's rapids proving so formidable that Powell once referred to the Canyon as "our granite prison."[2]

When speaking to the US House of Representatives about his explorations in the West, he advised that most land west of the one hundredth meridian—one of the first formalized delineations of the modern-day West—did not receive enough rainfall to allow for traditional intensive agriculture.[3] Running roughly through Abilene, Texas, in the South and

Bismarck, North Dakota, in the North, that line separated the humid from subhumid land in the United States. In other words, Powell argued these lands were relatively worthless for development and that they would—and should—only allow limited settlement throughout most of the West.

. . . .

Powell's expeditions and subsequent report coincided with a shift in the United States' tangled relationship with wilderness. Until that point, as Roderick Frazier Nash describes in *Wilderness and the American Mind*, much of the country's history had been an effort to conquer wilderness and vanquish the unknowns it contained.[4] The frontier, in the minds of American settlers, was always a promise of new beginnings. This both stemmed from and fostered a religious zeal to develop land. Even from the founding of British colonies in the early 1600s, the so-called New World was likened to an Edenic paradise and colonists to God's first people.

But, as Nash described, the promise of the New World "quickly shattered against the reality."[5] Especially for those living on the edges of society, involved in the backbreaking labor of farming and tree felling, the forest was likened to the desert of the Old Testament.[6] Contending with this enemy was a test of their faith.

This changed in the mid 1800s. The United States had grown from a ragtag assortment of colonies to a transcontinental empire. Forests and Native peoples had been forcibly removed. Western lands were still being divided up for settlers. In the midst of all this, people started to wonder what was being lost. The loudest voices—influential writers, scientists, travelers, and others not engaged directly in the process of clearing space—rose above the din of falling trees and dynamite blasts. In the 1850s, author Henry David Thoreau was one of many who reversed notions of what needed protection, calling attention to the "little oases of wildness in the desert of our civilization."[7]

Environmentalists, however, won few advocates when arguing the recreational, ecological, and cultural significance of setting aside land. While John Muir, who would go on to found the Sierra Club to lobby for environmental protection, believed that "between every two pines is a door leading to a new way of life," members of Congress saw actual doors.[8] Between every two pines was fifteen hundred board feet of lumber, perhaps a fifth of what was needed for a home at that time.

So, the environmentalists changed their pitch. When seeking passage of the Yellowstone Act of 1872, fourteen years after Ives passed through that "altogether valueless" region and as Powell was held captive by that "granite prison" of the Grand Canyon, proponents of preserving these spaces learned to exploit that language. They convinced Congress that the land was useless for development and would be most profitable if made into a tourism attraction. The railroad industry saw an opportunity to turn Yellowstone into a vacation draw on par with Niagara Falls.[9]

Politicians and influential figures saw the possibilities in creating attractions and a source of national pride. For a young nation lacking the kinds of cultural sites found throughout Europe, national parks became natural "monuments" to rival human-made ones across the Atlantic.[10] Yellowstone, pockmarked with geothermal activity, became the first national park. Next came Yosemite. Then Sequoia, Mount Rainier, and many more. It wouldn't be long before tourism's value would challenge that of traditional industries such as mining and railways, part of the process of rewriting the rules that governed the entire economy.

• • • • • • •

Throughout much of the 1900s, environmental determinism ruled the field of geography. Under this theory, an area's topography, resources, climate, and general geography were understood as its destiny.[11] Someone could take an inventory of all current resources within a place and determine whether or not the population would grow. This was on full display in the Old West: mines brought miners, ranches brought ranchers, and every town with a valuable resource became a boom town.

This would not last. As extractive industries in the western United States relied on increasingly powerful technology and competed within a global market, they produced fewer jobs for surrounding areas.

Eventually, the resource either ran out or its extraction ceased to be profitable. Then came the bust. Every collapse of a mining operation meant the collapse of a population. Every scarred landscape meant an eventual ghost town.

But that was the old economy. It's now been replaced by economies focused on knowledge production and service industries, what geographers David Gibbs and Rob Krueger refer to as the "new economies."[12] Rather than luring companies based on surrounding resources, the goal of cities has become luring people based on surrounding amenities. Exceptions exist, with cities still offering massive tax breaks and friendly regulatory environments in instances like Amazon's search for a second headquarters, but even in these instances, cities tout amenities far beyond the business's bottom line. The companies—the jobs—go where those seen as the most valuable workers want to live. The growth of remote work has flipped the old economy script: instead of jobs bringing people, it's people who bring jobs.

The West is a prime example. Pointing to the apparent rise and fall— the boom and bust—of industries in the West fails to take stock of the larger picture: western state populations throughout the twentieth century continued to grow far more rapidly than the rest of the country. Even in the 1980s, when the oil industry so integral to the West suffered severe losses, geographer Bill Travis notes, "All eleven western states . . . ended . . . with more people (and less open space) than they had at its start."[13] People stayed in the region even though the resources had dried up.

None of this made sense. As John Wesley Powell had noted, rainfall was too scarce throughout much of the region to allow for any sizable population to live. And yet, around the turn of the twentieth century, the West was becoming home to some of the largest cities in the country. And more people were arriving every day.

These cities—places such as Denver and Phoenix and Las Vegas— were what sociologist Harvey Molotch would call "growth machines."[14] They didn't grow in relation to nearby resources like water, as every populous city since the dawn of humanity had done. Instead, in these places, "growth itself attract[ed] water."[15] And this growth attracted more growth.

A series of technological innovations made these cities possible. Railroads came through in the 1880s and 1890s. Construction on Route 66, the first cross-country highway, began in 1926. Dams went up, providing seemingly endless supplies of cheap water and hydroelectricity. Air conditioning became widespread. Struggling to regain the identity it had lost when its extractive industries collapsed, the West packaged these factors into a product to sell: itself.

In the 1960s and '70s, with the country's population booming and affordable homeownership producing an-ever growing middle class, people headed west. Ski towns emerged. A series of paradigm-shifting public land acts passed. Intense city marketing campaigns, what Travis called "boosterism," took off.[16]

. . . .

This boosterism was on full display in 1981. That year, while the oil industry sputtered and jobs grew scarce, reporter Joel Garreau wrote extensively about the "empty quarter" of the intermountain or interior West, the slice of the West containing Flagstaff, St. George, and Bozeman.[17] Just ten years later, Garreau described the incredible growth of cities such as Tucson, Salt Lake City, Denver, Boise, and Phoenix in *Edge City: Life on the New Frontier.* This influential book was followed up with *Time Magazine*'s 1993 cover with the headline Boom Time in the Rockies. A few years later came *Newsweek*'s emphasis on "Pacific Northwest Paradises."[18]

This buzz became inseparable from the frenzy of future growth. In this case, the buzz around fast-growing cities generated more growth, which these cities then used for expansive, intentional advertising campaigns. It was as though a "Limited Time Offer" sign hung outside these cities and regions. People came in droves.

. . . .

Cities built around the New West model, what Travis referred to as an "economically diverse postindustrial regime of services, [information technology], light manufacturing, tourism, and retirement," have taken hold across the region.[19] A 2007 study led by rural sociologist Richelle Winkler identified several defining features of a transition to this New West economy. Among these features were in-migration, particularly of college-educated residents, increased seasonal housing, and rising housing costs. In other words, the New West was a regional version of the "new economy" trend taking hold throughout the country.

In examining this transition in the heart of the intermountain West—Idaho, Montana, Wyoming, Utah, and Colorado—Winkler and colleagues demonstrated that most New West expansion was happening near high-amenity, high-visitation public land sites. Of the places they identified as model New West communities, 26 percent were within an hour of a national park. The same was true for only 4 percent of Old West communities, those built around extractive industries. Colorado, Utah, and Montana topped the list for states seeing the most communities transition to the new economic drivers.[20]

Although the new economy's viability could be considered more stable than the past dependence on rapid extraction of nonrenewable resources, cities' newfound reliance on outside dollars requires them to be "growth machine[s]." In this environment, large infrastructure projects are undertaken to attract more tourists, partial-year residents, and new residents. These projects, Travis explains, are "passed off as simply 'catching up'" to the infrastructure projects previously deferred.[21]

Government officials and tour companies and businesses of every size aggressively market themselves, sculpting the city's image to maximize the number of visitors and new residents. This creates an extremely competitive environment. Recent research showed that towns in Europe found an enormous growth in tourism by simply updating their Wikipedia pages.[22] New economy towns and cities depend on gaining every possible edge to grow their economy through tourism and new higher-income residents.[23] When one city stops growing or reaches its boundary line, another is waiting to take its place. It becomes imperative that they keep growing.

A Beautiful Lie

Cities align environmental goals with this imperative by operating under the banner of "green growth" or "sustainable development." These declarations allow city officials to do the impossible: appease businesses and real estate developers while also protecting the environment. They issue directives and reports that identify specific, individual actors and specific, localized impacts.[24] But the truth lies just beyond the aesthetic.

A walk along Atlanta's BeltLine, a path built along an old rail corridor, feels environmentally friendly, as long as you don't stop to question what came before the plethora of new luxury-priced condos and apartment buildings. Rather than retrofitting existing homes in the area, these new structures altogether replace them. Those that didn't get torn down have sometimes doubled or tripled in value. In fact, the BeltLine is being paid for partially from the promise of an astronomical rise in nearby housing prices.

Atlanta is like New York, Minneapolis, and so many other cities whose governments build "greenways" and LEED-certified skyscrapers under the guise of reducing their city's environmental footprint. Particularly in the West, when held up against the plain-sight ecological impact of the old economy—the clear-cut forests, the strip-mined mountaintops, the dynamited rail tunnels—this new economy appears quite committed to environmental stewardship. And their advocacy may be heartfelt—but it is preached only as long as it's politically expedient. Enmeshed in a global economic system predicated on continual expansion, the goal of governments which tout green growth is ultimately to make their cities more appealing for high-spending tourists and new residents and investors. Their environmentalism is a performance.

While cities preserve the aesthetic of untouched wilderness at their edges, resources like food, water, timber, steel, and a host of others are imported from hundreds and sometimes thousands of miles beyond. This is because new economies are not simply built upon the idea that mountains, rivers, fields, and forests should be protected. They are built upon the idea that protecting them is more profitable than pillaging them. For locals and visitors seeking solace in nature, there is no discernible difference. Why there are mountain views or outdoor recreation opportunities galore is less important to most people than the fact that they are there. But for the long-term health of plants, animals, and entire ecosystems affected by these fast-developing areas, the distinction between short-term preservation and long-term sustainability could not be any more profound. Their presence in these environments is always precarious, secured only as long as it's viewed as profitable.

In these places, the environmental aesthetic is often elevated over the environmental impact, ironically making the human world feel separate from the natural world despite their inherent and endless entanglement. This separation is artificial, the boundaries created, observed, and controlled by humans. Or, as scholars Richard Peet and Michael Watts explained, "The environment is an active construction of the imagination."[25] Every aspect of the environment has been sculpted in some way by human hands. The reverse is also true. Whether living in huge cities or isolated farms and ranches, the built environment is simply a reassembly of what gets called the environment or natural world.

Most people have been so far removed from the processes through which this occurs that the end result just seems to materialize. The impact of mining limestone never enters the mind of someone walking along cement sidewalks. The impact of mining copper never enters the mind of someone flipping a light switch. The impact of mining coal never enters the mind of someone pushing a button to turn up the heat. The labyrinth of roads and power lines that weave between structures of plaster and steel has the effect of making us feel cut off, independent from the environment. The reality is that we are deeply intertwined.

The UN's 2017 "Global Status Report" identifies buildings and construction as being responsible for "36% of global final energy use and 39% of energy-related carbon dioxide."[26] This is especially pronounced when housing is viewed as a commodity. With locals unable to afford market rates, developers devote their attention to building for nonresidents. They build luxury-priced condos and large houses in the woods, catering to their clients' preferences for privacy and beautiful views. This means less in-fill and more sprawl.

With the city zoned for single-home dwellings and businesses to be largely separate, tourists stay in short-term rentals in residential areas and drive extended distances to reach businesses and attractions. This means more congestion on roads and more pollution. As more developments are left sitting empty to house nonprimary homeowners or future high-income residents, more developments take shape outside town, away from city services. The city constructs roads and utility lines to these new neighborhoods, tearing up trees and disrupting ecosystems in the process.

Full-time residents, who typically live in smaller, more integrated homes than nonresidents, are instead forced to "drive until they qualify," moving further from work and school and city services. At every turn— as more roads are built and more energy is used, as more people arrive and more houses go up—greenhouse gas emissions rise. These emissions have already wreaked havoc on climate patterns, ecosystems, and human life, becoming visibly destructive through increasingly powerful and frequent disasters.[27]

Everything we do has an impact on our environment, because we exist within it. The growing power that we give to financial institutions and unfettered markets to decide how we eat, move, work, and run our built environment—what can be understood as financialization—has a huge impact on the surrounding environment. As environmental historian Jason W. Moore explained, "The scarcities induced by [financialization] (through commodity booms) are neither more nor less directly connected to all of nature than crop failures, species extinctions, and climate shifts."

It is sometimes easier to see the social impacts of global economic policy than the environmental impact. As an Oxfam report asserts, every thirty hours during the two years since the COVID-19 pandemic began, a new billionaire emerged and nine hundred thousand more people fell into extreme poverty somewhere in the world.[28] For every Elon Musk or Jeff Bezos or Sam Bankman-Fried produced to dominate headlines and move markets with single tweets, nearly a million more people struggled to meet their basic survival needs.

These economic policies have equally massive environmental impacts. Moore explains simply that "Wall Street is a way of organizing nature."[29] As is Amazon. As is cryptocurrency. As is a city. When we fail to see the connection between profit-focused housing and environmental change, we are left reeling as our worlds collide.

· · · · · · ·

Climate change is not the only way this happens. Robert Watson, chair of the UN's 2019 Intergovernmental Science-Policy Platform on Biodiversity and Ecosystem Services (IPBES), argued that our negative impacts go far beyond the effects of burning fossil fuels. Watson opened the IPBES meeting by stating, "The evidence is incontestable. Our destruction of biodiversity and ecosystem services has reached levels that threaten our well-being at least as much as human-induced climate change."[30]

Even if we believe plant and animal species have no intrinsic worth and never step foot outside our constructed environment, expanding human society through development and agriculture wipes out the environments that provide our food, water, air, shelter, disease treatment, and disease protection. In other words, in developing every available acre of land and mining the surrounding environment for every resource under the sun, we are not simply creating an unsustainable world for countless plant and animal species; we are threatening our own.

In a study published in February 2022, researchers of wildfire risks "found that while the number of people living in the wildland-urban interface overall roughly doubled from 1990 to 2010, the population in its highest-hazard regions grew by 160%."[31] In addition to creating more possibilities for fire starts, ranging from rogue electrical sparks to fireworks to bonfires, building in these regions also puts more people and properties at risk of fire, demanding more resources to stamp out fires that were once naturally occurring, ecologically necessary events. Add in the materials for building homes, roads, powerlines, sewer lines, and scarce water resources and the environmental aesthetic of a second home in the desert or a short-term rental in the woods crumbles.

By valuing expansion above all else, we are hastening our own destruction. The thousands of Paradise, California, residents who lost their homes to a wildfire in 2018 and the thousands of western Kentucky residents who lost their homes to a tornado in 2021 signal that the age of climate refugees is not some theoretical future. It has already arrived. All these people need to live somewhere.

• • • • • • •

On the surface, the vastness of the West—with 46 percent of land protected in some fashion by the federal government—seems to show incredible restraint, supporting a narrative of environmental protection. But much of this land is still leased to ranchers grazing cattle, private operations extracting minerals, and irrigation networks supporting large farms and ever-expanding metropolitan areas. The public land protection has also spurred massive development on its edges.

A 2009 study led by Volker C. Radeloff of the University of Wisconsin showed that twenty-eight million housing units were built between 1940 and 2000 within approximately thirty miles of protected lands, nearly one million inside national forest boundaries. With this construction far outpacing other development efforts, the study argues that "housing growth in and near US protected areas has been strong for 6 decades, and that lands near protected areas are attractive for development." They added, "If development continues unabated, it will further limit the conservation value of protected areas, and biodiversity will be impoverished."[32]

More than a decade later, development shows no sign of slowing. Although the US population in 2021 grew by just 0.58 percent—the smallest increase in the last half-century—people have never stopped moving West. In the 2010s, every western state's population grew by at least 0.4 percent. This was not true for any other region.

Even when the land itself is set aside as wilderness or a contained ecological environment, the impact of human activity—often centered around highly consumptive tourism—is enormous. Guiding companies and public land agencies actively seeking to bring more tourists to the area to experience a touch of wildness can further the degradation of the region—wittingly or unwittingly—by encouraging unsustainable travel and development.

Mirroring cities' push for more visitors and high-income residents, the National Park Service (NPS) has become increasingly dependent on visitation to keep up maintenance. Annette McGivney wrote in an article for the *Guardian* in January 2022, "According to the not-for-profit National Parks Conservation Association, National Park Service staff has shrunk by 14% over the last decade, primarily due to federal funding cuts. Total visitation to all national park properties has increased 20% during the same period."[33]

More and more park superintendents are finding that the "NPS can't compete with Vrbo and Airbnb for housing" for its own employees.[34] The situation surely isn't being helped by the 2020 joint marketing campaign of Airbnb and the National Park Foundation, NPS's official nonprofit partner.[35] While recent federal investment in the NPS appears poised to address limited and neglected employee housing, the fact that it got to this point forces a troubling question. If an increasingly large percentage of people cannot afford to live near, work in, or travel to these places, what does it really mean for them to be considered public lands?

· · · · · · ·

At first glance, the BeltLine in Atlanta and High Line in New York suggest a desire to preserve some "wildness," and thereby an effort toward "the preservation of the world," as Henry David Thoreau wrote in the mid-1800s.[36] Like the Coconino National Forest surrounding Flagstaff and Snow Canyon State Park bordering St. George, they offer up narratives of restraint, assurance that the days of extraction and ecological destruction are behind us. In reality, the destruction has just been moved out of sight.

The Old West reliance on extractive industries—on jobs attracting people—led to a cycle of booms and busts. In the New West, cities again used nearby nature to attract outside money, this time preserving that nature to lure tourists. This scheme brought new jobs, new residents, and a new desire to protect natural spaces. But it stemmed from an old idea: growth at all costs.

Politicians and economists regularly cite the need for the economy to grow by 3 percent in terms of gross domestic product (GDP) every year. The modern GDP metric became widespread in the wake of the Great Depression, when economist Simon Kuznets presented it as a means of monitoring the country's total economic output and thereby economic stability. As it was understood, if GDP growth was too small, companies could not hire more people and people could not buy more things. But too much growth was also concerning, producing a bubble similar to the runaway economic growth of the Roaring Twenties and similarly liable to pop. From the beginning, Kuznets worried about the statistic being emphasized too much, writing in 1934, "The welfare of a nation can, therefore, scarcely be inferred from a measurement of national income.[37]

Kuznets's initial warnings—and subsequent warnings—were ignored. Since that time, GDP has ruled any discussion of the nation's well-being. A guideline to remain close to 3 percent growth became a mandate to achieve at least 3 percent growth. Anything outside this statistic—the income's distribution, the quality of what was produced, the environmental impact of this production—came to be seen as irrelevant.

As economic anthropologist, climate scientist, and author Jason Hickel notes, maintaining this level of growth means the economy doubles in just a little over two decades, a pace which the global economy has exponentially exceeded, with GDP doubling six times since 1960.[38] If all else stays the same, the amount of minerals extracted in a 3 percent growth society doubles every twenty-four years. The same is true for the fossil fuels burned, the clothes bought, the food eaten, and the overall things discarded.

In the United States, this doubling of stuff slowed between 1960 and 2018, as we more fully transformed into a service- and information-based economy and faced multiple severe recessions. And still the total amount of municipal solid waste—all the car tires and single-use plastics and used diapers left to congeal in a landfill in the heat of the sun—had increased by around 331 percent. And it wasn't just the result of population growth. As the amount of trash rose from 88.1 to 292.4 million tons, the amount produced per person reached 4.9 pounds per day, nearly double 1960 totals.[39] Green growth is an aesthetic, not an ethic. It's beholden to market valuation, not values.

This exclusive focus on market valuation has left us flailing when faced with the current scale of environmental damage. As Mathis Wackernagel and William Rees, the creators of the ecological footprint concept, put it in 1998, "The politically acceptable is ecologically disastrous while the ecologically necessary is politically impossible."[40]

A quarter century later, this situation has only worsened. Species are dying out faster than we can identify them. Our answer is to grow the economy. Kids' waning interaction with the natural world has been repeatedly linked with increased mental health issues.[41] Our answer is to grow the economy. We crash satellites into the moon and litter the oceans with microplastics. The sound from our deep-sea mining operations disrupts the life cycles of sea creatures hundreds of miles away. The light from our mega-cities does the same for land animals. Our answer is to grow the economy.

Something has gone horribly wrong with our species. We have found ways to detect slight changes in light at the far reaches of outer space but cannot see the harm we cause in our own backyard.

Waking Up

In August 2021, I woke to find myself covered in a thin layer of ash. Remnants of a fire approximately fifty miles west had drifted through the night and covered the Oregon forest where I slept. I was working as a youth backpacking guide and wondered if the kids on the trip would be scared or disturbed by this evidence of nearby wildfires, but, if they were, they didn't show it. They'd grown used to it the summer before, when smoke filled the air and produced an eerie, red-orange sun. For a few weeks, they'd been unable to play outside. This was just the new normal.

I don't know when I first entered into this so-called new normal. Was it when I saw the scale of national disasters like Hurricane Katrina in 2005? Or BP's Deepwater Horizon oil spill in 2010? Was it when disasters hit close to home, like in 2020 when half of the Northern California town where I'd previously worked on a wildfire crew burned? Or when fires threatened Flagstaff in 2019 or 2021 or twice in 2022? Or when heavy rains, no longer restrained by vegetation, flooded neighborhoods? Was it when weather became so strange that my vocabulary had to expand yearly to include terms like derecho, bomb cyclone, polar vortex, atmospheric flood, and nor'easter?

More likely, this became the new normal when society barely blinked. Katrina was one of the deadliest hurricanes in history, disproportionately killing and displacing both poor and Black residents in New Orleans. Huge percentages of these populations never returned and the rebuilt city became richer and whiter.[42] BP was fined $20 billion for its negligence in the Deepwater Horizon oil spill, one of the largest-ever environmental disasters. They wrote most of this off as a business expense, the bulk of the fine instead being paid by taxpayers. BP not only survived but is today more profitable than it's ever been.[43]

In that thousand-person Northern California town, hundreds who've called the place home for generations cannot afford or even find an insurer to protect their homes. Those buying mansions as second or third homes in the fire-prone foothills of Southern California do not face this problem. In Flagstaff, the city is working with the Army Corps of Engineers to reroute the fire-worsened flooding. Some of the few neighborhoods left affordable in Flagstaff are home to a high percentage of the city's Latino, Black, and Native population. Property values there are set to skyrocket when the flood protection project is completed. Rent and property taxes will do the same. It's one of the reasons the city agreed to it.

. . . .

Addictions start slowly. Over time, the effect of a beer or a glass of wine wears off. Two suffice for a while but soon prove inadequate. As the dopamine receptors in the brain grow accustomed to artificial highs, three are required. Then four. The body grows dependent. The mind grows dependent. No matter how much we've had, when the bartender asks if we've had enough, the only answer is one more.

As a society, we are addicted to more. More stuff, more houses, more money, more content. And because it's oil and gas we use to get more, we are addicted to oil and gas. As with other addictions, it is all too easy to blame this situation on individuals. Individuals who drive trucks and SUVs, who take helicopter tours and transcontinental flights, who seem to compulsively consume and fail to recycle, become subjects of scorn rather than sympathy. Activists deflate the tires of strangers' SUVs and throw soup on famous paintings, demanding that everyday people stop ignoring the changing climate.

Some see this thinking as flawed. They realize that a single transcontinental flight emits more greenhouse gases than most people in the Global South, the ones who are shouldering most of the burden of climate change, do in an entire year. But these system-minded people are far more concerned by the minimal scrutiny applied to the companies marketing the most gas-intensive vehicles and vacations. They realize that a growing number of people in younger generations feel like it's immoral to bring kids up in this world, believing that these kids would face a tortuous, if not entirely inhospitable, environment. But they see these efforts as misguided when politicians are actively entrenching and even subsidizing a future dominated by fossil fuels. In the eyes of those focused on systemic change, these systemic actors deserve society's undivided attention.

A false dichotomy emerges between blaming individuals and blaming the system, between advocating for individual action and advocating for collective action. It's true that the richest people in the world are responsible for a disproportionate amount of total greenhouse gas emissions, with the wealthiest 1 percent responsible for 11 percent of all housing emissions and 13 percent of total emissions. It's also true that the purchases of everyday people are funding this concentration of wealth.[44] It's true that just one hundred companies are responsible for 71 percent of all emissions produced between 1988 and 2017. It's also true that these emissions stem in large part from everyday people taking more flights, driving more SUVs, and investing more money in some of the most fossil-fuel-dependent companies.[45]

Individuals are not just consumers. These high-emitting companies—particularly the five largest of BP, Shell, ExxonMobil, Chevron, and Total, which have been shown to spend as much as $200 million each year to "control, delay, or block binding climate-motivated policy"—have an inordinate amount of power in lobbying elected officials. And everyday people are electing these officials.[46] All of US society is built in a way that makes people dependent on fossil fuels, thereby entrenching the emissions polluting the air, worsening disasters, and wiping out entire species and ecosystems. And the structure of US society is reinforced by the individual vacations and jobs and investments of everyday people who refuse to acknowledge this fact; who refuse to acknowledge the power they have to change any of it.

Growing up in the Midwest, I learned to stand up for what I believe in but also to not cause unnecessary tension. I developed a tendency of smiling or nodding or letting my face go blank when I didn't know what to say, traits that made me blend in to my surroundings. But, over time, this has become untenable. I know and am reminded daily that our way of life—the convenience, the individualized culture, the affluence, the opulence, the willingness to kick every problem we see down the road to the next town or generation—is erasing everything we hold dear.

I'm supposed to talk jovially to seemingly honest, well-meaning people who are reinforcing—even making a fortune off of—these problems and yet manage to walk through their days without the slightest moral turbulence. I used to be agreeable, likable, someone who wouldn't rock the boat. The boat has capsized.

Scientist and author Rachel Carson spurred a mass revolt against the harmful effects of DDT in her book *Silent Spring*. She wrote about the dangers in humans attempting to manufacture their environments. But she also wrote extensively, as one of her other books was called, about the importance of cultivating *The Sense of Wonder*. As she put it, "Those who dwell . . . among the beauties and mysteries of the earth are never alone or weary of life."[47]

Carson was right. There's something in watching the wintry waters of the Mississippi cut through layers of ice, something in listening to the rise and thrum of bats escaping a cave at dusk, something in the descending trill of a canyon wren and the incomprehensible stature of a redwood and the rugged power of a bison that leaves me still.

The chill of an Oregon alpine lake reminds me that I'm alive. The strength of a Mid-Atlantic summer storm reminds me that I'm small. The hypnotic glow of a Montana sunset reminds me that I'm part of something. When the horizon swallows the sun and darkness takes hold, when the leaves begin to rustle and my thoughts begin to race, I turn my gaze skyward. Something in the sight of stars—in the deserts of West Texas and the backwoods of Minnesota and my backyard in Flagstaff—provokes my sense of wonder in a way that city lights have failed to. I do not know why; I know only that I will do anything to protect it all.

· · · · · · ·

We have been slow to address our own impacts on nonhuman life, but the environment's impact on us is becoming harder to ignore. Fires, heat waves, droughts, flash floods, landslides, hurricanes, and more have increased in both regularity and intensity in recent years, touching every corner of the country.

The year 2021 was particularly devastating. The fire that sprinkled our camp with ash was preceded by a heat wave like the Pacific Northwest had never seen. Summer temperatures in Portland reached 117 degrees, a double-digit increase from the previous high. Tree roots fried beneath blistering pavement. Air conditioning became crucial for not simply staying cool but staying alive. Massive wildfires, which included Colorado's most destructive ever, continued to plague both human and nonhuman environments in the West, leading to landslides and potentially lethal air pollution.

In 2021, heat waves were both more severe and less predictable. Between 44 and 56 percent of the country experienced a drought. Four tropical storms battered the Southeast and East Coast, causing tremendous damage. Ten states, especially in the South and Midwest, saw their hottest-ever Decembers.[48]

This type of extreme and erratic weather is becoming more common. There were 193 tornadoes in December 2021 alone, nearly doubling the previous high set in 2002, although the extent of the link to climate change remains uncertain. Disasters, especially when so unexpected, can have deadly consequences, as was seen when the weather plunged below freezing in Texas and caused the electrical grid to fail in 2021. More than two hundred people died and millions were stranded without power or running water. Altogether, an annual report by the National Oceanic and Atmospheric Administration (NOAA) calculated twenty distinct billion-dollar climate and weather disasters during 2021. Directly responsible for at least 688 deaths, these events were estimated as causing $145 billion in damages, making it the third-costliest extreme weather year on record.[49]

Temperature increases are the underlying factor in most of these climatic changes. According to the National Aeronautics and Space Administration (NASA) and NOAA, nearly a quarter of the world's population experienced the hottest year in 2021 and the global average temperature was the sixth-hottest ever recorded. The Earth is heating up, this increased temperature is being driven largely by humans' burning of fossil fuels, and it's leading to a breakdown of both human and nonhuman environments. Neither our reliance on fossil fuels nor our development in some of the most vulnerable places has waned.

· · · · · · ·

In the West, cities and agriculture operations have grown large. San Francisco, Los Angeles, Denver, Phoenix, and San Diego are just some of the many places that would not have reached a fraction of their size without damming and diverting massive amounts of water from rivers hundreds of miles away. In order to support growing populations, ranching and agriculture require nearly 80 percent of the water taken from the Colorado River. The maintenance and incessant expansion of these industries degrade the soil, decrease biodiversity, and altogether diminish the long-term health of the environment. So, too, does the sprawl of development.

While General John Wesley Powell's 1870s warnings about large-scale farming and development in the West have been forgotten, Powell himself has not. Instead, one of the most prominent human-made lakes created by damming the mighty Colorado River now bears his name. In February 2022, Lake Powell, which provides large amounts of both water and electrical power to Arizona and California, and critical but far smaller amounts to Nevada and Mexico, had been reduced to less than 25 percent of capacity. In addition to the forty million residents in the region who are dependent on the river, people across the country are dependent on crops grown with the elaborate irrigation system permitted by the dams.[50] A single inordinately dry winter could spell disaster.

All this creates a cycle of unsustainability. In addition to flooding the ecosystem immediately upstream, dams disrupt the ecosystems downstream, particularly in areas like the Southwest. They alter predator-prey relationships, water temperature, and the dynamic qualities of a free-flowing river. But their biggest impact is allowing more human growth, which requires further water usage, which allows more growth, a cycle that seems determined to continue until the reservoirs runs dry.

Author and environmentalist Edward Abbey argued, "There is no shortage of water in the desert but exactly the right amount, a perfect ratio of water to rock, water to sand, insuring that wide free open, generous spacing among plants and animals, homes and towns and cities, which makes the arid West so different from any other part of the nation. There is no lack of water here unless you try to establish a city where no city should be."[51]

• • • • • • •

This amenity-driven migration seems to only be increasing.[52] Sparsely populated residential areas beyond cities and suburbs, what are often referred to as exurbs, are blurring the boundaries of where development ends and expansive natural spaces begin. People hungry for untamed space run into others hungry for the same thing.[53] Ironically, as geographer Bill Travis puts it, "The one force that might defeat the [western] region's success in the postindustrial economy is, simply, a loss of that regional charisma."[54] In other words, it becomes more difficult to maintain a conception of standing at the edge of a vast, uncharted frontier when surrounded by everything from interstates to RVs to flying drones to gift shops.

Nature is protected on the outskirts of Flagstaff, St. George, and Bozeman for the same reason it's protected in cities like Atlanta and New York: it's profitable. A log-cabin style mansion in the exurbs looks environmentally friendly until we consider the forest razed to make space for it. New LEED-certified apartment complexes, farm-to-table cafes, and electric bike shops seem to champion environmental values until we consider that these are just the tastes of a more affluent demographic. As this population moves in, existing residents are forced out. As long as everything built reinforces the current economic structure—as long as all the shops and homes and services as well as the roads, powerlines, piping, and mass transit systems that facilitate the heightened movement of workers, customers, and goods are built around turning a profit—environmentalism is a sham.

If what was ecologically sustainable guided every development effort, these cities—the entire country—would look very differently than they do. This is because government officials' main priority is attracting high-income visitors and new residents—along with the necessary food, water, energy, and infrastructure to support them—from across the country and world.

Richard Peet and Michael Watts, scientists in the growing field of political ecology, emphasize that this pattern of development happens because it exists within a political landscape that emphasizes short-term political and economic benefits above all else.[55] This economic rationale has profound environmental consequences, one of which is making the places we call home hotter, drier, and sometimes downright unlivable.

It is not too late to change, though the level of societal change needed is so unprecedented that it can feel that way. As Watson, the chair of the UN's 2019 biodiversity conference, explained, "Through 'transformative change,' nature can still be conserved, restored and used sustainably," with "transformative change" meaning "a fundamental, system-wide reorganization across technological, economic and social factors, including paradigms, goals and values."[56]

Put simply, we have to believe in something more than making a dollar.

Unaffordable Housing

"No moral code or ethical principle, no piece of scripture or holy teaching, can be summoned to defend what we have allowed our country to become." [1]
—Matthew Desmond, *Evicted*

IN JUNE 2018, A FENCE WENT UP around Arrowhead Mobile Home Park in Flagstaff. By that time, any remaining mobile homes were empty. Some of them were still adorned with the faces of their past residents, murals painted by local artists as a final protest. The residents themselves had lost their years-long fight to remain in their homes.

Most of the residents had originally moved in because a mobile home offered the cheapest type of shelter around, a common theme across the country. As of 2017, 70 percent of homes sold for less than $100,000 in the United States were categorized as mobile homes.[2] But this name is a misnomer. With cities vying to close these communities down and remaining parks unable to accommodate additional trailers, most trailers are old and not structurally sound for moving at all. In Arizona, it is illegal to move trailers constructed before 1977, a fact that resulted in almost every one of the fifty households at Arrowhead being forced to leave their trailer—their home—behind.

Many of the families at Arrowhead had immigrated to the United States from Mexico decades before. They had carved out lives in Flagstaff, working jobs in the service industry—at hotels and restaurants and stores—that were critical to the town's tourism-driven economy. As Jorge Garza, a master's student at NAU at that time, observed, these residents had formed a tight-knit community at Arrowhead. It was common to leave doors unlocked and for residents to rely on each other for repairs and child care. Kids played together and went to school together. For many, it was the only home they'd ever known.[3]

Eviction shattered these families' lives. Like most mobile home residents across the country, they were at the mercy of the landowner. When the land was sold to Kings House, a real estate developer with plans to build student housing complexes, Arrowhead residents were given six months to vacate the land. This was the minimum amount of notice required by Arizona law and far from what was adequate to upend their lives. As Garza wrote,

> *Residents continually spoke of losing sleep, fits of anger, family discord, illness, anxiety, and feelings of weakness throughout the experience of displacement. Many had to walk away from organizing, reading mail, or connecting with their families. They could not participate in any way with the reality of losing their homes because it was detrimental to their mental health. One resident said displacement had "aged" them and made them lose faith in themselves and in the community.*[4]

More than four years later, these residents are long gone from this land. While many are dispersed across Flagstaff, others have left the area entirely. Some who'd come to the United States seeking greater stability and freedom have returned to Mexico. The land that once held this community remains a vacant lot.

The former Arrowhead residents don't need to be told that housing is being auctioned off at a global scale. They don't need to be told that residents looking for housing options are being pitted against people from metropolitan areas with far higher income pools. They are already forced to spend more of their income to simply pay for a roof overhead. They know that this means less to spend on savings, education, starting a business, spending in the community, or any other pursuits because they are experiencing all this firsthand.

Though perhaps not facing an imminent threat of eviction, millions of people across the country can see similarities between their own situation and that of former Arrowhead residents. They don't need an assessment of the damage that comes from facing fast-rising rent or property taxes, perhaps struggling to find any housing at all; they're living it. Similarly, they don't need subsidies or promises from representatives who listen only long enough to gain a vote; their trust has worn thin. They want to know how we got into this mess. More important, they want to know real, tangible ways to get out.

But many people have come to very different conclusions about the current situation. They may see the rise in short-term rentals in Flagstaff, second homes in St. George, and general growth in Bozeman as part of a larger pattern. They don't dispute the rampant construction of luxury-priced housing or the notion that housing has become dominated by people who see it as nothing more than a way to turn a profit. They may even acknowledge that this focus on maximizing return on investment instead of producing stable homes is undermining our communities. But rather than asking how we can change any of this, they ask why they should care. Or more pointedly, if they have the money, why shouldn't they go out and buy a second home in one of these places right now?

I know because they've said so. They've told me that they envy Scott Shatford's story of making $6,500 per month with less than twenty hours of total work. They've told me that they want to make a passive income, to make their money work for them. In other words, they want to make a lot of money by doing a negligible amount of work, too. There are many words thrown about for people who don't want to work, who don't make a meaningful contribution to their community or society more generally. They're called lazy, reprobates, and leeches. But if they start with a lot of money and actively restrict other people's access to something as fundamental as housing, they're called investors, entrepreneurs, and sometimes even philanthropists.

I've ruined perfectly good conversations by pointing this out, by suggesting that we should change how we think about housing. It hasn't always made me fun at parties. I've continued because, for every conversation in which someone mentions their vacation rental or boasts of rising property value, I've had several others in which people wonder if there's a place for them. In tourism towns, it's often said half-jokingly that people "either have a second home or a second job." It seems we're all in that town now.

Beyond Boom and Bust

We are taught to think in binaries. *The market is booming or busting. The world is made up of haves and have-nots. We are profiting or losing.* But COVID has further revealed the cracks in this simplistic thinking. A July 2022 article in the *New York Times* profiled the town of Sun Valley, Idaho, explaining how an influx of wealth made housing increasingly unaffordable for existing residents. The Hunger Coalition, the group operating the food bank in nearby Bellevue, had seen demand skyrocket from just two years ago, from roughly "200 families each week to nearly 500 with the number still climbing." Brooke Pace McKenna, a leader at the Hunger Coalition, said, "More and more, we are seeing the teachers, the policemen, the fire department."[5] It's whoever actually lives and works there.

The housing boom that began in 2020 would seem to benefit a lot of people. City and state governments, buoyed by a huge flow of federal assistance and an influx of high-income, high-spending residents, would be obvious beneficiaries. Except that a December 2020 report from the Brookings Institute noted city and state governments across the country had continued cutting large numbers of jobs.[6]

Those buying a home, who gained the security of homeownership and could someday make a windfall from reselling their new house, would also seem to gain. Except that July 2021 calculations from the Center for Housing and Policy at the Federal Reserve Bank of Atlanta show the typical median-income homebuyer was paying a thirteen-year high of 32.1 percent of income on housing.[7] In other words, new homebuyers have been increasingly likely to meet HUD's definition of housing-cost burdened.

Of course, real estate companies would have appreciated the boom, until the number of people buying houses dropped in 2022. And those selling their homes benefited immensely, just as long as they could find somewhere else to live. For the vast majority looking to remain in a place, however, faced with rising rents or home prices or property taxes, losing the identity they'd long-attached to their home, there is no question of what to call it. This is a bust.

They face a dwindling and increasingly desperate set of choices. In order to cover the ballooning property tax, a retired couple on a fixed income forgo badly needed medical check-ups and prescriptions. Unable to afford housing elsewhere, a young mother stays in an abusive relationship. Seeking a way out of expensive and unstable rentals in a dangerous neighborhood, a couple with two kids puts half their monthly income toward a mortgage. With the walls closing in, a resident who's called the town home for years or decades or generations—who plays in a local band, who volunteers at the food bank, who is planning to start a family—moves to a new city.

The pattern repeats across the country. The housing system becomes increasingly oriented around profit, with those who benefit—or believe that they will benefit—critiquing those who suffer. Those who benefit from the boom become more skilled at obscuring their role in the concurrent bust. Government officials claim their hands are tied by the state or by the market or by voters. Besides, aren't they doing enough on housing already? Investors, developers, and landlords are just following the market. Wouldn't they be fools to not extract every possible dollar out of a house? Homeowners who will someday reap the benefit of staggering price increases worked hard to afford their investment. Why shouldn't they get what's rightfully theirs?

The beneficiaries of housing booms cling to these justifications as their communities flail. As government officials defend their market-oriented fixes to the growing unaffordability of housing, evictions rise. As real estate agents revel in the windfall of growing market demand, the unsheltered population grows. As homeowners vote down funding for affordable housing projects—or any multiunit housing projects—the city sprawls further outward.

Eventually, the lead server at the neighborhood café leaves town. Then a beloved teacher. Then the best local handyman. As powerful voices across the city shout their allegiance to the market, echoing the post-Enlightenment mantra that this is "the best of all possible worlds," many of those who once felt insulated from the unaffordability of housing have begun to feel the effects. They've seen store prices go up. They've felt their neighborhoods growing fragile, hollow, static. As they listen to the stories of a friend or daughter or employee struggling to make ends meet, they start to question whether the rising tide of economic growth actually lifts all boats and fortunes. They start to wonder if this logic is actually just causing more people to drown.

Despite this growing realization, government officials routinely argue that housing affordability has been a problem for a long time. Even if it's worsened in recent years, they challenge, "What can we do?" Indeed, Friedrich Engels termed the deterioration and unaffordability of working-class housing "the housing question" nearly 150 years ago.[8]

But the lengthy history of this struggle should give us more resolve to address it, not less. It should force us to confront the economic logic that connects the issues of the past with the ones we face today. And this economic logic is seldom clearer than in moments of crisis.

· · · · · · ·

Early on in the COVID-19 pandemic, as millions lost their jobs or saw their incomes and savings dwindle, government officials feared that failing to protect housing would plunge the national economy into a deep, prolonged depression. To prevent a tsunami of evictions and foreclosures, four major federal policies were implemented on a temporary, emergency basis including more robust unemployment payments, increased rental and mortgage assistance, an eviction moratorium, and record low interest rates.

As of October 5, 2021, COVID was killing approximately 1,259 people per day, a rate that made it the year's third-leading cause of death.[9] In terms of lives lost, every fifty-seven hours was another 9/11. Meanwhile, the protections initially deemed warranted by COVID's effects—additional unemployment, rental, and mortgage assistance—had long since expired. Many politicians and business leaders blamed these policies, which they said should have been less generous and expired sooner, for spurring average consumers to spend more money and contributing to inflation.

But they said little about the fact that rock-bottom interest rates did not budge for another six months. During this time, everything continued to be extraordinarily cheap for those with the resources. With the market low, the wealthiest segment of the country bought commercial and previously residential properties, grew their businesses, and invested heavily in the stock market, all with the express purpose of making a fortune when the market was high. They hoped that the price of everything would rise dramatically. They were counting on inflation.

Comparing the eviction moratorium and interest rate cuts demonstrates the federal government's priorities. The moratorium was only for those who met strict income and eligibility requirements and did not forgive a cent of unpaid rent. Additionally, it didn't stop landlords from refusing to renew leases, attaching fees or penalties, or raising the price on tenants. In other words, it was narrowly applied, strictly enforced, and temporary. The low interest rate was intended for any business or individual seeking to make large purchases, such as buying a home. In other words, it was broadly applied, accessible to anyone with sufficient funds, and would continue indefinitely.

Far from the narrative of rental prices dropping dramatically as people left urban areas during pandemic times, the market kept going up. Data taken from real estate site Zillow and analyzed by the *Guardian* showed that 82 of the 101 largest US cities saw rents increase at least 5 percent from February 2020 to June 2021. Just seven had decreased.[10]

An October 2021 report from JPMorgan Chase offered one potential reason for this. The data showed that landlords lost money initially in March and April of 2020 when tenants were unable to make payments but largely made that up by the summer of 2020 through back paid rents and, crucially, by delaying payments themselves. Landlords enrolled in government programs like mortgage forbearance and delayed renovations and repairs, all expenses that would eventually come due.[11]

Renters across the country have faced an uncertain future. Between these increased costs and the end of the eviction moratorium, the continued globalization of housing seen during COVID forced them to compete with tourists, second homeowners, high-salaried remote workers, and investors. If they were part of the 15 percent of renters behind on payments—double the rate before COVID—any unpaid rent carried as debt affected their credit score.[12] They may have lost their jobs when the industry collapsed or been hospitalized with COVID themselves, but the rent was still due on the first of the month. Missing a payment made it more difficult for these people to afford future rent or consider the prospect of homeownership.

· · · · · · ·

Residents in cities and towns have amplified the pressure on public officials to do something about the unaffordability of housing. As a result, government officials have been forced to realize that failure to act will result in workers moving away, in-migration slowing, or perhaps even being voted out of office. Typically, however, these realizations come about only after affordable housing has become downright unattainable. Many of the measures undertaken are designed to have little chance of changing the factors making housing unaffordable in the first place.

Flagstaff offers a prime example. In December 2020, Devonna McLaughlin, the CEO of Housing Solutions of Northern Arizona, brought a resolution before the city council to declare a housing emergency. The resolution spurred the city to formally acknowledge the severity of the situation. When the city council adopted the measure, they tasked the housing commission with meeting and developing strategies for making housing more affordable.

Over the course of the next year, the commission updated a ten-year housing plan that detailed the various reasons housing is unaffordable and presented an extensive wish list to the public for feedback. This wish list highlighted incentives meant to encourage the private market to build more affordable developments and a large bond measure, to be voted on in November 2022, allowing money to be collected over the course of 2023 if the measure passed.[13]

Meanwhile, according to real estate analysis by Redfin, the November 2021 median sale price of a house in Flagstaff had risen to $570,500, up 24.6 percent from a year prior.[14] Rental rates remained exorbitant. The emergency declaration and any subsequent action had come far too late for the dozens of residents in the Arrowhead Mobile Home Community who had been forced from their homes to make room for a vacant lot. As city officials applauded their apparent emergency efforts, I wondered how many more people had been evicted from their homes or forced from the area entirely.

The fault does not rest with city officials alone. A November 2021 report by Arizona State University's Morrison Institute for Public Policy supported the argument that state laws have disrupted affordable housing efforts, restricting municipal changes to property tax, short-term rental, and zoning laws.[15]

But these excuses in Flagstaff are not so different from those offered by officials in St. George related to the rising market valuation of building and land or by officials in Bozeman related to growth. City officials in each of these three places consistently argue that the biggest issues are those in which their hands are tied. The overwhelming theme is that housing could be affordable if only for one thing outside that city official's control.

This is a trend. Although there are many ways in which each of these cities is restricted from carrying out all desired policies, many ways in which state and federal law require changes, there are also many ways in which their governments can act but choose not to on the basis of economic incentive. They choose not to create policies that challenge state law for fear of invoking a lawsuit. They choose to promote tourism that actively feeds the short-term rental population. They choose to bring in high-income remote workers who force existing residents to compete with Silicon Valley or Wall Street salaries.

City officials—like county, state, and federal officials—do all this because they are in thrall to the market. When turning a profit is the only priority, why would a developer build a $200,000 house for a couple making $70,000 a year when he could instead build a $500,000 house for a remote worker making $140,000 a year? Why would a landlord rent a unit for $600 per month to someone who worked in the tourism industry when she could instead rent it to a tourist for $100 per night?

But people need housing like they need healthcare like they need food. If the housing market is driven by external demand and the cheapest adequate shelter for locals is half their monthly income, they'll be forced to pay it. If the healthcare market is very near a monopoly and life-saving insulin rises 300 percent from one year to the next, someone with diabetes has no choice but to pay it. If the grocery market doesn't see an impoverished area as profitable enough for a store, local residents will likely be forced to buy less nutritious and more expensive food from the gas station. The market is built around turning a profit, not meeting needs.

This has dire consequences. In housing, every effort to increase affordability is first viewed through a lens of how to keep developers and homeowners happy. Officials make deals with developers, fast-tracking the approval of luxury condos so long as 10 percent are listed at what's considered the fair market rate for those who make 80 to 100 percent of the area median income. They then feign surprise when this fails to keep up with the affordable housing needs of their population, where one-third to one-half of residents are burdened by ever-rising market rates. And, knowing the money they can make catering to the increasing external demand, many developers cease to view these government incentives to house locals as worth it.

Instead, developers do not build affordable housing for locals but investment properties for investors, weekend retreats for nonprimary homeowners, and, increasingly, large homes and luxury condos for people able to work remotely and not tied to the local labor market. Housing is being used to generate profit and lodge short-term visitors while residents struggle to find affordable—sometimes any—housing.

Echoes of History

This story is not new. The excuses made in Flagstaff are not so different than those made by other cities dealing with an influx of new visitors. They are not so different from the way in which government at all levels in the United States has historically enabled wealthy, outside settlers to move in, a fact that has consistently had the worst effect on non-White people. Government has perpetually maintained this stance, even as it forced Native peoples from their land and prevented most non-Whites from claiming land offered through the Homestead Act of 1862.[16]

This preferential treatment for both Whiteness and wealth remained through the twentieth century as government prevented all non-White races from accessing the Federal Housing Administration's homeownership subsidies, spurring massive urban disinvestment in majority non-White areas followed by massive reinvestment to bring back more affluent, overwhelmingly White residents.[17] And it was perhaps most visible during the Great Recession when cause and effect were collapsed into a short window of time.

Legislators and media put out no call to action when the Center for Responsible Lending proclaimed in 2006 that the pervasiveness of subprime mortgages was set to wipe out a generation of Black wealth.[18] The government only responded when the stock market crashed in 2008 and millions more were unable to pay for their mortgages, rents, or other goods and services. It then propped up the very same companies responsible for the dismantling of the economy and the largest loss of non-White wealth in history. There was no eviction moratorium. Rather than going to jail, the executives of the banks most instrumental to the crash took home bonuses. The goal was not to rescue people; the goal was to rescue the economy and restore it almost precisely as before: driven by scarcity and the whims of the wealthy.

Without real and lasting intervention, all this repeats itself. During the Great Recession, the housing market's widespread institution of subprime mortgages resulted in a landslide of foreclosures when mortgage rates rose and millions of people were unable to pay. HUD sold hundreds of thousands of these foreclosed homes to private equity firms, particularly benefiting the Blackstone Group.[19] Blackstone bought up and repaired these and thousands more homes under the name Invitation Homes, becoming the largest owner of single-family rental properties in the country.

After selling its stake for a $7 billion profit in 2019, Blackstone purchased Home Partners of America and its seventeen thousand single-family homes in the two following years.[20] Blackstone's profits from the sale of its homes in 2019, many of which came from HUD originally, could have funded all of HUD's efforts to ensure fair housing and equal opportunity in 2022. And for forty-two years after.[21]

These profits are a small sum of Blackstone's annual gains. Blackstone owns American Campus Communities, which builds large housing complexes on the boundaries of college campuses such as NAU in Flagstaff and MSU in Bozeman. It's owned thousands of Hilton hotels and iconic office buildings such as Chicago's Willis Tower. It's even had control of the pensions of public employees throughout California.

Blackstone promotes its investments as important efforts to address low housing supply, growing inequality, and environmental degradation, but its primary goal is not a secret. As CEO and cofounder Steve Schwartzman said in 2015, "We have a performance record that is . . . pretty much in a league of our own, we've compounded [returns of] around 18% after fees."[22] Between 2007 and 2015, Blackstone quadrupled its assets and planned to double them again by 2023. This growth had made Schwartzman worth around $11.6 billion in 2015, the thirty-eighth richest person in the country at the time according to *Forbes*.[23]

With an estimated net worth of $27.8 billion in 2023, Schwartzman is just one of many investors on *Forbes*'s annual list of billionaires.[24] In the same way, although Blackstone is one of the most prominent benefi-ciaries of increased home buying during the pandemic, it is not alone. A July 2021 report from Redfin shows that the number of properties purchased by an investor, defined as "any institution or business that purchases residential real estate," hit a record high in the second quarter of 2021.

The percentage of homes purchased by investors now hovers around 15.9 percent, down slightly from the highwater 16.1 percent prepandemic level but showing the mark of the steady influx of investors in home buy-ing over the course of the last two decades. In the same quarter of 2000, less than 6 percent of homes were bought by investors.[25] The nation's fastest-growing metropolitan areas, cities like Atlanta and Phoenix and Miami, are some of the hardest hit, with investors buying at least one of every four homes sold in the first quarter of 2022.[26]

While these are partially based upon multiunit properties, both single-family homes and condos are becoming more popular purchases for investors. Additionally, while the evidence shows that investors have increased their purchases of high-priced properties, it is low-priced prop-erties that they are especially after. Investors purchased 20.8 percent of all low-priced properties sold in the first quarter of 2021.[27] Many of these low-priced properties are being put toward what's sometimes billed as a new solution to unaffordable housing: rent-to-own contracts.

These contracts are primarily split between lease-option, which offer renters the chance to buy the house at the end of their lease, and lease-purchase, which typically require renters to buy, usually at an agreed-upon price. Offering an apparent path to homeownership, renting to own has attracted a lot of attention, even being heralded as a creative solution to housing issues by celebrities such as Jay-Z and Will Smith. But massive investments by private equity firms like Blackstone signal that potential homeowners might want to study the contracts carefully.

In some contracts, the home sale price is agreed upon beforehand. In many cases, it isn't. Some contracts stipulate that monthly rent paid goes toward a down payment. In others, it's lost. Some stipulate that the home-owner will provide maintenance on the property until the renter takes over. In others, the renter is responsible. Overwhelmingly, the monthly rental price is higher than rent for a comparable unit.

Buy-to-rent housing has produced rent-to-buy housing. But, with the profit incentive still looming large, that does not mean it's any more affordable.

Meanwhile, demand for nonprimary homes had risen 177.9 percent from April 2020 to April 2021, vastly outpacing the 77.8 percent seen for primary homes.[28] The Federal Housing Finance agency announced in January 2022 that it would increase upfront fees for many high-balance or second home loans starting in April. Acting Director Sandra L. Thompson said this would allow government housing loan agencies "to better achieve their mission of facilitating equitable and sustainable access to homeownership."[29] In addition to the fact that this appears two years late for the present crisis, many people looking for second homes can secure private loans, if they need loans at all.

Just how many of these new second homes ended up being listed as short-term rentals is unknown. But a February 2021 report by Airbnb, showing that new hosts had taken in $1 billion in the year since the first COVID lockdowns were initiated, suggests this number is not insignificant.[30] When housing is bought up by nonresidents, government officials frequently meet these findings with surprise, as if the market has gone awry. In reality, the market has done exactly what it was designed to do: it turned a profit.

Beyond Individualism

Although many financially secure homeowners may sympathize with those who struggle to afford housing, they also can't help but breathe a sigh of relief that they got in at the right time. Those who didn't buy homes soon retreat to places they can afford. But what they call a retreat is perceived by existing residents as a sort of invasion.

All this has had the cumulative effect of homogenizing neighborhoods. As sociologist Doug Massey's research shows, an average poor family in 1970 lived in areas of 14 percent poverty. By 1990, that number was 28 percent. Rich households have gotten richer and poor households have gotten poorer, but the same thing has also happened to neighborhoods. And, with that, access to good schools, jobs, medical facilities, parks, trails, counselors, lawyers, stores, food, transportation, and houses has become increasingly dependent on one's wealth.[31]

As William Brune, the tourism official in Flagstaff stated, "If you can't afford to live here, you can't afford to be working here."[32] The upshot for places like Flagstaff, which are already bound by either political boundaries like neighboring cities or Native reservations or geographic boundaries like forests or mountains—places with nowhere else to go—is that people move away from the region entirely.

These people are left in a curious situation. They know that it's their jobs, in construction and food service and hospitality, that keep the community going. And yet, their wages frequently fall far short of allowing them to remain in the community. As they commute farther and farther to work, they begin to resent the tourists and remote workers and investors who marvel at the ornate building designs with no sign of the builders, who congregate in the beautiful parks with no trace of the landscapers, who move from shops to stores to markets that are staffed by a smaller and increasingly transient staff. They wonder if these visitors and newcomers who now occupy the place they once called home prefer it that way. An attractive collection of bricks and latchkeys. A beautiful façade propped up by ghosts.

In the third quarter of 2021, the national median home price rose beyond $400,000 for the first time ever.[33] Those struggling to make ends meet did not come anywhere near the means needed for a downpayment on a house.

Just one year later, as the median price bordered $480,000, the number of people left out has only grown. In this context, many resort to alternatives such as variable-rate mortgages that start low and then rise dramatically over the coming years. Commonplace in the early 2000s due to deregulated housing and banking industries that insisted on market growth at all costs, banks used these variable-rate, or subprime, mortgages to target the most vulnerable populations, purposely misleading people into believing that there was little risk. But these mortgages were incredibly risky, if not outright doomed. And the bankers knew it.

In 2007 and 2008, the higher mortgage rates kicked in for millions. Inevitably, they fell behind on their monthly payments and defaulted en masse. The inflated price of housing dropped out and the stock market crashed. The global economy entered a tailspin, affecting everything from retirement accounts to business stability to the price of housing to credit access. As for the banks themselves, they received a massive taxpayer-funded bailout. They have little incentive for operating any differently fifteen years later.

All this is not to say that a housing crash is imminent, though many people—especially renters in their twenties and thirties who've been priced out of the possibility of homeownership—are praying for that to be the case. It is instead to say that, just as stock prices may now rise during a recession and executives are likely to receive large bonuses from board members and shareholders while laying off thousands of employees, we may not recognize a housing crash because housing has become divorced from actually housing people. Every home is instead investment material, an asset, mere real estate.

The market is "crashing" or has "crashed" for millions and millions of people already. The fact that politicians and media outlets and developers and homeowners across the country view these stories as separate from their own shows that, barely more than a decade on from the last housing crash, the housing system—like the economy as a whole—remains unchanged.

Catching Up

Time and again, city officials in Flagstaff, St. George, and Bozeman articulated a belief that the housing market would self-correct and that it simply had not yet had time to do so. They referred to their city's affordable housing issue as a "supply and demand" issue, wherein housing costs are rising simply because demand outpaces supply. The problem, they argued, was low inventory, to be solved by building more homes.

This is a common justification. As Bill Travis wrote, additional building is frequently "passed off as simply 'catching up.'"[34]

Despite advocating for more development, there seemed to be little interest on the part of elected officials in what was actually being built. Nobody seemed to question whether efforts to increase construction and development were simply inducing more demand for nonlocals able to pay far more than locals. A fall 2016 article in Flagstaff's local newspaper, the *Arizona Daily Sun*, for instance, listed thirteen ongoing residential and hotel projects that would add just shy of six thousand total units in the city.[35] That is nearly one-fifth of all 31,369 housing units that now exist within the city.[36]

And yet, in 2020, after all these units were built, Flagstaff officials continually cited a housing shortage as a fundamental reason for high prices. How many units would it take to catch up? They estimated another six thousand. The housing shortage in Flagstaff, like that throughout the country, is a manufactured shortage. Scarcity is profitable.

Where these homes went is not a mystery. SmartAsset, which describes itself as "an online destination for consumer-focused financial information and advice," listed Flagstaff as the fifth-best secondary home market in the country in 2021, citing that 28.21 percent of all 2019 mortgages there had been for second homes.[37] A percentage of these are then offered up as short-term rentals.

Meanwhile, Northern Arizona University (NAU), like Montana State University (MSU) in Bozeman, has seen a major influx of students in the last fifteen years. Between the fall of 2008 and the fall of 2018, the number of students erupted from 14,766 to 23,140, a nearly 57 percent jump.[38] Like many universities across the country, efforts to grow enrollment began as a means of making up for diminished state contributions in the aftermath of the Great Recession. Though the crisis passed, the state's contributions to the higher education budget never returned to prerecession size, and the growth never stopped.

Large-scale student housing complexes built to accommodate this growth were referred to by multiple interviewees as "monstrosities." They argued that the four-, five-, and six-story buildings worsen congestion, alter existing character, and block the view of the San Francisco Peaks. And these officials were not the only critics. Around town, it's not uncommon to see bumper stickers stating "Flagstaff: A Suburb of NAU."

Finally, Flagstaff has seen enormous growth, especially among people able to work remotely. Many officials in cities throughout the intermountain West realize that they "have an incredibly tasty product," as St. George tourism official John Feely put it, in terms of outdoor amenities.[39] Similarly, officials in larger cities seek to attract individuals through more jobs, events, restaurants, bike trails, coffee shops, and an endless list of things that compound with the constant growth of the population. The city itself is for sale. And no city has any intention of ceasing to market itself as long as there is a buyer, no matter what this does to affordable housing efforts.

In a select few places across the country, failure to build may really be the biggest reason for housing unaffordability. In the San Francisco metropolitan area, for instance, the 2023 population remains almost unchanged from 25 years before. This signals that new residents working for high salaries in the booming tech industry have largely displaced low-income residents.

In most places, however—especially a town like Flagstaff—the problem is not low housing supply. Rather, the problem is that there is an insatiable demand, in many cases driven by those who aren't actually full-time residents in these places. O. M. Kerney wrote about this in his 2007 study of workforce housing in the West, with Flagstaff one of his three case study cities. As he stated, "Why the development community would build modestly priced housing for the relatively modest local wage earners when they can build homes that cater to a national audience of homebuyers with almost unlimited earning (and spending) potential is unclear."[40]

The View from Flagstaff

Kerney was a master's student at NAU when he wrote that. Twelve years later, I experienced all this firsthand. I saw new housing complexes devoted to the growing undergraduate population at NAU. I saw the glut of mansions masquerading as cabins in the woods. And I saw the sea of tourists milling about downtown, many of whom would stay in potential homes that had instead been converted into short-term rentals, potential homes instead owned by investors and nonresidents.

Like a lot of incoming residents, I had moved to Flagstaff as a result of a connection to NAU, in my case to begin a master's program in geography. A teaching assistantship had offered the prospect of making ends meet without taking on further debt. This was only possible with three roommates and devoting 60 percent of my monthly income to housing expenses, but I felt lucky. After all, the married couple we were renting from was on a research sabbatical for the year and could have easily charged more or rented their home out as a short-term rental. That they didn't was an individual decision, a small act of kindness in an otherwise ruthless housing landscape. But it made all the difference in the world to us.

In the three years since, my three roommates have left town. So have dozens of other friends and acquaintances. They left Flagstaff for many reasons ranging from the desire to be closer to family to seeking better job opportunities, but the feeling that the town was too beholden to the dollars of tourists and influence of developers was high on the list. Many of them talk about missing the small-town feel and the sense they were part of a community. They talk about missing little things like their favorite breakfast burrito or their favorite brewery, missing the access to hiking trails and the way the high-elevation night sky seemed to swallow them up.

Though it's hard to continually say goodbye to so many people, there are many reasons why I stayed. I love living in a mountain town. I feel most at home when I'm backpacking through the woods and most like myself when I'm around others who understand this feeling. But the biggest reason I'm still here is much more straightforward: after a decade of moving from place to place, I was just desperate to find somewhere I could call home. The more housing costs increase and the more people leave town, the less I feel like I've found that. The less I feel like I'll ever find it.

The unaffordability of the housing market, like the precarity of the economy more generally, turns choices of where to live and what to do for work into existential ones. The only path to stability seems to be by treating the world as a zero-sum game in which one's gains come at another's expense. Dog eat dog.

For some, including many investors and the ultrawealthy, this quickly becomes more than simply an effort to find stability, instead being usurped by the all-encompassing goal of accumulating wealth. They claim that their charitable donation or board membership or philanthropic foundation is not just a tax break or ego boost but a way of truly changing things. A growing number claim that they'll really be able to change things when they die rich, with their wealth going toward causes that help the poorest.

This notion of helping is built upon the flawed idea that their money and prestige have put them in the best position to determine what others need. Dr. Lilla Watson, an Aboriginal Australian scholar and activist, refuted this belief at the 1985 United Nations Decade for Women Conference, articulating a commonly held but seldom-respected attitude from marginalized people across the globe. As she put it, "If you have come here to help me, you are wasting your time. But if you have come because your liberation is bound up with mine, then let us work together."[41] Nearly forty years later, the most affluent continue to be lauded—and given huge tax breaks—for their commitment to helping. And nowhere is the harm of this worldview clearer than the dysfunction and inequality of the global economy.

In the interim between Kerney's 2007 study and my 2021 graduation from NAU, the housing market imploded once and the economy as a whole cratered twice. With no fundamental reforms to how the economy operates, my generation, like the one that follows, knows that the development community has no intention to "build modestly priced housing for the relatively modest local wage earners." Expecting the housing market to self-correct its appeal to higher-spending populations is utterly antithetical to its profit-oriented design.

• • • • • • •

Commentators nationwide who argue that we need to build more housing are not wrong. Building has been forestalled by exclusionary zoning laws that demand mandatory lot sizes and restrict multiunit properties, arduous permitting systems which can take years to navigate and ensure only the largest developers can gain access, and a continual ceding of public regulatory authority to private interests. This is particularly true in the large cities—San Francisco, New York, and DC chief among them—in which these commentators tend to reside.

But the fact is that housing has not been built because it has not been viewed as profitable. A litany of groups including developers, investors, homeowners, and politicians has had an entrenched interest in ensuring that the price of housing remains high and keeps getting higher. While the interests of these groups sometimes conflict, each of them maintains a perpetual seat at the table. They are often the only ones.

When housing has been built, it's overwhelmingly been used to house new, higher-income residents, provide investment opportunities for individuals and private equity firms, and lodge tourists. Time and time again, we have seen that more housing does not equate to more affordable housing. We've seen that more housing does not equate to more homes.

The data bears this out. Months of supply—the number of months it would take for all available homes to sell based on current trends—is commonly used as a metric for gauging the health of the real estate market. According to Redfin, four to five months is considered average, with less inventory typically increasing prices and more typically causing a decrease.[42]

For new homes, Federal Reserve data did indeed show a drop below four months of supply for the five-month period between June 2020 and October 2020. But this was the first time that had happened in seventeen years, and the supply has not dropped below that point since. In November 2021, there were 6.5 months of new house inventory available.[43]

The same is true when it comes to apartments. Although updating zoning codes is necessary to accommodate more units, this tends to especially benefit childless adults. As Matt Lewis, a spokesperson for California YIMBY (Yes In My Backyard), said, "Yes, there's been a build baby build' attitude because we're so far behind, but there are big asterisks and caveats to that. If you just do zoning, you will end up with a whole lot of one- and two-bedrooms."[44]

The market favors those who will pay more. Investors and those who proclaim building as a panacea for all housing ills are no longer able to argue that investors have a small impact on housing. This is particularly true in areas with the biggest concerns about affordability. As Laura Brenner, president and CEO of the Greater Port of Cincinnati Development Authority, testified before the US Senate in August 2022, "We've been told by institutional investors that they only own about 1 percent of single-family homes; however . . . this could mean 50 percent of houses on a single street. When the geographical impact is so concentrated, it has a game-changing impact on what it means to live in that neighborhood."[45] The impact is even larger when factoring in smaller investors, those with fewer than one hundred properties. Without any firm rules requiring residency or maximum income amounts for occupants, additional housing built is likely to cater to higher-income people.

This is nothing new. Although investors' role has heightened in recent years, developers have been opting to build fewer affordable homes for decades. A May 2021 report prepared by governmental housing loan agency Freddie Mac showed that both the percent and number of entry-level, or starter, single-family homes have fallen to their lowest levels in at least the past half-century. As households have gotten smaller, houses themselves have gotten larger. In 1981, around 39 percent of new homes built were less than fourteen hundred square feet. By 2001, less than 15 percent achieved that standard. In 2021, only around 5 percent did.[46]

Simply incentivizing the market to build more homes will likely do little to alter the current $440,000 price tag of homeownership. Though seldom acknowledged, this is partially by design. Of all the interviews I conducted, the only person who touched on this issue was Devonna McLaughlin, the CEO of Housing Solutions of Northern Arizona. She explained:

I mean, I think we all agree that we don't want our markets to crash either, right? Like when you're talking about affordable housing, it's crazy, but if we went to a place where housing prices decreased by 25 percent, that would create a whole different world of hurt problems. So, from . . . the real estate perspective, steady and appreciating prices are good. It creates buyers and sellers and stability in the market.[47]

Profits fall when supply outpaces demand or fixed costs are too great.[48] In other words, in small cities with a $350,000 median home price, building one hundred new homes and selling them at $200,000 would destroy the exaggerated return on investment enjoyed throughout the entire industry. Politicians know this when they create years-long committees to address so-called housing emergencies. Developers know this when they advocate building as a silver bullet for making housing affordable. Homeowners know this when they oppose affordable housing in their neighborhoods. They may say that they want others to have affordable housing, but their commitment stops when it affects their campaigns or bottom lines or retirement plans. In their eyes, caring about other people is a bad investment.

The Economy Reigns Supreme

Overwhelmingly in Flagstaff, St. George, and Bozeman, it was nongovernmental planners and housing officials who voiced the most major objections to the unaffordability of housing. On the surface, this makes sense. It's far easier to draw attention to an issue that one is not responsible for fixing. It also shows a deference to growth and market forces among many government officials that fails to inspire hope that these problems will be addressed.

Rachel Grant, a city councilmember in Flagstaff, mused about the cyclical, short-term thinking around housing, "We're like this little hamster."[49] Government officials remain beholden to half-measures and repeat empty promises. Trapped with the same constraints—return on investments and economic growth—they cannot come up with a single new idea. They speak on behalf of economic growth no matter the cost to the health, happiness, and stability of the community they claim to represent.

Against this backdrop, people are setting up tents on sidewalks in Portland and squatting in abandoned houses in New York. They are sleeping in trees in Atlanta and chaining themselves to foreclosed homes in Detroit. They live in converted vans in forests outside mountain towns and under bridges in river towns. Increasingly, in cities ranging from Spokane, Washington, to Evansville, Indiana, they are being purposefully arrested in order to get off the streets. People make a home wherever they are, including at the margins of society.

Flagstaff, St. George, and Bozeman are microcosms of a larger story playing out across the country. Cities are seeking to avoid the vulnerabilities of the old economy, in which resources were oversupplied and cheaply sold in order to appease the rapacity of the market. This resulted in a proverbial "race to the bottom," leading to an economic bust. Now operating in the mindset of the new economy, they have embraced the notion of endless growth. The city is branded, packaged, and sold to the highest bidder.

Nowhere is this more visible than in the sprawl of the country's largest cities. If we ran a twenty-year time lapse from the center of each, we would see they've grown drastically both in terms of population and infrastructure. They've grown up, they've grown out, and they've grown through the development of every lot within. But this development has been neither random nor even.

Though growth is often a city's most hotly debated issue, many community members are shut out of the decision-making process. Approximately 74 million people—nearly one in every four people in the United States—live in HOAs, with this number growing all the time. In 2021, 82 percent of all new single-family homes sold were part of an HOA.[50] These planned communities have incredible autonomy to establish and enforce rules within their boundaries to which every member is legally bound. Homeowners who do not conform to these covenants, conditions, and restrictions, the CC&Rs, can be monitored, fined, and even evicted with very little legal recourse.

CC&Rs range from the mundane, such as the number of yard signs residents are allowed to have, to monumental, such as what developments are allowed. While these rules are typically enforced by boards which are elected by members, it's not uncommon for the HOA's daily affairs to instead be handled by outside management companies. But residents within HOAs are not the only ones affected by their rules. As they determine what is allowed within their boundaries—thereby determining who is allowed within their boundaries—these rules have a ripple effect in the surrounding areas. As HOAs prevent short-term rentals, they are concentrated in the bordering non-HOA neighborhoods. The same goes for second homes and multiunit properties and a host of other types of development.

The result is that, as some neighborhoods are protected as homes, others are opened to outside investors. Through exclusionary zoning laws and city marketing campaigns and the proliferation of HOAs, neighborhoods of single-family homes are reinforced as the desired form of development, what Black studies scholar George Lipsitz would likely recognize as the "privileged moral geography of the nation."[51] Meanwhile, the housing of renters and cost-burdened households grows evermore precarious.

For this reason, just as the shape of cities has changed, so has their makeup. They've sought to attract high-income earners and spenders in order to fund new roads, new businesses, new everything. Competing to attract the same high-income populations, cities have grown more and more similar. If you're from there, this similarity will probably mean something lost in the way of local stores, untamed patches of nature, and neighbors. If you're not, that will probably mean something gained in the way of recognizable shops, perfectly manicured hedges, and tall, rectangular towers of steel and glass. The mom-and-pop diner becomes a Denny's. The school becomes an outlet mall. The signs have become more numerous, the streets have grown wider, and the place has come to feel like home to anyone who doesn't intend to be there very long. Anyone who does is left with a sense of loss so deep that it feels like betrayal.

This happens because the market demands it. Just as sites like AirDNA utilize algorithms to quantify and promote the most profitable places to operate short-term rentals, a Texas-based company known as RealPage has done the same for long-term rentals. Although just one of many rent-setting software companies, it is by far the largest, the first choice among property management companies like GreyStar that oversee hundreds of thousands of units.

In an October 2022 article, *ProPublica*'s Heather Vogell concluded what RealPage was already proudly promoting: the company is one major reason for skyrocketing rents across the country. Andrew Bowen, a Real-Page executive said, "I think [our software's] driving it, quite honestly. As a property manager, very few of us would be willing to actually raise rents double digits within a single month by doing it manually."

The company's role in driving up housing costs does not stop there. Far from simply publishing their recommendations to customers—which former RealPage employees argue are accepted 90 percent of the time—the company has created private work groups that bring together landlords who would otherwise be in competition with each other. Vogell notes that, "RealPage discourages bargaining with renters and has even recommended that landlords in some cases accept a lower occupancy rate in order to raise rents and make more money."

If residents had anywhere else to go—if property managers were actually competing to offer something better—this would make no business sense. It only makes sense when property managers use the same software and operate under the same rules and sit in the same working groups to further refine the same business strategy.

As RealStar has come to dominate the market for rent-setting software, the multiunit housing market has become dominated by fewer property managers. According to the National Multifamily Housing Council, which surveys buildings with five or more units, the fifty largest property managers alone oversaw 4.2 million units in 2021.[52] That amounts to nearly one in every five of these residential buildings throughout the country. RealStar was sued for collusion within days of the *ProPublica* article's publication.[53]

Dominated by algorithms and huge corporations, places begin to lose their identities. Beneath the seasonal trends and the few landmarks giving definition to the city, Miami is not so different from Chicago is not so different than L.A. And beneath the proximity of public land and historic main streets, Flagstaff is not so different from St. George is not so different than Bozeman. Because the architecture is guided almost entirely by utility with facades of glitz. Because the people are almost invariably from somewhere else. Because the goal of the place has become whatever the market demands.

Former UN Special Rapporteur on Adequate Housing Leilani Farha saw this. As she explained in the housing documentary *Push*, this issue is not confined to the US West or even the United States as a whole. She explained, "This is what I'm seeing happen around the world. The buying up of land, the displacement of the poorest people, and the putting up of luxury units that are not actually for the people who live in the community."[54]

. . . .

With the remote work boom, cities have gained an additional wealthy demographic to seek out. In places ranging from Bloomfield, Iowa, to Tulsa, Oklahoma, officials are paying incoming remote workers up to $10,000. Even cities that have admitted to struggling to keep housing affordable are not ashamed to admit wanting more remote workers to move there. In public land–bound Flagstaff, my landlord stood in my kitchen and told me that was the city's goal. His dual identity as a full-time city employee and landlord, like the teacher who had served as my last landlord, offered evidence that Flagstaff wages were not enough to afford the city's cost of living. When I asked why the city was interested in remote workers, he answered honestly that "they typically make more money."

He then added something about these workers having a lower environmental footprint, a way of justifying the practice despite having virtually no evidence to back it up. Although these remote workers will not need to commute to work or occupy office space in town, more residents typically translates into further sprawl and their higher salary typically translates into larger houses. If the remote workers take advantage of their digital freedom to take one more cross-country or international flight than their in-person counterparts, they negate any supposed advantage of not commuting to work, particularly if they would have bused, biked, or walked. At best, the environmental impact of recruiting more remote workers is uncertain.

The social and economic effects, however, are straightforward: this influx of new residents will price out people who make local wages addressing local needs. City officials don't care. The economy must grow.

Eventually, short-term rentals and timeshare properties will abound, acknowledgment of the fact that the price of housing is only attainable by dividing it up among many people. When this ceases to meet the bill, it's possible that corporations will begin buying up properties en masse, offering short-term stays in coastal and mountain towns as a benefit for remote-working employees. Or perhaps the day will come in which homes are traded directly on the stock market, divorced from the function of housing people altogether.

That day seems to have arrived in China, where an estimated 90 percent of households are owned and 20 percent of homeowners have at least two houses. Data from the 2017 China Household Finance Survey showed that 65 million homes—21 percent of all homes in the country—are empty. China is home to dozens of so-called ghost cities, but there's a difference between these and the abandoned towns that dot the US West: China's ghost cities have never been occupied. The houses are simply assets to buy and sell.[55]

At some point, this race to the top will be revealed as a lie. There will be no one left who is willing or able to buy. With homes seen as mere investments, hot potatoes to be tossed around, there's little recognition that the buzzer could sound at any moment. For many, it already has.

II
where we've been

7

Blank Space

STRIKE A MATCH AND ITS SMOKE will emanate outward, filling every available open space. Any gas will follow this pattern, entering a stage of frenetic energy as its molecules expand outward until they bump against an impermeable surface, at which time they must find a state of equilibrium within the enclosed space. We often understand the history of the United States as operating the same way.

We take an individual event, perhaps the 1607 arrival of English settlers at what became known as Jamestown, Virginia, or perhaps the 1776 signing of the Declaration of Independence, as the lit match. We then take the present-day borders of the continental United States that we know so well—the Atlantic and Pacific Oceans in the east and west, the forty-ninth parallel in the north and the Rio Grande in the south—as the room. In this mindset, the expansion of the country gains an air of inevitability, of destiny even. The peoples who occupied the space for millennia, facing the very real threats of cultural and actual genocide, seldom enter the national consciousness. We are taught one US history, belonging to the descendants of Western Europeans who were willing to brave the unknown and carve out an existence in a new land.

When we tell this story, the land is blank, a stage set for the human drama about to unfold. We tell the story of a people longing for a freedom the world has never known. With a stubborn, unified resolve, the people throw off the yoke of an empire and forge a nation under the highest of ideals, "that all men are created equal." The people venture west into the great unknown, guided by an unbreakable faith in the promise of tomorrow. Ever committed to this promise, this country has been a city on a hill, a light to counter the darkness of history and unchecked power. It's a fantastic story, the one on which we are raised and to which we come to owe our most sacred identity as Americans. The only problem is that it's a lie.

• • • • • • •

There are times when David Bustos is so soft-spoken that I have to strain to hear him. But the story he's telling dismantles the dominant view of human history. The most prevalent theory of the first human arrival in what we now know as the Americas is that they used a land bridge formed during the last Ice Age to cross the Bering Strait, walking from modern-day Russia into modern-day Alaska approximately ten to twelve thousand years ago. But as the resource program manager at White Sands National Park in southern New Mexico, Bustos has worked with scientists from across the country and Native nations from across the region to study fossilized human footprints embedded on the shores of an ancient lake bed within the park. And their findings are changing everything.

Using radioactive dating to assess the age of grass seeds found within these footprints, they've revealed that human habitation in the area dates to between seventeen and twenty-three thousand years ago—at least. The human footprints are interspersed with those of now-extinct mammoths, giant ground sloths, and North American camels. The presence of some of these prints shock scientists, revealing creatures they never knew existed in the area. But not everyone is surprised. As Bustos explains, Native peoples in the area had millennia-old oral histories of hunting megafauna such as camels and sloths. As has happened in other public lands sites, the scientific evidence is merely confirming what Native peoples have consistently held to be true.

The prints are so well defined that they show evidence of hunting strategy, of children playing in the mud, and even of a woman shifting a young child from hip to hip as she walks. Bustos sees these signs of shared humanity as the most important aspect of the finding:

> I think to me the greatest thing that we sort of see is people are people. . . . You know, at the end of the day, all cultures, all nations, all people throughout time, we're sort of the same. If you get to the very bottom of us, we care about our family, . . . you have to interact with the environment. . . . It's neat to see what we all sort of came from and, I think, at the core of all of us, is still alive. You know, you take a kid out from anywhere in the world and put a big puddle in front of them and they know what to do.

Bustos said that nearby Native nations will sometimes laugh when talking about the significance of the find, saying things like, "Ah, we've always known we've been here! What are you talking about? It's not a big deal."[1] The exact dates give context to human history in the area, but they are less important than the fact that humans have resided in this area and across the Americas for thousands of years.

These humans lived in families, tribes, and nations. They were interwoven and isolated, warring and pacifist. They lived in elaborate, sedentary societies with highly specialized labor forces, nomadic bands in which everyone was engaged in the daily rhythms of survival, and all variations between. They spoke thousands of languages, held extraordinarily unique, complex understandings of the cosmos, and established trade networks from the Rockies to the Pacific and Central America to the Canadian border. In short, people developed radically different ways of meeting their basic needs of living and loving and dying across the entirety of what is now the United States.

It's for this reason that the word many tribes and nations used to describe themselves translates simply as "the people." But there was not one people. Those who left their footsteps at White Sands were just some of many peoples carrying on one of many ways of life built around deep relationship with the surrounding environment. These peoples were sometimes connected through trade and marriage and conflict but mostly just connected by the sun and moon and stars overhead.

The Doctrine of Discovery

All this changed a little less than six hundred years ago. Nation-states across the European continent were growing rapidly. To support the appetites of their growing populations and the avarice of their rulers, the nations developed sophisticated systems of trade and relied upon increasingly specialized labor. They competed for resources with others in the region, seeking out new frontiers for scarce and luxurious goods. Promised extraordinary wealth by extraordinarily wealthy kings and queens, Spaniards and Frenchmen and Brits and members of every European nation-state sailed beyond the edge of the known earth. And when they reached the shores of these distant lands, they found them already occupied, home to thriving civilizations all their own.

Had the goal been mere survival, it's possible that an exchange of knowledge and goods between the two peoples could have benefited both. But the European nations were not after survival; they were after domination. To justify forced and permanent access to foreign occupied land, Portugal turned to the divine proclamation of the Catholic pope. In 1455, Pope Nicholas V issued the papal bull Romanus Pontifex, thereby granting the first Christian nation arriving in a land the "right to 'grant,' 'discover,' 'subdue,' 'acquire,' and 'possess' and permanently control non-Christian indigenous peoples, along with their lands, territories, and resources."[2] This international legal pact established the rules of conquest for all European nations, later becoming known as the Doctrine of Discovery.

The "conquering" nations were permitted and even encouraged to remove any sign of Indigenous peoples' presence, what Anishinaabe Ojibwe historian Jean O'Brien refers to as "firsting and lasting."[3] In simpler terms, "finders, keepers" was valid only for Christian Europeans. No matter non-Christians' numbers or the extent of their settlement, the logic of the Doctrine of Discovery nullified their claim to territory. While many places became sites for the extraction of resources, others became sites for settlement. What are now known as the Americas became both.

In 1491, the Americas were home to thousands of Old Worlds, thousands of distinct cultures, peoples, and civilizations that had been spreading throughout the hemisphere since before the last Ice Age. A year later, in the name of their Christian God and in service to a distant crown, invading Europeans sought to destroy these Old Worlds to create what they would call the New World.

· · · · · · ·

In the 1600s, English Protestants began creating colonies along the Atlantic Coast, away from the Old England which many had come to view as overtaken by wickedness. They sought "a new and sacred beginning in a new and sacred land" and believed themselves to be chosen for this.[4] It was this mindset which allowed John Winthrop, the first governor of the Massachusetts Bay Colony whose influence on the direction of the US government would later lead him to be regarded as "America's forgotten founding father," to describe the smallpox decimation of Native populations as an act of divine intervention. [5][6]

In the 1630s, Winthrop argued Native peoples had no civil right to land since they had not enclosed it, settled it, or in any way improved it.[7] He wasn't alone. In his Two Treatises of Government, John Locke argued that a man's property was made up of the land he improved.[8] Locke's ideas were revered by many leaders in the colonies and would prove central in establishing the US system of government. His belief in a natural right to life, liberty, and property would be rewritten as "life, liberty, and the pursuit of happiness." Property was not guaranteed.

But the first colonists at Jamestown were not focused on expansion; they were just trying to make it through winter. Starving, sick, and freezing, it was only through the knowledge and trade of Native tribes that any settlers managed to survive. Until the early 1700s, Natives vastly outnumbered the British colonists and every New England settlement was made through treaty or purchase.[9] But after the Revolutionary War, as the US population grew exponentially, the new government began invoking the philosophy of *vacuum domicilium*—their "obligation to cultivate the earth"—to dispossess Native nations of their lands.[10]

This justification, however, could only go so far. After all, it could hardly be argued that the Native nations in the eastern woodlands which formed the Iroquois League—whose system of governance was used to inform the one developed by the young United States—did not have an organized society. It could not be said that these partially agriculture-based societies had not done anything to improve the land they held.

The justification again fell apart in relation to societies like the Cherokee, with sophisticated systems of government, thriving economies, and a written language. There could be no taking of land for the purpose of "civilizing" an already-civilized people. Indeed, the Cherokee—along with the Creek, Choctaw, Chickasaw, and Seminole—were commonly referred to as the "Five Civilized Tribes."[11]

But, as historian Henry Rosenthal notes, "The American right to buy always superseded the Indian right not to sell."[12] This idea was enshrined for all time in the Supreme Court's 1827 Johnson v. McIntosh ruling. While continuing the previous British prohibition of private sale of land—tribally owned land—west of the Appalachian Mountains, the Court gave exclusive purchasing rights to the federal government.

Evidence shows this was not a typical case. The plaintiff attorneys had hired the defense attorneys, manufacturing this courtroom conflict. The Supreme Court ruled that Native peoples could not buy or sell land privately—only through the federal government.[13] Chief Justice John Marshall, despite holding arge amounts of real estate in the territory, did not recuse himself. Instead, he wrote the unanimous decision, arguing that the Doctrine of Discovery gave "'an exclusive right to extinguish the Indian title of occupancy, either by purchase or by conquest.'"[14]

But the federal government, in making no firm stand against encroaching settlement—even arguing it was incapable of preventing settlers from claiming that space—had been making its decision for decades.[15] Failure to act is itself an action. The 1827 Court decision merely reinforced the de facto, if unwritten, policy of the United States. By the 1820s, Cherokee land once covering five states had been reduced to mostly within Georgia state lines.[16] Then, in 1827, the same year that the Supreme Court made its ruling in *Johnson v. McIntosh*, prospectors found gold on Cherokee land.

As land-hungry settlers grew louder in their calls for the removal of Native nations, *Johnson v. McIntosh* gave the federal government the absolute and exclusive power to terminate tribal claims. There would be no more shirking the issue. In the years following, President Andrew Jackson echoed settlers' cries in endorsing expansion and development of western land. In his 1830 inaugural address, he asked the crowd, "'What good man would prefer a country covered with forests and ranged by a few thousand savages to our extensive Republic, studded with cities, towns, and prosperous farms, embellished with all the improvements which art can devise or industry execute?'"[17]

That same year, Jackson signed the Removal Act, paving the way for what would later be known as "The Trail of Tears," which forced the "Five Civilized Tribes" from their ancestral homeland.[18] Alexis de Tocqueville observed this policy in action as he traveled the United States gaining insights for his highly acclaimed book *Democracy in America*.[19] In no uncertain terms, he described seeing a large band of Choctaws seeking to cross the Mississippi River in wintertime. "I saw them embark to pass the mighty river, and never will that solemn spectacle fade from my remembrance. No cry, no sob, was heard amongst the assembled crowd; all were silent. Their calamities were of ancient date, and they knew them to be irremediable."[20]

De Tocqueville's writing places the ubiquitous nature of the Doctrine of Discovery on full display. He takes pains to describe how the societal value placed on education and religious devotion allowed the

United States to prosper.[21] From the first pages, he marvels at the equality achieved amongst people across the United States and cites this as the reason for democracy's spread in Europe.[22] But Native peoples were not part of this equation.

From these early examples, a contradiction emerges. The federal government repeatedly claims an inability to protect local populations from outside settlement and then invokes its overwhelming force to clear that space. More moderate politicians of the time like former Presidents Adams and Monroe epitomized this contradiction, paying lip service to a policy of limited settlement decades before while quietly speaking favorably of Native removal. While it was Jackson who ultimately signed the bill and ordered this removal, the policy had been made possible by the inaction and tacit backing of prior administrations.[23]

All this would repeat itself. The following decades would be marked by military campaigns and coercive economic treaties, almost entirely clearing unsettled country of Native nations and foreign powers. As David Getches and other researchers wrote in their sprawling *Cases and Materials on Federal Indian Law*:

> *It was not long before waves of immigrants encountered Indian country in their quest for a new life in the West. They coveted tribal lands and natural resources that were legally off-limits to settlement. So more lands were demanded by homesteaders. The US lacked both the tactical ability and the political will to hold the boundaries of the large western reservations.*[24]

The Doctrine of Discovery marched west, attempting to erase the footprints of all those who came before and all those who sought another way.

"The Same Old Stupid Plan"

But other paths have remained. Karen Begay's very existence testifies to this fact. When I interviewed her, I barely needed to ask any questions.

She is a Navajo woman building a traditional *hogan—home* in Navajo—about fifty miles northwest of Flagstaff. I just wanted to know why. Begay told me her clans: Nakai Diné and Ta'neeszahnii. She told me her grandmother was a rug weaver and her grandfather was a medicine man. She told me they're from a place known as Smoke Signal. She told me where she got the logs—the nearby San Francisco Peaks—and the labor—working with a steady stream of volunteers from a mutual aid organization known as Kinlani, the Navajo name for Flagstaff. And I realized that these were not simply biographical facts; they infused everything she did.

Begay was building the hogan as a home but also intended for it to be a gathering place for Native ceremonies and rituals. She used natural materials and emphasized the importance of having everything one day collapse back to the earth. The site was blessed and established as a place where the Navajo community could get in touch with its roots. Begay said she was trying to live the Native way: "thinking seven generations ahead."[25] She belonged to this place.

She did not stop there. After building her own hogan, Begay began building homes for others on the Navajo Reservation. Some of these structures use modern materials such as vinyl siding on the exterior and dry wall on the interior. Some have electricity and ceiling fans and other amenities. Regardless of their features, she relies on monetary donations, donated materials, and the help of future residents to keep the costs of building a hogan low. She also works for free.

In Begay's eyes, a hogan is "some place you can always go back to." It's connected to a larger community of people whose lives are intertwined, a place inseparable from the surrounding landscape. She started building hogans for other people because she saw the increasing unaffordability of housing in Flagstaff and how restrictions on the Navajo Reservation—for home-site leases and inspections and surveys—made building difficult. She saw that her sense of place was under threat and felt the responsibility of protecting it.

I just feel like that this housing crisis is not going to go away any time soon. . . . I'm trying to make a little bit of a difference, maybe not in everybody's life but maybe even if it was just ten homes that I built, that would be ten families that are no longer living in the street or ten families that now have a house. I think we could wait forever for the government. Really!

She laughs as she talks about the prospect of waiting for the government to act, noting the political dysfunction that grips the country, but her laughter seems to be a coping mechanism. It's a way of acknowledging how easily government and tribal officials are "blinded by greed," as she sees it. It's a way of dealing with the consequences of this greed, like the hundreds of unsheltered Navajo people in Flagstaff and the surrounding area or the rising cost of housing throughout the nation.

Karen Begay has grown accustomed to outside wealth and greed threatening existing communities. In view of the country's history, she isn't surprised by the continued commodification of the housing market. After all, Airbnb's mantra of "Helping anyone belong anywhere," providing a vacant space for people from across the country and world, is a business plan. If there is more profit incentive in providing space for short-term visitors over long-term residents and no restriction on doing so, it seems obvious what property owners with vacant spaces will choose. The present housing situation is written into the country's origin narrative.

According to that narrative, the land was blank when Western European settlers arrived. Every frontier involved the creation of blank space, of free land, of great profit for some. And each frontier involved the active displacement and erasure of others.

It's tempting to view this as something confined to the past. After all, the defining feature of the 1890 census, inspiring Frederick Jackson Turner's famous thesis on "The Significance of the Frontier in American History," was its failure to identify this blank space in the West.[26] But nearly a century later, in 1981, the intermountain or interior West was still being described as the "Empty Quarter."[27]

More than forty years later, this perceived emptiness continues to be invoked. Arizona is often referred to as "the Wild West." Utah's most-visited national park, Zion, translates to "paradise" or "promised land." Montana bears the moniker of "the last best place." Characterized by second homes and short-term rentals and new developments bought by high-salaried remote workers, it's not surprising that a 2018 analysis from data firm Moody's did not identify a single one of the eleven western states in the top half for housing affordability.[28]

It's also tempting to view this as something confined to the West. After all, the percentage of homes in large cities taken off the market for use as short-term rentals pales in comparison to those in many towns across the intermountain West. But, as Turner himself wrote, "The West, at bottom, is a form of society, rather than an area. It is the term applied to the region whose social conditions result from the application of older institutions and ideas to the transforming influences of free land."[29]

That's why a 2019 report from Harvard's Joint Center for Housing Studies identified 30.2 percent of nationwide households burdened by housing costs.[30] That's why barely half of US workers can afford a one-bedroom apartment on their current wages.[31] And that's why there is not a single state in the country where a person working full-time for minimum wage can reliably afford a two-bedroom apartment.[32] Meanwhile, according to five-year estimates by the 2020 American Community Survey, nearly one in every nine housing units nationwide is unoccupied.[33]

The frontier never closed; it merely changed forms. At first glance, it's difficult to see the link between eighteenth- and nineteenth-century covered wagons moving west across the United States and the large swaths of contemporary tourists flocking to tourism towns. It's hard to see the link between prospectors in a mining town in 1850 and developers in a metropolitan area in 2022. In reality, as Langston Hughes wrote in 1936, it's just "the same old stupid plan / Of dog eat dog, of mighty crush the weak."[34]

A closer look reveals that many of the factors cited for rising housing costs—from tourists to second homeowners to remote workers to students to investors to general residential growth—have something in common: they make the local housing market a global one. They empty out existing communities to make room for outsiders. And these outsiders are overwhelmingly wealthier and Whiter than the people they replace.

White Lies

The first thing that struck me was the silence. When I began interviewing people in June 2020, George Floyd, a Black man in Minneapolis, had just been killed by a White police officer kneeling on his neck for nearly nine minutes. Recorded and published by a bystander, Floyd's death came on the heels of Breonna Taylor's death at the hands of plainclothes police officers executing a no-knock raid of her Louisville home. This followed Ahmaud Arbery's death at the hands of three White men in Glynn County, Georgia. Their deaths ignited a summer of protests and the United States entered into what seemed to be the throes of a racial reckoning. But as I talked with city officials about housing inequalities, scarcely a word was said about race until I asked at the end of interviews.

The twenty-four interviewees with some link to housing policy—ranging from elected officials, planners, and compliance officials to real estate agents, researchers, and tourism representatives—were largely selected via email, phone, or referral. Collectively, they offered a snapshot of whose voices were heard and who had power in the cities of Flagstaff, St. George, Bozeman, their respective states, and neighboring towns. All of them were White.

Bozeman is 89.6 percent White alone, non-Latino; St. George is 80.5 percent. Although Flagstaff's population initially seems more diverse—with 64.5 percent White alone, 19.3 percent Latino, and 7.8 percent Native—this must be understood in a broader context. The overall state of Arizona population is only 54.1 percent White alone and this number remains the same within Coconino County, of which Flagstaff is part.[35] Additionally, the city is bordered by the Navajo and Hopi Nations, a constant reminder that the political boundaries and names that appear on maps are recent additions, violent attempts to erase previous peoples. The

Navajo Nation's 175,000 people represent by far the largest population on Native-held land.[36]

Despite existing on ancestral Native land and within relatively close proximity to Native reservations, the populations of Bozeman and St. George are so overwhelmingly White that talking about race relations is largely a hypothetical exercise. City governments frequently cite population growth as a means of increasing racial diversity. In Bozeman, elected official Pat Witton was optimistic that University and tech industry growth would drive greater diversity. But rapidly rising housing prices threaten to diminish all residential growth, especially that of non-Whites.

Elected officials do not exist in a bubble. Many, like Flagstaff city councilmember Adam Shimoni, are well-versed in the country's history of racism and rightly argue that the effects of racial discrimination through policies like redlining have lingered. They see, as Flagstaff city councilmember Rachel Grant sees, that governmental policy has an important role to play in addressing the racialized conditions that exist today, such as the prevalence of unhoused Native peoples in Flagstaff. But they do not discuss targeted housing solutions.

Officials in Flagstaff, St. George, and Bozeman are not so different than officials in cities across the country. They speak of housing largely without reference to race, preferring to use seemingly neutral economic terms like supply and demand. But housing is not racially neutral in these cities. In Flagstaff, one of the most prominent examples of displacement in recent years has been the removal of the largely Latino population of Arrowhead Mobile Home Park.[37] Though the residents were evicted in 2018, the area remains undeveloped. In Bozeman, the onslaught of evictions resulting from COVID has threatened to displace residents of the only predominantly non-White neighborhood in the city.[38] This is what happens when elected officials talk about housing without talking about race.

What "Race-Neutral" Means

These cities were part of a larger story. An examination of laws and policies across the country today will yield few explicitly racialized policies, perhaps especially related to housing. At the same time, statistics are telling. The 2010 Census found Black isolation or segregation to be 55 percent nationally and more than 70 percent in northern cities with large Black populations, especially Midwestern cities like Milwaukee, Detroit, Cleveland, and Chicago. Evidence points to much of the perceived integration as fleeting and resulting merely from gentrification in process.[39] In 2013, Whites' median net worth ($141,900) was thirteen times that of Blacks ($11,000). This was the largest gap recorded since the late 1980s.[40]

Meanwhile, even though the law forbids discrimination, a National Bureau of Economic Research study undertaken in 2020 revealed rampant discrimination against potential renters bearing Black- or Latino-sounding names. Researchers found property owners across nearly all fifty of the top metropolitan areas were more likely to respond to names appearing to represent White people than their Black or Latino counterparts.[41] The absence of racial language in policies today does not mean race is no longer a consideration in housing. Instead, race is invoked through reference to habit, economic status, immigration status, procedural knowledge, and a whole host of other signifiers.

Understanding the unaffordable housing landscape in the United States today requires unifying two seemingly disparate facts: ostensibly nonracial policies and rampant racial inequality.[42] When real estate officials refer to supply and demand and economic trends, they seem to speak of immutable laws. When people in positions of power speak about being bound by geographic barriers or market trends, they give an impression of being apolitical. But it's typically the most apolitical narratives that contain the most political agendas.[43] Justifying the way things are is inherently political.

The fact that Western European settlers populated what is now the United States was not inevitable. Neither was the manner in which they did so. Rather, the series of massive migrations involved was made possible by far-reaching laws and extensive government support. And it was always reinforced by violence or the threat of violence. The entire history of land, housing, and race in the United States has produced a highly "racialized space."[44] Such spaces, once produced, remain stubbornly in place, no matter the harm done.

This history has created what philosopher Charles Mills refers to as the "geography of whiteness."[45] That this history has been forgotten or distorted is evidence of not only present-day racial prejudices in a purportedly postracial society but also something far more insidious and difficult to track: racialized power structures. Throughout the history of the United States, racism has been codified by federal legislation and local ordinance, by national organization and neighborhood norm. All this has combined to produce the present situation, what Black studies scholar George Lipsitz has referred to as "the racialization of space and the spatialization of race."[46]

Lipsitz describes this landscape as the White spatial imaginary. As he puts it, "The white spatial imaginary (WSI) is innately ahistorical. It accepts the prevailing imbalances of wealth and power between racialized spaces as a baseline reality that should not be disturbed, as an accurate register of the achievement and worth of the people who live in those spaces."[47] The WSI, like environmental determinism, cannot imagine the world existing in any other way. It requires a very selective view of history, one that prizes individual achievement and adheres to a belief in individual destiny while ignoring the unearned advantages of structural, systemic racism.

Squaring race-neutral language with highly racialized spaces requires challenging the politics and history that produced the world that now exists. The links between race and economics are frequently dismissed as the result of hard work and circumstance, but a deep history of US land and housing policy shows that the gaps between Whites and non-Whites in education, employment, homeownership, wealth, and so many more material categories result from other factors. Race and class come to be seen as overlapping—even sometimes interchangeable—because politicians and citizens have done little to alter the world order from which they emerged. Instead, they've reinforced it.

• • • • • • •

Determining the "winners" and "losers" from an influx of tourists, second homeowners, or new residents is not difficult. In an environment in which housing is simply another commodity, the so-called winners are those who profit from owning property and the losers are those who struggle to afford it.[48] Those bound to lose, in other words, are those for whom housing is home, not real estate.[49] Beyond the strict binary of those who profit from rising real estate and those who must pay higher sums to maintain residence, there exists another category: those already displaced. These people cannot vote, speak before a city council, or sit down for an interview about the difficulties in managing the cost of housing; they do not exist within the bounds of these cities at all.[50]

This is not simply a matter of economics. Particularly in the West, frontier imaginaries have involved the intentional unsettling of preestablished populations, which has overwhelmingly fallen upon racial lines. The United States' land and housing policy has continually privileged White money, bodies, and mobility, and this history lies at the core of the West's construction as a frontier.

Places are not naturally segregated along lines of class and race but this segregation has been and continues to be reinforced in a myriad of ways. Harold Ickes, head of the federal government's 1930s-era Public Works Administration, or PWA, operated under a "neighborhood composition rule" that favored racially homogenous neighborhoods. It was this policy that served as a blueprint for future housing law.[51] Of those who are able to stay in increasingly unaffordable places, non-Whites—particularly Native and Black people—are far less likely to own property or hold office. As a result, White voices often dominate the housing conversations.

Race and wealth are tightly bound across the entire country. As the market becomes a stand-in for deciding who gets to belong, the expensive housing market itself ends up reproducing Ickes's policy on a municipal scale. Built upon and still bordering Native land, infused with generations of low-wage Black and immigrant labor, it's not surprising that the western mountain towns that I set out to study became enclaves of Whiteness and wealth.

Housing is a commodity in the United States. In this context, short-term rentals promise higher profits than long-term rentals and second homes promise higher returns than other investments. Long-term residents can only look on as investors and high-earning residents buy up homes. Strangers replace neighbors and housing becomes unaffordable, facts that become viewed as regrettable but unavoidable consequences. That non-Whites are the least benefited and most vulnerable to displacement is scarcely given mention.

· · · · · · ·

Since the 1960s, hopeful commentators have pointed to particular events—the passage of the Civil Rights Act, the passage of the Fair Housing Act, the election of the first Black president—as evidence that the United States has become a postracial society. And each time, widespread racial disparities and subsequent events have proven them fantastically wrong. People confuse exceptions for rules, data points for trends. The success story of one non-White person comes to mean that race is no longer a determining factor in anyone's success. In the same way, Michelle Alexander, the author of *The New Jim Crow: Mass Incarceration in the Age of Colorblindness*, explains that everyday racism seems mild or even nonexistent compared to the most malicious and outright discriminatory acts:

> *When we think of racism we think of Governor Wallace of Alabama blocking the schoolhouse door; we think of water hoses, lynchings, racial epithets, and "whites only" signs. These images make it easy to forget that many wonderful, goodhearted white people who were generous to others, respectful of their neighbors, and even kind to their black maids, gardeners, or shoe shiners—and wished them well—nevertheless went to the polls and voted for racial segregation. . . . Our understanding of racism is therefore shaped by the most extreme expressions of individual bigotry, not by the way in which it functions naturally, almost invisibly (and sometimes with*

genuinely benign intent), when it is embedded in the structure of a social system.[52]

In recent years, the racism that characterizes the United States has been harder to ignore. White supremacists have found new avenues of connecting and recruiting. Acts of racial violence, from both private citizens and police, have been captured on video. Public officials' racial prejudices have been captured on audio recordings. This has led some to ask difficult questions about unearned advantages, prompting uncomfortable answers and sparking efforts toward meaningful change. Mostly, these examples of overt racism have enabled us to ignore the many hidden and insidious ways that race factors into our lives. We see racism personified in a politician or viral video rather than the determining factor in where we live, what we do for work, and what we inherit.

Millions upon millions of White people today would argue that they try to be good people and that being a good person means not being racist. By extension, they cannot be racist. The country is full of well-intentioned people who believe racism is something from the past or something happening somewhere else at the same time that the country remains fundamentally unequal.

What follows is that residents in Flagstaff and St. George and Bozeman—like residents in Minneapolis and Seattle and Portland—are joining anti-racist book clubs and classes as their homes remain White enclaves. Corporations that widen racial wealth and health gaps run ads promoting equality. Universities where students of color bear the brunt of reduced funding and insurmountable loans advertise their commitment to racial diversity. Politicians with histories of advocating policies with especially harmful effects for people of color cast opponents as racist.

And across the country all-White neighborhoods are peppered with lawn signs saying HATE HAS NO HOME HERE in six languages. But when efforts to address racial disparities like building affordable housing or multiunit properties are proposed in the neighborhood, many of these existing residents make it clear that they oppose new residents having a home there either. We have, as sociologist and former president of the

American Sociological Society Eduardo Bonilla-Silva titled his book, *Racism Without Racists*.

"Only Secondarily a Nation"

The history of the US is scarred by the violent displacement of Native peoples from their homes. It's stained by the theft of Black Africans from theirs. It's similarly tarnished by the continual coercion of immigrants into dangerous and unstable work for low wages. Racism was the glue used to build an empire. It was the rope used to tame the frontier.

Back in 1896, in reiterating his argument regarding the implications of the United States' western frontier, Frederick Jackson Turner quoted Professor Emile Boutmy, the French political scientist and sociologist. Boutmy argued:

> [The United States'] one primary and predominant object is to cultivate and settle these prairies, forests, and vast waste lands. The striking and peculiar characteristic of American society is that it is not so much a democracy as a huge commercial company for the discovery, cultivation, and capitalization of its enormous territory.[53]

Forced to compete on a global market, more and more residents today are pushed to the city's edges or far-flung suburbs. In the West, they are being forced into precarious living situations on surrounding public lands, as outlined in an October 2021 *HighCountry News* feature by Sarah Tory.[54] Many now live permanently out of their vehicle, a lifestyle that gained international attention through the 2020 Oscar-winning film *Nomadland*. Fittingly, the movie is dedicated "to the ones who had to depart." Even more appropriate, its inspiration, the investigative book *Nomadland* by Jessica Bruder, is subtitled *Surviving America in the Twenty-First Century*.[55]

Boutmy likely would not have been surprised. As he concluded, "The United States are primarily a commercial society, and only secondarily a nation."[56]

The Latest Frontier

The housing situation we see across the United States today—the rise in rent, home sale prices, houselessness, remote workers, second, third, and fourth homes—is inseparable from this history. Our country has continually built new frontiers, new spaces imagined as empty, free, and profitable. The end of one frontier and beginning of another can be marked out by specific events or new trends but they blend together into a patchwork of histories. As historian and sociologist Lewis Mumford said in 1925, "'The movement of population . . . come[s] as successive waves, and while one wave recedes as the next comes foaming in, the first nevertheless persists and mingles with the second as an undertow."[57]

Each frontier has occurred through the direct exclusion or displacement of people who were there already. As such, these frontiers have required many defenses, ones that have changed depending on the time. First came the New World, justified by the Doctrine of Discovery. Then came the West, mandated by Manifest Destiny. Next came the suburbs, enshrined as the hallmark of the American Dream. After that followed gentrification, defended by the invisible hand of the market.[58] Finally came the iteration we see today, what Manuel Aalbers called the "financialization of home".[59] It's been met with a shrug.

Every frontier carries on the mission of creating empty space for outside capital, always at the expense of those who previously called a place home. Past settlers have invoked divine providence, destiny, and economics to explain their frontier and the displacement it caused. Mostly, they argued the primacy derived from their guns. Today's settlers argue the primacy derived from their funds.

In describing the taking of the West, historian Anders Stephanson struck the same ambivalent tone, writing, "I have tried to avoid moralizing. Perhaps it had to happen the way it did."[60] Government officials interviewed were quick to echo this sentiment, throwing their hands up and asking, *What can we do?* After all, they explained, affordable housing was a problem a long time ago.

We call ourselves the richest country on earth while a third of our households are burdened by the cost of the roof overhead. More than a half million are unsheltered entirely.

We call ourselves the freest country on earth while racial segregation is rampant in schools, neighborhoods, and workplaces. More than one in every hundred adults, including a far higher percentage of non-Whites, are incarcerated.

We call ourselves the best country on earth while the children being born today are part of a wave of generations expected to face more frequent disasters, earn less money, and live shorter, sicker lives than their parents.

All of this informs the tired, dishonest housing conversation in this country. The truth is that we all exist within an overarching system that has prioritized particular outsiders at the direct expense of current residents. Overwhelmingly, this has fallen along racial lines, and today these lines mirror economic ones. These twin plagues of poverty and racism have persisted because governments at all levels have continually abdicated their responsibility to act on behalf of every person in the country, refusing to do anything more than appeasing and enriching a wealthy, overwhelmingly White subset of the population. Because, as a society, we have allowed this. The system we have today is just a new iteration of the one we've had for 570 years.

Winning the West

"The men of capital and enterprise come. The settler is ready to sell out and take the advantage of the rise in property, push farther into the interior and become, himself, a man of capital and enterprise in turn." [1]

—John Mason Peck, 1837

Manifest Destiny

IN 1845, REPORTER JOHN L. O'SULLIVAN dubbed movement west to be the "fulfillment of our manifest destiny to overspread the continent allotted by Providence for the free development of our yearly multiplying millions." He was describing a long-simmering shift. The "New World" offered to Europe through the Doctrine of Discovery had given way to US expansion "allotted by Providence."

Increasing in military might, the United States grew rapidly in the decade following O'Sullivan's proclamation. The country fought and gained control of a then-independent Texas, purchased today's Pacific Northwest from Great Britain, and successfully challenged Mexico's claim to all land west of the Rio Grande. In the span of just a few years, the United States had grown by more than 50 percent. The once-fledgling nation seeking escape from empire had become an empire itself.

Manifest Destiny, with origins in the idea of a Promised Land for God's chosen people, provided a justification for westward expansion.[2] It was hardly needed. As "Father of Texas" Stephen F. Austin once said, stopping expansion would be like trying to dam the Mississippi River.[3] Settlers sought new lives and "extend[ed] the [nation's] sphere" of influence west, just as James Madison had argued for in the nation's founding.[4] It is no coincidence that the decades-brewing battle over slavery finally bubbled to the surface. Slavery, however, was only part of this equation. With the prospect of free land in the 1860s, the fight over how that land would be regulated boiled over and nearly led to the dissolution of the country.[5]

Up until that point, Whiteness informed every aspect of life in the South. Whites owned the land, owned the labor, and made the laws. When the Civil War ended in 1865 and millions of previously enslaved Black people suddenly walked free, White Southerners did not just see the threat to their identity but, rather, their entire way of life. They did everything in their power to retain control.

First came the land. In the months leading up to the end of the Civil War, Union general William T. Sherman had developed a far-reaching land redistribution policy known as Special Field Orders No. 15, with forty acres and a mule going to every person who'd been enslaved. During what would become known as the Reconstruction period after the war, President Andrew Johnson nixed the policy. The move, resulting from the influence of White plantation owners, lawyers, and political leaders, is commonly understood in retrospect as dooming any possibility of economic equality for Blacks in the South.[6]

Next came the labor. When slavery was abolished upon passage of the Thirteenth Amendment, it came with an exception: slavery would be permitted in cases of crime. In the years following the Civil War, the law ensured many Blacks were released from the bounds of slavery only to be enmeshed into a system of low-wage sharecropping and convict leasing for petty and often manufactured crimes.

Unchanged 160 years later, this law now allows for a disproportionately non-White prison population to be forced into labor ranging from stitching military gear to fighting wildfires. With compensation as low as twenty-five cents per hour, this practice has created such an incentive to build and fill prisons that a school-to-prison pipeline has opened. Students in predominantly non-White and impoverished schools are more likely to be severely penalized and criminalized for perceived behavior issues than students in predominantly White and affluent schools.[7]

As sociologist Forrest Stuart noted, the Reconstruction had similarities with "the enclosure period of the English countryside in which large landowners converted peasants' common lands into private pastures in order to raise sheep for the burgeoning textile market."[8] In the US South, Whites began using new anti-vagrancy and anti-loitering laws to retain Black labor. Black people, whether never enslaved or recently emancipated, could be imprisoned and forced into unpaid labor at the hands of the state for simply staying in one place for too long.

Finally came the law. Based on their numbers and fragile coalitions held with disaffected Whites, Blacks immediately gained political power in the South. Between 1865 and 1877, 16 Black men were elected to Congress in addition to hundreds in state legislatures and local government positions. They were able to do this because they were protected by federal troops in the South and a committed Congress in Washington. But a Supreme Court decision removed the potential of disrupting key White-owned monopolies. Political alliances frayed. Federal troops left. In the wake of these events, racial discrimination and violence took hold. Black political power in the South and across the country quickly disintegrated.[9]

Yet, no matter how hard White Southerners worked to hold onto power and keep Black labor working on White land, it would have all been for naught if Black people could find better conditions in other regions. Quickly, the racial hierarchy that had defined the South was enforced through violence and enshrined in law far beyond the Mason-Dixon Line. When Confederate General Robert E. Lee had surrendered at Virginia's Appomattox Courthouse on April 9, 1865, it seemed clear that the North had won the war. But as the Confederacy saw its worldview and way of life reproduced throughout the country, it seemed to have won its own victory.

This was especially true in the rapidly settling West. Local and state governments in the West passed a litany of racially restrictive policies, with some places banning Black people entirely. One of the most blatant examples was the state of Oregon, which was founded as an all-White state in 1859. Policies like these had lasting effects, with Oregon resisting Black residents until 1926.[10] Even nearly a century later, the makeup of Oregon's population has hardly changed. Just 2.3 percent of the state's 4.2 million people are Black.

But the federal government was always at the helm. One of the primary ways that Whites retained control of the West was through the Homestead Act of 1862, which offered 160-acre parcels of land to citizens willing to manage and "improve" them.[11] Although a small number of Blacks and Latinos secured land on the frontier, specific policy and enforcement always favored White settlers.

In May 1865, just one month after the Civil War formally ended, General Ulysses S. Grant sought to merge Confederate and Union forces in order to invade Mexico and go to war with the French armies occupying it, even sending tens of thousands of soldiers to the southern border in preparation. Historian and Grant biographer Ron Chernow wrote, "With Mexico, Grant played a dangerous game, hoping to reunite North and South under the banner of a popular foreign war."[12]

Although that invasion never happened, the North and South would find common cause in clearing the western frontier of Natives. In this way, while westward expansion eased the tension still afoot in the East, its continued settlement was neither random nor inevitable. The US army waged continual wars against Native nations, killing Native peoples under the banner of Manifest Destiny and driving them off their ancestral lands from the Plains to the Pacific. These lands then became the homesteads of White settlers.[13]

Just as Sherman's land redistribution policy offers a glimpse into an alternate history, the 1869 Board of Indian Commissioners offered two potential ways forward in federal-tribal relations. Issuing their report in the same year the transcontinental railroad was completed, the board seemed ready to break with tradition. They wrote, "The history of the government connections with the Indians is a shameful record of broken treaties and unfulfilled promises."[14]

But truly renegotiating these relationships would mean undermining every justification the US had made to this territory, especially in the West. The board quickly added, "When upon the reservation, [Native peoples] should be taught as soon as possible the advantage of individual ownership of property."[15] They went on to discuss the importance of divesting tribes of communal lands.

Whereas taking Native lands had previously been justified on the grounds of converting Native peoples to Christianity, this marked a shift.[16] Land theft was now being justified as necessary to convert Indigenous people to a different creed: the preeminence of property. As more and more settlers moved west, it would not be long before the board's stated intentions would find their way into policy.

In 1887, Congress passed the Dawes Act, or what would become known as the General Allotment Act. Under this policy, tribes were forced onto far smaller reservations, with much of their land being made available for private ownership to those settlers pushing west.[17] This would lead to the loss of approximately ninety million acres of tribal lands—an area roughly the size of Montana—in less than fifty years. It is no coincidence that this started almost precisely at the time the West was beginning to "fill up" and the frontier would soon be pronounced "closed" in the 1890 Census.[18]

The Changing Face of the Nation

When the frontier was formally recognized as "closed," 87 percent of Black Americans worked in agriculture or domestic and personal service. Whites in the agriculture-dependent South did not fear that Blacks would compete for their jobs, because Whites owned the land. Whites in the North did not initially fear Blacks competing for their jobs, because they were few in numbers and worked in separate industries.[19] A common folk axiom at the time noted, "The South doesn't care how close a Negro gets just as long as he doesn't get too high; the North doesn't care how high he gets just so he doesn't get too close."[20]

The North stringently enforced segregation laws. In 1910, Baltimore passed a law preventing Blacks from buying homes on blocks with White majorities. Whites, similarly, were not allowed to move into majority-Black blocks.[21] Facing external judicial and public pressure, the city merely revised the law to apply to blocks already made up of one race. This law would be emulated to varying degrees in many Southern and border cities. In 1915, the NAACP's sixth annual report highlighted the segregation that still existed in neighborhoods and entire cities.[22] This would only worsen when then-Secretary of Commerce Herbert Hoover championed economic zoning plans in 1921. He used the Baltimore law as a blueprint.[23]

These zoning laws effectively blocked any potential integration in the North. But White people in the North found they faced other competition. Between 1880 and 1920, twenty-three million people entered and spread to every region across the country. As of 1910, 58 percent of all factory and mining workers were immigrants.[24]

This influx of immigrants would not be allowed to last. In 1924, the Johnson-Reed Immigration Act reduced the total number of immigrants allowed into the country from more than 387,000 to less than 187,000. But one of the most lasting effects of the law was not simply limiting how many immigrants were allowed in; it was dictating where they came from, severely restricting any foreign-born populations whose country of origin was not already well-represented in 1890. In 1921, 222,000 Italians entered the country. Between 1925 and 1930, there was an average of fifteen thousand each year. The law effectively banned Asian immigration altogether.[25]

But Black people could not be sealed out. The perhaps-subtler forms of racism seen previously in the North gave way to more overt forms as the Great Migration began around 1916. By 1919, with immigration halted in the early days of World War I, half a million Black people had left the South for better employment and legal protections in the North. In the 1920s, a million more would do the same.[26] And with Black migration came White violence.

In 1917, as World War I raged in Europe, cities across the US erupted. It started in the heart of the country: East St. Louis. Scores of people were killed and thousands of Black residents displaced. The violence then hit Houston. Two years later, it hit Chicago. And Omaha, Washington, D.C., and Elaine, Arkansas.[27] The violence against incoming Black residents was so widespread in the summer of 1919—striking at least twenty-six cities—that it was deemed the "Red Summer."[28] In 1921, White mobs ransacked and firebombed Tulsa's Greenwood District in Oklahoma, what had become known as "Black Wall Street," after a later-dismissed allegation against a Black man. Hundreds of Black residents were killed and thousands more were forced from their homes.[29]

The Great Migration period from 1916 to 1921 was rife with racial terror, but it only signaled what was to come. In each of these instances, governments did not pursue charges against those who assaulted Black residents or destroyed their property. Insurance companies did not honor payouts.[30] Many Black residents rebuilt their homes and community, but they were sent a clear message that they were on their own. During the next decade, encouraged by the absence of accountability for perpetrators of race massacres like these, the Ku Klux Klan and other White supremacist organizations grew rapidly.

Far from fulfilling the stereotypical image of the Ku Klux Klan as an impoverished, uneducated mob, historian Timothy Egan shows in his book *A Fever in the Heartland* that the White supremacist organization was overwhelmingly made up of members of the middle-class.[31] Beneath the white hoods—or often gathering without them—were teachers, policemen, and store owners as well as doctors, lawyers, and politicians. As Egan says, "Governors, including Oregon's, were elected with the full backing of the Klan. Four members of the United States Senate, up to seventy-five members of the House. So it wasn't some little bunch of guys in a basement."[32]

As the history of the Ku Klux Klan makes clear, the violence of this time period was not a Southern or Northern phenomenon but one that gripped the entire country. The height of its activity was in the Midwest and West, with membership highest in Indiana (240,000) and Ohio (195,000). In the 1920s, Oregon had the second-highest membership rate in the country, trailing only Indiana. It grew out of a backlash against immigration and women's rights, but the threat of Black in-migration to the Midwest and West was its driving force.[33]

The Klan's membership reflected that. Whites had grown accustomed to exclusive access to land and economic opportunities, seeing these as their birthright. As Blacks migrated from the South and immigrants traveled from around the world, Whites perceived this privileged status to be slipping away. They ridiculed, fought, and imprisoned immigrants from Ireland, Eastern Europe, and Southern Europe. Still, as these immigrants integrated in the workplace, in housing, and in language, they eventually gained acceptance as "Americans."

People from outside these regions, including Black people who'd been in the United States for centuries, often found it far more difficult or were prevented from ever doing the same. Many of these recent immigrants turned hostile toward Blacks seeking to establish residence in an area.[34] These newly White Americans were in the throes of the intoxicating power of free land and would do anything to secure it, even if that meant embracing racist ideology. Nowhere was this more visible than in the West, which was changing from a region of homesteading to a region of cities resembling the size and structure in other parts of the country.

The West, with its stated promise of equal opportunity, maintained its racialized space through laws, real estate policies, acts of violence, and a mountain of interpersonal offenses. As in other parts of the country, all these combined to encourage if not altogether mandate segregation. When these tactics failed to stop the steady influx of Black migrants, cities—especially smaller ones apprehensive of large population increases—often turned toward regulations and outright bans. Like Baltimore and St. Louis, Denver and Los Angeles passed segregation laws that greatly impacted the racial makeup of the entire region.[35]

But settling the West required extensive labor. To meet this need without altering the racial hierarchy, cities and states passed sundown laws and laws against interracial marriage. During the day, Black people and recent immigrants worked side-by-side felling trees, laying rail, and working the mines. But after dark, Black people were banned from town.[36] Their labor was needed, but their settlement would not be tolerated.

In the following decades, many Western states actually became less racially diverse, even as the United States as a whole became far more diverse. In Montana, 3.4 percent of the 1910 population in the state capital of Helena was Black. As of 2020, the population was 0.7 percent Black. The city in 2021 had roughly half the total number of Black residents (232) as it had more than a century before (420). Statewide, despite growing by nearly 12 percent between 2010 and 2021, just 0.6 percent of Montana's population was Black.

This history is familiar throughout much of the country but had been willfully forgotten in the West. Recent research, such as historian Quintard Taylor's 1998 book *In Search of the Racial Frontier: African Americans in the American West 1528–1990,* have started to change this. Deeply researched and articulating both the number and significance of Blacks in the West, Taylor's work seeks to force a reckoning with the commonly accepted narrative of White settlers as the sole pioneers on a rugged and empty frontier.

* * * * * * *

Local discriminatory laws and individual acts of violence were instrumental in segregating the West and the entire country, but many people allowed this violence to proliferate. Industry leaders were often in lock-step with government officials and prevailing White opinion when it came to segregation. The National Association of Real Estate Boards (NAREB), for instance, had rules against residential mixing in 1913. As Stephen Grant Meyer wrote in *As Long as They Don't Move Next Door*, "The weight of evidence demonstrates that [policies] reflected a popular unwillingness on the part of whites to have African Americans living in their midst."[37] The same year, Woodrow Wilson approved segregation across federal offices.[38] Policies reflected White racial animus—and then amplified it.

In backing the removal of Native peoples in 1830, Senator Benjamin Leigh of Virginia, may have accurately described the prevalence of White resistance to living with another race.[39] Similarly, in advocating for segregated neighborhoods a century later, real estate companies may have been accurate in saying prices could drop in suddenly integrated neighborhoods because some White residents would flee.[40] But Leigh's policies favoring removal and realtors' policies favoring segregation cannot be understood as simply reflecting the will of the masses. Instead, these statements belie the influence of these entities in shaping the will of the White populace and, in so doing, continuing to shape the racial landscape.

At this time, race was seldom invoked directly or publicly in relation to federal housing policy. In fact, the federal government said little about housing at all, instead allowing city and state governments as well as real estate companies and boards to determine their own policies. When these nonfederal actors sought to create or preserve segregated neighborhoods, the federal government remained silent. And this silence spoke volumes.

Better Homes in America was a nominally private group with so much political clout that it operated essentially as an arm of the government. In its announcement within the October 1922 issue of the *Delineator*, the fledgling organization refers to itself as "a nation-wide campaign conducted in cooperation with national and state officials." The campaign was built around increasing homeownership, branding "the home as an investment," as its first president, then-secretary of commerce Herbert

Hoover, entitled the article he wrote for the magazine. Hoover argued that there was a "primal instinct in us all for home ownership."[41]

Hoover was joined by other powerful figures including sitting Vice President Calvin Coolidge, who served as chair of the advisory council, and future president Franklin D. Roosevelt, then president of the American Construction Council. Better Homes in America's 1923 "Demonstration Week," in which recently constructed, idealized homes were on display in cities across the country, had the support of governors from 30 states plus the territories of Hawaii and Alaska.[42]

Although these demonstrations were often explicitly segregated, Better Homes in America was typically coyer on racial issues. Instead of explicitly promoting racially segregated neighborhoods, they advertised "'restricted residential districts'" as a way to ensure homeowners "'protection against persons with whom your family won't care to associate.'"[43]

Particularly within the post–World War I landscape, homeownership had become a badge of patriotism.[44] The rapid movement of Black citizens from the South and entrance of immigrants from throughout Europe and Mexico had crowded Northern cities and led to calls for more housing construction. And, with the news of Russia's Bolshevik Revolution still fresh in everyone's mind, any federal plan which advocated for cooperative or public housing was seen as political suicide. Amid heavy lobbying from the real estate industry, the detached, single-family home became the idealized form of homeownership.[45]

In the same stroke, multiunit properties became villainized. This view would only grow stronger in the wake of a 1926 Supreme Court ruling which upheld the right of a Cleveland suburb to restrict apartments from an area of single-family homes.[46] Being an American meant owning a home—a detached, single-family home. There was just one problem: homeownership was prohibitively expensive.

At the time, a 50 percent down payment was standard when buying a home. Additionally, full loan repayment was typically required in just five to seven years. For much of the population, Whites included, homeownership was all but out of reach.[47] The stock market crash of 1929 and the ensuing Depression only heightened this difficulty. If the federal government wanted "a nation of homeowners," as Vice President Calvin Coolidge had called for in 1922, it would have to expend a massive amount of effort and money to make it possible. And that is exactly what the federal government did.

Dreaming the Suburbs

In 1870, there was one major railway in the Western United States, running from Omaha to San Francisco. By 1890, there were hundreds, leading to the fateful 1890 census report that the western frontier had closed. In the decades after, technological and demographic changes dramatically altered the landscape of where people lived and worked. Industrial jobs supplanted agricultural jobs as the main economic engine for the country. The routes people traveled frequently remained the same as those taken by Native peoples on foot thousands and thousands of years before, but foot travel was replaced by wagons and then replaced by train and then automobile. People could now live further from work. With twenty-three million people entering the country between 1880 and 1920 and work being concentrated in industrial areas of cities, it could be argued that they had to.[1]

These demographic and economic changes further distorted what, until the Civil War, had been a clear, rigidly enforced racial hierarchy in the United States. Suddenly, with immigration from outside western

Europe growing dramatically, who was White and who was not was no longer always clear. In the suburbs, the "small parts" around "cities," it would be made clear again.

The suburbs began to take shape in 1934 as the Federal Housing Administration (FHA) provided a system for insuring mortgages and vastly increased the possibility of homeownership. As part of this program, the FHA mapped areas they deemed worthy or unworthy of credit. Those dubbed most hazardous or the biggest credit risks were outlined in red—redlined. Building on several court cases that had defined Whiteness, race was a primary feature of the FHA. Credit—and therefore the possibility of homeownership and upward mobility—became almost entirely inaccessible to non-Whites.[2]

If someone wanted to point to the moment Whiteness took on its modern construct—when it grew to include those with ancestry from western, southern, and eastern Europe, when it suddenly covered Australians and New Zealanders, though not the Aboriginal or Māori, when it excepted those of Middle Eastern, North African, or Polynesian origin—this was it. And this was the moment when this modern construct of Whiteness became synonymous with wealth. As with the genocide of Native peoples and the enslavement of Black Africans, as with racialized immigration policies at all ports of entry and racial segregation throughout the country, this group of people, author James Baldwin observed, "brought humanity to the edge of oblivion, because they think they are white."[3] Between 1934 and 1962, the US government underwrote $120 billion in loans. Less than 2 percent were granted to non-White people.[4]

These maps, like many racialized policies surrounding housing, were deliberately obscured from the public eye.[5] This was the lie, a lie that worked because the White population was more than willing to embrace the belief that homeownership marked success in a free market.[6] It was the lie cultivated by an already long-standing ideal of individualism. Historian Frederick Jackson Turner himself realized the intoxicating allure of individualistic thinking in the United States, writing, "We cannot lay too much stress upon this point, for it was at the very heart of the whole American movement."[7]

. . . .

Similar to justifying the removal of Native peoples on grounds that they had not "improved" the land, White people in the mid-twentieth century would often point to urban "slums" as reasons Black people were not fit for homeownership. And similarly, these justifications do not stand up to the slightest scrutiny. In the mid-nineteenth century, tribes with advanced governments, languages, and economies were viewed as the greatest threat and some of the first to be sought out for forced removal.[8] More than a hundred years later, it was common to see documents such as the 1943 national real estate manual that advised against what it viewed as the three biggest threats to neighborhoods: "prostitution houses, bootleggers, and a colored man of means who was giving his children a college education and thought they were entitled to live among whites."[9]

Success of non-Whites, particularly in close proximity to Whites, demonstrated an ability to overcome systemic obstacles and laid bare that even poorer Whites had been granted priority over wealthier Blacks. The "market" was not simply based on who could afford it but on what political scientist and Black studies professor Cedric Robinson referred to as "racial capitalism."[10] These examples punctured the myth of the self-made man that was so central to the frontier imaginary for White settlers in the nineteenth century and White homeowners in the twentieth.

. . . .

World War II scrambled the map, forcing people of all races into close proximity. Between December 1941 and March 1945, fifteen million people—approximately one in every nine—in the United States changed their county of residence. Especially for Black Americans, much of this migration was to cities with war plants such as Detroit, Baltimore, Los Angeles, and San Francisco.[11] This migration during and after World

War II dwarfed the already-massive number that had moved three decades before, at the start of World War I.

Instances arose across the country of Whites blocking temporary housing for Black war workers.[12] It was common at the time for Whites to argue that Blacks didn't want integration either. President Truman, speaking to the National Colored Democratic Association in the late 1940s, attempted to strike a balance, saying, "I wish to make it clear that I am not appealing for social equality of the Negro." It was his opinion that Black leaders wanted "justice, not social relations."[13] When Supreme Court rulings in *Shelley v. Kramer* (1948) and *Barrows v. Jackson* (1953) banned racially restrictive housing deeds and covenants, this argument was put to the test.

The Supreme Court determined in 1954 that "separate educational facilities are inherently unequal." The same was true of housing. Despite Truman's rhetoric, Black families sought affordable housing irrespective of the neighborhood's racial composition. In a 1956 Urban League poll, 84 percent of 678 polled Black families in Los Angeles said they would move to nonminority neighborhoods if they could.[14]

In Los Angeles suburbs such as West Adams, Crenshaw, and Compton—as in many across the nation—entrance of Black residents triggered racist responses ranging from vandalism to bomb threats to beatings of the White homeowners who sold to them. The resistance to integration was not common to all races; housing, perhaps more than any other facet of US society, crystallized the ways race and class had been fused together.[15] Integration represented a threat to a system predicated on the basis of White supremacy.

During the Great Migration, White residents killed thousands of recently arrived Black residents and displaced tens of thousands—if not hundreds of thousands—more. A quarter century later, efforts to integrate the suburbs faced similar mob violence from Whites. Collectively, these acts served as warnings that those spaces were reserved for Whites only. As Lipsitz noted, "Widespread, costly, and often counterproductive practices of surveillance, regulation, and incarceration become justified as forms of frontier defense against demonized people of color."[16]

The judicial rulings that opened the door for integrated neighborhoods were given little enforcement to back them up. Police were on hand in some instances but did not intervene, only serving to reinforce past efforts aimed at achieving segregation.[17] This White vigilantism was so widespread and yet is now so sparsely spoken of that it has been described as the "hidden violence" of post–World War II.[18]

This trend was not restricted to suburbs. In a practice described as "Whitecapping," Whites routinely used terror tactics to force Blacks from homes in the country and take possession of these spaces.[19] Whitecapping was tolerated and reinforced by what historian Pete Daniel refers to as the government's "passive nullification" of Black farmers' right to land. In *Dispossession: Discrimination Against African American Farmers in the Age of Civil Rights*, Daniel details the government's discriminatory patterns, which eventually contributed to the loss of 93 percent of Black farmers between 1940 and 1973. The number of Black farmers plummeted from more than 680,000 to fewer than 46,000, less than one tenth of 1 percent of the total rural population.[20]

White Flight

If terror campaigns and government complicity failed to remove Blacks from areas, Whites moved from these integrating areas en masse, further populating suburbs and creating new ones beyond. This is commonly referred to as "White flight."[21] Many claimed fears of plummeting property value as their reasoning. The prevalence of violence and migration, however, pointed toward underlying racial animus.[22]

As was true prior to this entire period of homeownership, the real estate industry both reinforced and fostered these fears. Realtors engaged in blockbusting practices of reiterating these concerns and creating an urgency for White residents to leave. When they did, the price was raised for incoming Blacks who had few other options.[23] Real estate agents also held their own internal codes. If an agent sold to non-White buyers in White neighborhoods, they were blackballed, punished with restricted access to listing services.[24]

Just as in other areas, this internal code did not simply materialize from within the real estate industry. As head of the Public Works Administration (PWA) and secretary of the interior, Harold Ickes instituted a "neighborhood composition rule" that emphasized maintaining the existing racial makeup of areas. Such a rule was almost identical to the one espoused shortly after by the FHA's 1935 Underwriting Manual.[25] Ickes created an interracial workforce that built trails, dams, bridges, schools, and other infrastructure projects across the Depression-era United States, especially the West. He would then commonly determine whether an area was White or Black and order segregated workforce housing to match his perception.[26] While White communities continued to rely on non-Whites' labor, they were openly hostile to non-Whites and even outlawed their presence outside of work.

When Congress ended the PWA in 1937 and localities established their own agencies and construction plans, those agencies were federally funded by the United States Housing Authority (USHA). One of USHA's primary stipulations was that "the aim of the [local housing] authority should be the preservation rather than the disruption of community social structures which best fit the desires of the groups concerned."[27] The 1940 Lanham Act financing housing for workers in defense industries echoed this effort to maintain segregation. Ickes's "neighborhood composition rule" continued.

Every push toward integration seemed to be met with backlash. A 1949 Housing Act passed Congress only after proposed amendments to integrate any newly built public housing had been removed.[28] Despite the sea of policies slowly moving to prevent housing discrimination in cities and states across both the North and West, most lacked enforcement and many seemed to offer mixed federal support at best.[29] It was the same nonresponse the federal government had given when faced with the rampant encroachment of settlers on Native land 180 years prior.[30] That the federal government had created the frenzy for land in both instances did not force a strong affirmation of change. Whether complicit or feeble, the result was the same: a federal statement of not condoning such actions with little to no effort to alter them.

• • • • • • •

Some of these efforts to continue racializing space were formalized with policy. The 1950s, for instance, saw a combined 330,000 Black migrants moving to the three largest West Coast cities: Los Angeles, San Francisco, and Seattle.[31] Despite a homeownership boom, public housing—either government-built or government-sponsored housing—had remained a common residential option across races since the passage of the Housing Act of 1937. It kept housing affordable for those unable to afford the higher costs of private development, which had no interest in providing affordable housing for low-income people when it had a higher-income market available.

When the Housing Act of 1937 passed, the government stipulated that the units created as public housing would be exclusively for low-income residents. Additionally, every unit created would also dictate that poor-quality units already in existence—slums—would be torn down. Neither of these things had to happen. The first was agreed to so as not to disrupt the profit margins of private developers. The second was agreed to so as to appease cities, which court rulings determined to have oversight over the building of public housing, as opposed to the federal government.[32] [33] But the fact that these stipulations were included ensured that public housing would operate at a loss. The government would become the slumlord.

For nearly two decades, public housing remained popular with tenants and the broader public, at least compared to the scant alternatives. They even housed some people who would have been considered part of the middle class. But buildings also remained segregated. And over time, as more White residents secured loans and bought homes and more housing for Black residents fell into disrepair or economic dead zones, this became more and more difficult to justify. Vacancies in White public housing grew alongside the wait lists for Black public housing. Finally, it reached a breaking point. In 1954, the California Supreme Court decided in *Banks v. Housing Authority of San Francisco* that the same standards must apply to all who were eligible for public housing, regardless of race.[34]

Almost overnight, public housing became taboo and politically unpopular, synonymous with where Black people lived.[35] Twelve states passed constitutional amendments requiring local referendums for building low-income family public housing. The Supreme Court upheld the practice.[36] The real estate industry, always opposed to public housing, was quick to draw attention to the government costs in public housing while further obscuring the far more massive government subsidies involved in suburbanization.[37] Homeownership, almost explicitly reserved for those identified as White, was reinforced as the model of success in US society.

Tension Rising

Cases like this and shifts in the economy underscored the US population's continued movement West. By this point, Native peoples had largely been forced to give up their lands or been relegated to far smaller and less economically viable reservations. The Hoover Commission of 1949 called for "complete integration" and termination of tribes and federal recognition. This resulted in the termination of 109 tribes and bands, especially smaller ones, but even those not formally terminated were deeply affected. Most tribes endured intrusive assimilation policies, leading to the "continued relocation programs to encourage Indian migration from the reservations to urban areas."[38]

New laws were ostensibly opening the West to non-Whites, a phenomenon leading one paper to refer to the region in the 1950s as the "'New Frontier' of racial tension."[39] This statement came as large populations of Blacks and other people of color, especially immigrants, entered cities previously carved out to be majority-White in the West.

When the 1887 General Allotment Act had wiped out two-thirds of Native land, reducing reservations from 138 million collective acres in 1887 to 48 million acres in 1934, race had scarcely been mentioned as a factor. With much of the remaining acreage poor for farming, Native peoples were left with few options but to seek out work in increasingly urbanized areas.[40] In other words, "racial tension" was noted when non-Whites searched for stable housing, jobs, or schools in predominantly

White areas. When Whites entered predominantly non-White areas, it was just the market at work.

The 1968 Fair Housing Act, passed to quell the violence and despondency that had boiled over in the days following Martin Luther King Jr.'s assassination, signaled a monumental shift. No longer would housing discrimination on the basis of race be tolerated.[41] But even this was tempered by a lack of enforcement. The first HUD secretary, Robert Weaver, requested $11.1 million to hire 850 investigators White and Black "housing testers" who would compare treatment in home-buying efforts and address discriminatory practices. With approximately one investigator for every 240,000 people in the country, they would face an uphill battle but would at least be able to maintain a presence across the country. The 1969 budget instead allocated funds for forty-two.[42]

As detailed by reporter Nikole Hannah-Jones, HUD secretary George Romney famously described housing in the late 1960s as a "high-income white noose" around what were predominantly Black inner cities. Using the language of the 1968 Fair Housing Act, which instructed the government to "affirmatively further" desegregation in housing, Romney planned to refuse funding for towns and cities which were not adequately desegregating.[43]

His proposal was stopped by President Nixon, saying in a then-confidential 1972 memo, "I am convinced that while legal segregation is totally wrong that forced integration of housing or education is just as wrong." Every president of both parties for the next forty years followed suit and the policy was never enacted. As Martin Luther King Jr. said himself in 1967, "There is a tragic gulf between civil rights laws passed and civil rights laws implemented."[44]

A century prior, the Civil War had ended with the Union intact and Black Americans being officially freed from slavery. But the culture of slavery—the culture of White supremacy, of discrimination, of the fusion of race and economics—remained alive and well. As land ownership remained the same, Black people found themselves forced into the margins of society or back to the fields. Upon leaving the South, they found a diffuse, sometimes deadly level of prejudice and discrimination. Racism was embedded in the country's political makeup and economic engine, and White people in every region seemed determined to keep it this way.

A growing number were drawn to leaders like Marcus Garvey and Malcolm X who proclaimed Black nationalism and separation from Whites. They'd lost patience in waiting for a shared future. The majority who still held out hope of an integrated future staked this hope on the civil rights movement of the 1960s.

Activists did win sweeping advances that opened up society for all non-Whites. But these gains had not come easy. And, as the rights of Black people to sit at the same lunch counters, be educated in the same schools, and live in the same neighborhoods as White people were formally enshrined in law, the culture that had led to such discrimination pushed back violently. People such as Alabama governor George Wallace, who promised to defend "segregation forever" in 1963, changed their words but not their ideology. While campaigning for president in 1964 and 1968, Wallace scarcely mentioned segregation directly. Instead, he spoke primarily of freedom from government intrusion, the same argument made today by those seeking to obscure the significance of slavery as a reason for the Civil War.

The Confederate flag was suddenly flown in pockets of the country far beyond the dozen states which had seceded. This did not arise from nowhere. As historian Greg Grandin documents, the flag has reappeared again and again in US military operations abroad dating back to the Spanish-American War in 1898.[45] But it was during the Korean and Vietnam Wars—as racial integration and the civil rights movement dominated headlines—that the Confederate flag came to be seen as a symbol of a far more general resistance to change. Nowhere was this White resistance to change—this White entitlement—clearer than where they lived. And where they allowed non-Whites to live.

· · · · · · · ·

Decades on from the creation of the Federal Housing Administration, the United States had largely succeeded in creating a "nation of homeowners" based on their chosen criteria.[46] In addition to the psychological benefits that came from being secure in their home, tens of millions were rewarded with a slate of tax breaks ranging from mortgage interest to property tax to home repairs. Their monthly payments would not go to a landlord but instead toward something they would own. It would go toward an investment, an investment that was already skyrocketing in value. They would tell themselves all this was possible because they'd worked hard and been frugal, things that may have been true. But the truth was that none of it would have been possible if not for one thing: the government had decided they were White.

In declaring who was White, the government also declared who wasn't. This subsection of America was ruled ineligible for the government assistance suddenly accessible to White people. These people—with ancestry from Africa, Asia, and across the Americas—fought this discrimination at every turn, organizing marches and boycotts and sit-ins. They worked long hours at factories and on trains and in shops, usually working for White bosses and tending to White customers in order to pay their White landlords. Many non-White residents managed to make ends meet in underfunded public housing and cramped apartments in the city.

And then they started hearing about "urban renewal" and "revitalization." They started seeing men and women in suits beside men and women in hardhats. Politicians came. And cops. Rents started going up, often under the pretense of renovations. Seemingly overnight, the inner city had become a place of rapid investment, what its residents had wanted for years, sometimes decades. The problem was that it wasn't for them.

Reviving the City

Ruth Glass knew something about migration. One of thousands of Jewish people who fled to England just before the Nazi Party came to power, Glass became a sociologist specializing in Afro-Caribbean immigrant experiences in England and the rapid urbanization of countries throughout the Global South. Overwhelmingly, she wrote about the working class. But it was her observations on the movement of the middle and upper class for which she is remembered. In her 1964 book *London: Aspects of Change*, she traced the influx of these classes to working-class neighborhoods across London, noting how affordable restaurants became espresso shops and affordable homes became "elegant, expensive residences." And she gave this process a name: gentrification.[1]

Speaking so directly to an intimately familiar phenomenon, the word has outlived Glass. With some heralding its ability to bring new investment to an area and others bemoaning the displacement of longtime residents, gentrification has been characterized as "the most politically loaded word in urban geography."[2] So, it made sense that I received a wide array of answers when I asked a sample of people "What's the first word that comes to mind when you hear the term *gentrification*?"

One said complicated. Another said inequity. Two said Starbucks, four said White, the others said justice and poor and upscale and dangerous. Wealth. Profit. Discriminatory. Displacement. Class. Hipsters. Greed. Change.

No matter which word first comes to mind, most people understand gentrification only in terms of its effects. We think of flannel and overpriced coffee. We think of people working remotely and dogs wearing sweaters. We think of clean streets and Whole Foods and high rises and any number of other stereotypes. In this way, we miss how gentrification actually occurs.

The history of the word gives some insight into how we can make sense of it today. In 1969, five years after Glass coined the term and on the heels of the 1968 Fair Housing Act's passage, a White Brooklyn man named Everett Ortner brought the term to the US.[3] The founder of the Brownstone Revival Committee, Ortner touched off a debate that rages on today: just what does gentrification "revive"? Perhaps more important, for whose benefit?

To create space for wealth or so-called revival, the area must first be made blank. That's why gentrification is not simply richer people moving into an area; it's also poorer people—and those perceived to be less profitable—being pushed out. In contrast to popular beliefs on the subject, this process is neither natural nor accidental. As Neil Smith points out in his rent gap theory, "The economic geography of gentrification is not random."[4] Beneath the veneer of new businesses, less crime, and cleaner streets, this process is primarily about replacing what exists with something new.[5] As Glass explained upon first using the term, "Once this process of 'gentrification' starts in a district, it goes on until all or most of the original working-class occupiers are displaced, and the whole social character of the district is changed."[6]

Analogies abound for gentrification but both proponents and opponents often describe it in terms of a frontier.[7] The changing neighborhood is a place to occupy, to claim as one's own, to call home. Occasionally, it is even compared to colonization, an admission that the space suddenly occupied was not previously empty.[8] Jessi Quizar, an urban studies professor at the University of Washington, Tacoma, has studied both in depth. In an article about housing in Detroit, she noted that "although I am disturbed by an uncritical metaphor . . . that equates gentrification with settler colonialism, I am increasingly convinced that we must take the relationship between them seriously."[9] Historian Patrick Wolfe famously said of the colonization of the United States that "invasion is a structure not an event."[10] The same could be said of gentrification.

One major difference, a more modern twist on any comparison, is that the physical, more immediately visible forms of violence that allowed the United States to settle the western part of the "New World" are not the primary drivers of the gentrification of a city block. The violence is instead often psychological, coming about through the stress of poor building upkeep, the continued presence of crime, harassment by police, and the feeling of loss that accompanies a radical change in the neighborhood. It is also often economic, as seen in increased costs for commercial space and housing itself. But the threat of physical violence is always lurking, found in the presence of police or the potential for eviction.

· · · · · · ·

Back in 2016, I was working for a nonprofit tree work and landscape construction company in Minneapolis. I was a crew lead for a group of young adults who had barriers to employment that ranged from criminal records to learning disabilities to unsteady home lives. For the most part, I liked my job, with typical daily tasks involving mowing lawns, building boardwalks, and trimming trees. And then came the day that my supervisor informed us that our task involved clearing the encampments of the unhoused.

According to the initial listing, my job required a college degree. Additional certifications didn't hurt. The qualified applicant would take home thirteen dollars an hour and whatever it felt like to clear people's temporary homes.

I paused. I asked questions. I was told that, in the days prior, people had been informed we would be there and were being provided for by St. Stephen's, a Minneapolis-based homeless services group. I made it clear that I still didn't like it, that I saw no reason why people could not take shelter beneath the bridges that passed over the Minneapolis Greenway.

Some of the young adult crew members had faced unstable housing and evictions themselves. They knew what it felt like to have nowhere else to go. I made eye contact with one of them and wished I hadn't. I still felt his eyes on me as I looked back to my supervisor. For a moment, I thought about refusing, about what would happen if I did. About whether the crew members would feel pressure to do the same. About whether I'd be written up or simply fired. And then I was throwing mattresses, clothes, stuffed animals, and anything else into the bed of the truck.

I told myself that I didn't have much of a choice. Up until that point, my employment in Minneapolis had been less than steady. Despite spending the bulk of each day looking, I didn't find work before arriving or for the eight weeks after. Neither did my two roommates. With my savings dwindling rapidly, I lowered my sights and applied for a job at Jimmy John's. I knew I could get it, because I'd worked for the chain for years already. At minimum wage, my income was meager. To get enough shifts to make ends meet, I often worked late nights, sometimes closing as late as 4:00 am. Many of these nights, I delivered sandwiches by bicycle.

In the dead of Minnesota winter, I hit my breaking point. A light dusting of snow had covered the layer of ice beneath. I rounded a corner on my bike and lost control on a particularly slick patch, sending both my bike and my body into the road. But nobody was coming. I sat there alone on the ice for a minute, wondering what I was doing in that job, in Minnesota, in life.

In the following weeks, another job finally came through and I put in my notice. Things slowly got better. I spent my first year in Minneapolis working two, sometimes three, jobs that typically added up to more than forty hours a week. I had no benefits of any kind but managed to make things work by forgoing a car, instead putting the bulk of my income toward rent and paying down student loans. After more than a year of this, I'd finally gotten the job as a crew leader for the tree work and employment training program.

By most indicators—I was White, a recent transplant to the city, and had a college degree—I was part of the wave of gentrification sweeping through the city. I saw the rent going up and saw the changing face of the neighborhood, even knew I was the changing face of the neighborhood. But I told myself it hadn't been easy for me either, that I'd earned my presence there by sheer determination.

Earned. Merited. Deserved. The United States worships narratives like these, of individuals triumphing against all odds. Worst to first. Chump to champ. Rags to riches. These stories parallel the country's favorite creation myth about how an outmanned, outgunned army made up of everyday people with a dogged commitment to liberty gave birth to the greatest country in the history of the world.

We concoct similar stories about ourselves, of how we got to where we are, how others got to where they are. These stories form a philosophy of who gets to belong. Unsure where to put our faith, we cling to the sanctity of the market. We come to believe that we earn our place in a changing neighborhood, just like we earn our place in society. And that others can, too.

. . . .

Gentrification can sometimes be turned into an academic exercise. It is the result of liberal ideology within a postindustrial economy. It stems from the juxtaposition of an aesthetic of place and community with increasingly planned neighborhoods. The credit or blame rests with the proliferation of technology-dependent—and therefore less geographically bound—jobs, what we now call remote work.[11] Regardless, the critical element in understanding these frontiers of gentrification—understanding any frontiers—is that they are neither inevitable nor happenstance; they are built. And, as author Naomi Klein states, "The reason you build a frontier is always the same: nothing is more profitable."[12]

From its earliest entrance into the public vocabulary, gentrification was an intentional, often systematic process of change. Furthermore, it began long before individuals of higher perceived value ever entered a neighborhood. As was true for previous frontiers, on-the-ground changes began with policies and actions far removed from these places. Individuals are making choices about where to live, but these decisions are being guided and prompted by both the options that are economically available and the ideal that is internalized. These options and ideals are not created by brave developers or so-called pioneers to a previously undesirable space. Rather, in gentrification, spaces are made desirable as the result of policies that favor growth and wealth over community stability.[13]

Gentrification is only possible by the direct and indirect actions of government at all levels. The 1970s and 1980s saw the federal government cut massive amounts from social services, transportation, and affordable housing, leaving cities and states to make up the gap.[14] Unable to pay for road maintenance, social services, and a host of other issues, cities competed to attract residents who would spend more and contribute to a higher tax base. This resulted in severe disinvestment to poorer areas, especially those home to more people of color.

This disinvestment often paved the way for what journalist and author P. E. Moskowitz referred to as Stage 0: the use of real estate, tax, and zoning policies to clear previously disinvested areas in order to make room for new development. This so-called urban renewal translated into poorer, marginalized residents leaving and wealthier ones entering.[15] As author James Baldwin once quipped, "Urban renewal means Negro removal."[16]

Nowhere has this process been more visible than in the fight over public housing. In Chicago in the early 1970s, for instance, the Supreme Court ordered HUD to build public housing in predominantly White areas of the city as well as the majority-Black ones. Chicago's response was to stop building public housing entirely.[17]

This change signaled the collapse of one of the most significant defenses against rising housing costs. Public housing had been brought into existence by the refusal of the real estate industry to build adequate housing for working- and middle-class residents when wealthier, more profitable homes could be built.[18] When cities ceased to build public housing units or restricted them to the poorest residents, the message was clear: the market had free reign.

Racial segregation took hold. Parts of cities—sometimes entire cities—were intentionally cleared for outside wealth. Through tax breaks and zoning allowances, more affluent, overwhelmingly White, populations flocked back to the city. Settlements and federal court rulings found HUD and local government practices responsible for this segregation in cities ranging from Baltimore to Dallas to San Francisco.[19] Nevertheless, this process has continued, not so different from that seen in 1980. Geographers Richard Schaffer and Neil Smith saw this in their 1986 article "The Gentrification of Harlem." As they explained, "We are witnessing not a curious anomaly but a trenchant restructuring of urban space."[20]

This trenchant restructuring is more than a suggested aesthetic; it pervades everything about a place. Kids making up games in the street become kids following rules on the playground. The music spilling out of a nightclub becomes the hushed conversations of a café. People change. Sights change. Smells change. But, perhaps more than anything else, the sounds change.

In an article for *The Atlantic*, Xochitl Gonzalez described the myriad changes to the working-class Brooklyn neighborhood in which she grew up. And with these changes comes policing of these changes. As one example of the long history of this policing in New York, Gonzalez explained how the New York Police Department launched Operation Soundtrap in 1991 to fine and even confiscate cars emitting music that was deemed too loud. The police chief at the time said, "If they don't turn down the volume, we'll turn off their ignition." This program was most active in majority non-White neighborhoods.

In 2019, after reporting the most noise complaints to the city's non-emergency hotline, Brooklyn was named the loudest borough in New York by one data analysis. The vast majority of these complaints were not for offenses like construction work or car horns but more personal allegations like talking or playing music too loudly. But, as Gonzalez questioned, "Was it the noisiest borough? Or was it just home to the densest mix of loud people and people who wanted to control those loud people?"

Operation Soundtrap is part of a pattern of policing neighborhoods for anything or anyone seen as straying too far from accepted parameters. As the saying goes, "The nail that sticks out is hammered down." The phrase is usually understood to refer to more collectivist cultures like those found in East Asia, not individualist ones like the United States. But the individualism in the United States is a selective one, prohibiting panhandling and many home-based businesses and even houses below a certain size while offering virtually no limits to nepotism and corporate tax loopholes and the construction of mansions.

In fast-growing neighborhoods, city officials adopt rules and norms similar to homeowners' associations. They embrace a controversial criminology philosophy known as the "broken windows theory" and punish the "window breakers." They remove graffiti and punish graffiti artists. They crack down on broken taillights and drinking in public and loitering, increasing police power to take unilateral action.[21]

When determining who gets to belong, city officials apply rules unevenly. As high-end grocery stores move in, community gardens are criminalized. As developers of luxury condos get a tax break, existing residents see a rent increase. Those who fit the neighborhood's new aesthetic—one that's typically Whiter and wealthier and favors different credentials—are welcomed with open arms. Those who don't are shamed, reported, and fined, forced to choose between blending in and moving out. Gonzalez observed that, "The sound of gentrification is silence."[22] The truth is that it depends on who's making the noise.

The West and Gentrification

When Neil Smith said gentrification was producing a "new urban frontier," he was seeing a similarity between the blank, unregulated landscape of the West and the increasingly blank, unregulated landscape of cities.[23] This was more than an abstract comparison. As towns and cities across the West embraced technological innovation and transitioned to a service-based economy, the region began to see rapid growth. The new development and investment that spurred an overwhelmingly White and more affluent population to return to cities across the country also spurred their movement west. This westward trend has never ceased.

A frontier is inherently a political determination involving who is included and who is excluded. It bestows power to some individuals to make—or escape—the rules in a particular demarcated territory. Most important, frontiers do not begin as blank slates but instead are made into them.[24]

The need to protect nature has often been used as justification to make a place "blank."[25] In some instances, nature has been viewed as something needing "improvement," justifying its seizure by those willing or able to do so.[26] In others, it is something to be preserved, justifying land seizure by those who claim a desire to protect it, what has come to be known as the "conservation and control thesis."[27] The determining factor in which logic is used—"improvement" or "protection" of nature—is who stands to gain.

Westward expansion may have been driven by ideals of freedom, individualism, and new beginnings, but it was always grounded in something far less noble and far more tangible: it was profitable.[28] Each successive push west was enabled by federal governmental policy. Technology, labor, and the "discovery" of new material facilitated new ventures, and therefore new ways to accumulate profit.

So-called commodity frontiers followed the same westward march as towns grew around western US outposts for timber, mining, and large-scale agriculture.[29] Many were not equipped with the resources nearby needed to support this growth. In this way, despite the visible ecological impacts of these extractive industries, the western frontier has always created lines between development and nature, operating on an illusion of separation between the human and natural world.

In the 1970s and 1980s, many who had previously taken up residence in suburbs were spurred to relocate to city centers that were receiving massive investment. With striking advances in transportation, communication, and land development easing the "friction of distance," others sought out the original escape: the West.[30] The "small-town atmosphere and proximity to public lands" of so-called micropolitan western towns like Flagstaff, Bozeman, Bend, and Boulder easily evoked the frontier imaginary that was so embedded in the creation of the suburbs.[31]

Similar to large metropolitan areas orchestrating a "back-to-the-city" movement, the New West economy reversed the traditional calculus from jobs attracting people to one of people attracting jobs. Before people arrived, however, even before they had the capacity to handle the influx of people, cities branded themselves as tourism hubs.[32] Touting the climate, recreation opportunities, and aesthetic appeal of the surrounding area, the "New West School" sought to attract many of the same populations as cities: well-educated, monied or potentially monied, and mostly White.

· · · · · · · ·

In the face of these systemic, even global, forces, it becomes easy to cling to stories. The fledgling nation that became an empire. The "city on a hill" that became an example for the world. Children and adults alike are fed stories of superheroes, spies, the lone fighter in the ring. Overcoming all odds, finding one's way in a foreign and hostile land, becomes a sort of rite of passage.

This creates a strange dichotomy. To succeed is to struggle immensely, living perilously close to the edge but never going over. To succeed is to risk it all on what others deem a stupid investment, to live paycheck-to-paycheck in order to chase a dream, to buy up all the Monopoly properties and teeter on the brink, only to pass "Go" and live another day, earning a passive income each time others' land on our property. Though we were once weak ourselves, our willingness to exploit others' weakness becomes a sudden windfall.

The more difficult trick for those who succeed becomes justifying this inequality. In order to hold ourselves up as paragons of success against a backdrop of squalor, our molehills become mountains. Seeing others as competitors, we are quick to dismiss the odds they face with declarations that they should work harder. In our eyes, their mountains are mere molehills. Our stories, stemming from an obsession with a mythical self-made man, are distorted and self-serving, strident denials of the help we've received alongside righteous outrage at the help others request. In short, our stories are lies.

As was mine. The truth was that I'd waited a little too long before starting back at Jimmy John's. My first paycheck was delayed a week, until after our rent was due. With no credit card and no other way to pay, I grew desperate and borrowed the money from my girlfriend at the time.

Though I paid her back within a month, the memory still makes me feel ashamed in a way that I can't explain. I know that I did nothing wrong, but I also know that I wasn't supposed to ask for help, wasn't supposed to need help. In this sense, I'd failed. It's why, for eight years, I never told anyone about it. Since that time, I've lent money to others who've needed it. They've always returned it quickly, thanked me profusely, and never talked about it again.

I've gotten help a hundred, a thousand, an unfathomable number of times in my life. Most of these instances are not the difference between whether or not I make rent, but they've still granted me greater security in more ways than I could ever hope to articulate. I tell myself that many people have had such help, realizing at the same time that this help is much more readily available to people like me: White, college-educated people who grew up in safe, middle-class neighborhoods. But we are enmeshed in a system that pushes us to deny this, to hold fast to an ideal of total self-reliance. We act out of fear, then out of insecurity, then out of selfishness, rather than admit the help we've received. Rather than admit that we all need a little help sometimes. We offer up our humanity for the sake of making a living.

Prior to that day on the Greenway, I'd felt proud to be doing something good in the world. But on that day, it finally hit me that anything I did was embedded in the existing structure. I could work for a lower wage for a nonprofit whose mission focused on breaking cycles of poverty and racism only to find myself removing the homes of the poorest and most marginalized in society. They'd been considered eyesores for more afflu-ent bikers and walkers. I knew in that moment that I would need to leave the job and leave the city, to get as far away as possible from anything that forced me to destroy someone else's home for the sake of a consistent paycheck.

Moving Along

In 2018, a year after I left Minneapolis and two years after I'd cleared encampments along the Greenway, approximately three hundred people gathered and set up tents less than a mile from where I used to live. From 2015 to 2018, the unhoused population had grown by more than four hundred people, or approximately 11 percent.[33] Despite this encampment representing only a fraction of this total unhoused population, it was still the largest encampment in Minneapolis history, with a disproportionate percentage of Native people.[34]

On a return visit to the city, I drove past this encampment. I wondered how many people there had once made a home along the Greenway. While this 2018 encampment was temporarily bolstered with a litany of social services for housing and hygiene and mental health, people would eventually be forced from there, too. John Tribbett, a street outreach manager with St. Stephen's, said, "After [the 2018 encampment] closed, what we really saw was the atomization of people experiencing unsheltered homelessness throughout the summer of 2019 and frankly up until COVID."

This wouldn't last. In July 2020, more than five hundred people, many who had been removed from temporary shelter in a hotel, set up an encampment in Powderhorn Park. One of the largest in the city, the park became a temporary refuge. Leading up to this point, Tribbett said that people experiencing homelessness in Minneapolis had grown accustomed to displacement and were often "on the move all the time."[35] Like a lot of people without stable housing, they would have become used to being told by everyone from pedestrians to store owners to "Move along." If they were like populations elsewhere, they would have heard it most often from police. Perhaps, then, it's not surprising that Powderhorn is mere blocks from where George Floyd had been murdered by a Minneapolis police officer just two months prior.

. . . .

At its core, gentrification means people entering and people leaving. Some people are not simply forced from the neighborhood but from the area altogether. *Nomadland*, directed by Chloé Zhao and awarded the Academy Award for Best Picture, shines a light on the growing number of people who have taken to living out of vehicles, especially in the US West. Relying almost entirely on nonactors, the film gives voice to a widespread search for freedom and self-discovery. One poignant scene shows a teenage girl asking the main character, Fern, if she's homeless, to which Fern replies, amused, "I'm not homeless. I'm just houseless. Not the same thing, right?"[36]

But Fern's response, signifying a degree of choice, obscures the systemic conditions that led her and so many others there. As some people live in vehicles to seek adventure or a simpler life, working high-salaried remote jobs and turning their lifestyles into social media fame, others like Fern are there because they feel their backs against the wall. They live in their cars because they have no place else to go.

For the many without cars, forced from housing due to rising prices and medical debt and mental health issues and addiction and a host of other issues, they are without shelter entirely. Out on the streets, they experience the cruelest edges of our society, with almost everything they do visible and almost nothing they do understood in the eyes of a casual bystander.

In studying housing, I learned that, regardless of political identification, these casual bystanders tend to have a firm opinion about unhoused people. Often, these bystanders do not want their city to do more for these people; they want the city to do less. In their opinion, which studies have refuted, the city's services for people without housing were attracting unhoused people from other places. [37]

In these conversations, bystanders asserted that they had heard or observed or read somewhere that most people without housing choose to live that way. By justifying others' suffering, these bystanders felt no responsibility to intervene, to change these conditions. They felt no need to challenge whether the disdain they reserved for someone receiving a free tent or occasional shower—as though he or she had committed some monstrous crime—actually said something unnerving about themselves. Perhaps they recognize the real crime is that, in the richest country on earth, more than a half-million people can only afford whatever dignity is offered to them on the street.

Perhaps they also see something far more unsettling than a criminal or outcast when they look at an unsheltered person: they see themselves. As they walk by a person begging or freezing or inebriated or alone, bystanders' minds start to wander. What would they do if the economy slowed and their company laid them off? What would they do if their daughter's cancer returned? What would they do if the rent rose too much?

Anxious to rid themselves of these thoughts, bystanders join the chorus of people telling unsheltered people to move along, that they don't belong there. Eventually, this demand becomes official policy, reflected in cities across the country.

St. Louis offers one of the most extreme examples, issuing ultimatums to unsheltered people who panhandle or simply sit in certain areas of the city: they can pay hefty fines and go to jail or they can sign a "neighborhood order of protection" that bans them from entering entire neighborhoods. Chased out of housing and chased off the street, cut off from family, friends, and critical city services, their existence in the city becomes a crime.[38]

Unsheltered people become accustomed to being told to move along. The question they often ask in return is not for individual bystanders or city officials but a question to society as a whole: "Move along to where?"

"Belong[ing] Anywhere"

The Global Housing Market

IN 1896, FREDERICK JACKSON TURNER wrote, "For nearly three centuries the dominant fact in American life has been expansion. With the settlement of the Pacific coast and the occupation of the free lands, this movement has come to a check." He predicted this frontier would not cease but instead expand abroad.

A century later, in 1993, President Bill Clinton signed the North American Free Trade Agreement. In promoting NAFTA, Clinton invoked President John F. Kennedy, declaring that "this new global economy is our new frontier."[1] Expansion remained "the dominant fact in American life."[2]

Within this new frontier, local producers competed with far larger, less geographically bound ones and everyone was enmeshed in the same system. Just as the General Allotment Act had pitted Native peoples against wealthy White settlers more than a century before, NAFTA pitted small farms, or campesinos, in Mexico against multinational corporations in

179

the United States.[3] Goods would come from whichever place could provide them cheaper. Whether they were cheaper due to lax environmental, labor, or human rights rules was beside the point; the dollar was the only metric that mattered.

The widespread financialization of goods and services paved the way for the financialization of industries that had long been understood as requiring some level of government stabilization to maintain reasonable prices. With further deregulation of the banking and housing industries in the 1990s and 2000s, housing in the United States was set to follow suit. In the eyes of the market, the purpose of buying property was the potential gain in renting it out, a process that scholar Manuel Aalbers termed the "financialization of home."[4]

When the housing market crashed in the late 2000s, it sent shockwaves through the economy. By the time the dust settled, an estimated ten million people had been forced from their homes and more than $19 trillion in household wealth had been lost.[5] Housing was just like everything else: another commodity for sale on the global market.

But housing is not like other products. Outside of the rare collector's item or antique, everything from roller skates to laptops to cars loses value over time. Housing, however, like the land it sits on, determines access to everything from social interaction to clean air to a good education. Housing takes longer to make, is more resistant to severe damage, and is not treated as merely a replaceable product by those who actually use it. For these reasons and many more, housing gains value, often dramatically.

This is exaggerated when the map is opened up and properties are bought and sold by the wealthiest across the globe. The housing market is quickly divorced from what local people can reasonably pay because it's not confined to local people.

In this environment, someone who lost their job during a national crisis like the 2020 spread of a new and deadly virus and cannot produce three months of consistent paystubs can't compete against someone who didn't. It doesn't matter that at least twenty-three million people faced the same situation. Someone with a dog can't compete against someone without one. Neither can someone working a local, low-paying job educating kids compete against someone working a remote, high-paying job marketing stuff. Even when someone accepts that more stable housing will not be found and purchases an RV to park in a friend's driveway, a call will still be placed warning of eviction, for both the person living in the RV and the friends living in the house. The RV could be parked in the forest outside of town.

Between the fall of 2018 and spring of 2021, this was Amira Shweyk's life in Bend, Oregon. She had a college degree, had never been late on a housing payment, and had exhausted every avenue to find more stable housing in Bend. Eventually, she drove her recently purchased thirty-year-old RV into the Deschutes National Forest.

Shweyk fit the profile of everything that Bend, a fast-growing, tourism-driven city in the Cascade Mountains, made itself out to be. She'd worked as a wilderness therapy instructor, leading groups of youth and young adults with social, mental health, and substance abuse issues on multiday backpacking trips. She'd worked as an outdoor educator for youth, including as a mountain biking coach. And she'd worked in outdoor gear shops. In every job, her mission was in some way tied to helping people experience the natural world around Bend. And yet, this torrent of people—of visitors, temporary residents, and new, full-time residents working remote jobs—was driving up the cost of housing.

Even outside the city and living in an RV, this influx of people impacted Shweyk. During Memorial Day weekend, she returned to one of her usual sites in the forest and found it occupied. As was every other site. She drove around dirt roads and dispersed campsites in an endless loop: working in the same industry that was driving the city's growth, driving her own displacement. At the same time the city was reveling in the boom, she was one of many struggling with the bust.[6]

"Finance Is Like Mining"

The hypercompetitive housing markets produced by this financialization of home in places like Bend are part of a new but unsurprising chapter in the history of housing and land in the United States. Saskia Sassen, a sociologist and the author of *Denationalization: Territory, Authority, and Rights in a Global Digital Age*, noted this link in extraction. As she said in the 2019 housing documentary *Push*, "I always say finance sells something it does not have. And that means that finance is basically an extractive sector. Finance is like mining: once it has what it needs, it doesn't care what happens with the rest."[7]

But, just as with every previous frontier, this isn't inevitable. In the same documentary, former UN Special Rapporteur on Adequate Housing Leilani Farha was unequivocal on this point, saying,

> *In a human rights framework and through the UN system, it's very clear who was accountable: states. States are responsible. They have international human rights obligations, they sign treaties, and they make commitments to the international community that they will uphold international human rights, which include the right to adequate housing.*[8]

In the United States, the federal government has not simply failed to uphold these agreements but actively undermined them. It has passed laws and granted loans with the intent of increasing segregation. It has redlined, employed eminent domain, created the suburbs, and created zoning laws restricting smaller houses, certain businesses, and mixed-income properties. Altogether, the federal government's housing policies seem designed to eliminate any sort of "right" to a home that may have existed previously.

Much of this was not part of any formalized policy or process but resulted from an utter lack of policies relating to housing. Time after time, the federal government has ceded its role in housing policy to the whims of the market. Farha pointed to the wake of the Great Recession as evidence of this larger trend. She drew attention to HUD's heavily discounted auction of 180,000 delinquent mortgages, the majority of which went to private equity firms. Arguing for changes, it is no chance event that her two most unsparing letters in the US were reserved for the Blackstone Group, "one of the largest real estate private equity firms in the world," and the federal government itself.[9]

When policy has been implemented, it has often been designed to "encourage the institutional investment in housing as an asset class," as Farha put it. She summarized these actions by stating that "the United States of America has disconnected housing from its core social purpose of providing people with a place to live in with security and dignity," a trend that has been especially harmful to minority groups.[10] This entire philosophy can be identified as the federal government's embrace of the financialization of home.

State and local governments have often followed suit. What becomes clear from previous frontiers—the "New World," the West, the suburbs, the gentrified city, even public lands themselves—is that the frontier is another name for blank space. While this frontier logic has changed forms, it has always followed a similar pattern of producing blank spaces and systematically privileging the access of outside wealth.

* * * * * * *

The globalization of the housing market can be understood through geographer David Harvey's concept of "accumulation by dispossession."[11] In less academic terms, some people get more by taking from others. The rich get richer. The poor get poorer.

This happens through four steps. First, housing is privatized and made available solely based on who can afford it. Since 1976, for example, public housing has received progressively less funding, although the cost of its maintenance has grown.[12] The National Low Income Housing Coalition now finds that "fewer than four affordable and available homes exist for every 10 extremely low-income renter households nationwide.[13]

Second, through financialization, banks and concentrated wealth grow more dominant in these spheres.[14] Those who can afford the property are given preference over lower-income residents, regardless of whether it will be their primary home. Individuals buying second—or third, or fourth—homes or those looking to hold property temporarily and sell it for higher value have the same right to this space as a year-round resident.[15]

Third, in the wake of perceived crises, powerful entities use the urgency of the moment to enact previously untenable practices. The housing crash of 2008, for example, led to a $700 billion bailout of many of the very banks implicated in causing the economic recession.[16] Labeled "too big to fail," their flawed and outright criminal practices made visible by the financial crisis were excused in the name of stemming the tide of greater economic repercussions. As Michael Lewis wrote in *The Big Short: Inside the Doomsday Machine*, "[Wall Street] firms, which disdained the need for government regulation in good times, insisted on being rescued by government in bad times. Success was individual achievement; failure was a social problem."[17]

Finally, government redistributions favor the creation of capital to make up for budget shortfalls.[18] In the 2008 housing crisis, local and state governments found themselves short on funds and cut social services and education expenses, relying on private funds to fill the gaps.[19] In the absence of government assistance and infrastructure, individuals, companies, and local governments are left with limited options but to rely on investors and funding sources that have unforeseen consequences.

Naomi Klein referred to these last two steps as "the shock doctrine," the method by which those in power push through previously untenable policies and defund social services in the wake of disasters and chaos.[20] While many of the banks most responsible for the housing crash saw massive bailouts from the federal government, most people saw cuts to social services on which they had relied. None of this was new, just a new form of what Klein calls "frontier capitalism, with the frontier constantly shifting location, moving on as soon as the law catches up."[21] This system depends on the continual creation of frontiers.[22]

Normally, the local, on-the-ground conditions are tied into a system with far-reaching consequences, with the effects of one action typically obscured by the immensity of the web.[23] The shock doctrine, however, shortens the time span of cause and effect. By shining a light on the rash of policies pushed through in a chaotic time, the intended and unintended impacts become easier to identify.

Education was one of the first social services to suffer in the wake of the Great Recession. NAU in Flagstaff offers an example. Between the 2001–2002 and 2008–2009 school years, the amount of money budgeted by the state grew from approximately $112 million to more than $161 million, always at least 75 percent of the university's operating budget and at least $6,400 per student. Within three years, the state's contribution had dropped to less than the 2001–2002 total, an amount that has only been met twice since. Since that time, the state has never paid more than 50 percent of the university's operating costs, never devoting more than $4,500 per student.[24]

This mirrors a national trend in which public colleges and universities have become increasingly dependent on private funding. In many cases, there is little difference between the sources funding public and private schools. As in the case of the banks, the private sector's failures were the public's problem; the public sector's failures were a profiteer's dream.

At NAU, as at other universities, students and faculty bore the brunt of state funding cuts. NAU's enrollment grew massively to offset the lost revenue from the Arizona State Legislature. With thousands more students suddenly on campus and in need of housing, residents, unsurprisingly, pushed back against NAU's growth. Bumper stickers with "Flagstaff: A Suburb of NAU" became more common.

Students, already paying more to get the education seen as a prerequisite to landing a decent job, have felt this resentment. Allie Wilkins summarized this in a 2017 student editorial for *The Lumberjack*, the school paper, saying, "We didn't vote to get kicked off campus, we didn't ask for rent so expensive we have no choice but to cram eight people into a two bedroom, and we definitely didn't ask to be made the villain by a town we love just as much as the person who's lived downtown for 15 years."[25]

What set NAU's growth in motion was less state funding for higher education. In other words, many of the taxpayers who are upset about the influx of students and who may personally be paying thousands more each year due to the resulting housing crunch are also those who are paying less in taxes. Without this tax revenue, NAU's growth is one of the only things allowing the university to operate. Wilkins's article, then, was aptly titled: "Students Are Not the Problem with Housing: They're the Scapegoats."

In Berkeley, California, this tension between the growing student enrollment and the rest of the city came to a head in February 2022. That was when a judge ruled that the University of California, Berkeley would have to dramatically shrink its enrollment, meaning that the university would have to rescind thousands of acceptance letters to incoming students. On the surface, this decision seemed to offer a view that locals were reasserting control, but it raised the question of what it means to be a local, what it means to belong to a place. As Annie Lowrey of the *Atlantic* pointed out, the former investment banker who initially brought forward the lawsuit spent much of his time prepandemic in New Zealand and traveling. His house in Berkeley was just one of the places he called home.[26]

What's in a Crisis?

In 2009, in the context of the national housing crisis, UN Special Rapporteur Leilani Farha visited Los Angeles. After studying the situation, she pointed to both gentrification and the wave of foreclosures as primary causes for increases in houselessness.[27] But this was no coincidence. As tens of millions of people were forced into substandard housing or shut out of housing entirely, many of the wealthiest people and companies orchestrated a windfall. Of the nearly 180,000 delinquent mortgages sold by the US government at greatly reduced prices, "as much as 95 percent of these were bought by private equity firms." Many of these were then made into real estate investment trusts, or REITs, with extremely favorable tax conditions.

Farha observed, "National government policy focused on deregulation and the provision of tax benefits has facilitated the treatment of foreclosed homes as a means of wealth extraction for private equity firms and corporate landlords."[28]

The disparities resulting from crisis-induced policies are both profound and predictable. The single and multifamily dwellings organized as

REITs were worth more than $1 trillion on the New York Stock Exchange as of 2019. They were being traded actively in almost precisely the same way as mortgages had previously been packaged together and "securitized" without a thought for whether payments made by homeowners, or in this case tenants, could be sustained.[29] In other words, the rental market was seeing the level of outside investment recently seen in the homeownership market, investment levels that were directly implicated in the housing crash barely a decade before.

Prepandemic, through December 2019, the national homeownership rate stood at 65.1 percent, an increase from five years prior but still among the lowest rates since 1996.[30] With these diminished rates resulting in millions more people renting, affordable rentals became increasingly scarce, and therefore unaffordable. Between 2006 and 2016, the number of people making under $26,000 grew by 1.8 million while the number of affordable units shrunk by 500,000.[31] As of 2017, 31.5 percent of all households were considered cost burdened, spending more than 30 percent of income toward housing costs.[32] They would be more likely to struggle to afford medications and car payments and birthday presents for their kids. At the same time, 26.9 percent of households were owned outright, with no mortgage or debt.[33] They would be more likely to buy another property.

Who ends up in which category is neither random nor accidental. From the violent removal of Native nations in the 1600s to the Federal Housing Administration's refusal of homeownership to Black people, the United States has continually expanded because of a succession of frontiers expressly for the wealth of outside, overwhelmingly White, settlers.

Even when governmental policy was not directly to blame, it was the government's refusal to act that furthered the racist housing landscape. In 1964, as new civil rights laws were implemented that would have opened recreation centers and parks everywhere to all races, the Federal Housing Administration made it clear that the government favored private control over these areas.[34] When homeowners' associations, or HOAs, enacted racially restrictive rules, the government did not fight them. The 500 HOAs that existed quickly multiplied, reaching upward of 250,000 today.[35]

Government officials argue that the country has changed, that the racialized policies of the past have been struck down. But the virulent racist mobs of the past have largely been replaced by White politicians and homeowners who bristle at the slightest hint of criticism. Many HOAs claim to be built around creating more livable, inclusive communities. In reality, they function expressly as a means of maximizing property values within an area, a fact which increases the likelihood that they will continue to be the White enclaves so inherent to the initial spread of HOAs.

This denial occurs in all aspects of US society.[36] This was evidenced when the Supreme Court ruled in 2007 that, as Black studies professor George Lipsitz wrote, "modest school desegregation programs in Seattle and Louisville violated the rights of white children."[37] For anyone who has benefited from the country's history of violent displacement, enslavement, and segregation of non-Whites, desegregation feels like oppression.[38] Being forced to look in the mirror feels like oppression.

Without reflection and targeted policies to alter its effects, US history becomes a weight carried into the present. The 2020 Census revealed that 54 percent of all metropolitan areas were more segregated than they had been in 1990. Meanwhile, the ten most-segregated cities spanned the country, with the most segregated regions actually being the Midwest, Mid-Atlantic, and West Coast.[39]

Crises, and narratives of crisis, often produce decidedly racialized impacts. The housing market crash in 2008 was no exception. As Laura Gottesdiener relayed in her book, *A Dream Foreclosed*, the Center for Responsible Lending saw the danger in subprime mortgages and issued a statement in 2006 that "predicted that unless the government intervened, it was likely that bankers would directly cause 'the largest loss of African-American wealth that we have ever seen, wiping out a generation of home wealth building."[40] Warnings were everywhere; they simply were not heeded. The housing bubble finally burst, and the stock market crashed.

· · · · · · ·

The height of the housing market crash coincided with the spread of smartphones, allowing apps and digital platforms to further take hold. The Great Recession, in this vein, has been labeled "the Great Disruption" for further clearing space for the dominance of what's been termed platform capitalism.[41] When Airbnb was founded in 2008, short-term rentals seemed to meet a demand for cheaper travel accommodation options and provide supplemental income for residents unable to make ends meet in the unstable recession times. The number of Airbnbs, VRBOs, and other short-term rentals skyrocketed. The frontier had gone digital.

The map was now open. For investors and real estate agents and tourists and anyone with enough money, every space became accessible. For people like Amira Shweyk, there was suddenly nowhere else to go. Looking back on it in August 2022, more than a year and a half later, Shweyk said, "That's the point. We're so cornered. . . . What else am I supposed to do? I can't—I tried living in a house, didn't pan out. Tried living in an RV. That's not panning out. Do you want me in a tent on the street? Because that's my other option. That's still illegal."

Shweyk noticed that she'd "started feeling very resentful" toward Bend itself. The city seemed to be advertising itself directly to people like her who were young and had a dog and loved the outdoors but then seemed content to leave them "scrapping" for housing.

It was common for Bend residents to resent anyone new moving there, a feeling summarized in bumper stickers reading, "Bend sucks. Don't move here." Shweyk didn't feel that way toward incoming residents, though; she knew the forces that had kept her from finding stable housing were far larger than their individual decisions.

Even still, as she approached the summer of 2021, Shweyk felt like she faced a stark choice between the possibility of housing somewhere else and retaining her community in Bend. It soon failed to feel like a choice at all. She felt guilty for what she described as "freeloading" off of her community in order to meet her basic needs and started to drift away from people. With her mental health suffering, staying no longer felt worth it.

And then a job came through, what Shweyk saw as a well-paying job using her past experience. She'd be working as the director of a summer camp. If finances had been the sole reason for not previously securing housing, she could have finally found housing. But it had never been that simple. Instead, working seasonally, she'd been denied the possibility of rent countless times for not having a consistent income history, a fact that made it harder to maintain a consistent income. Ecstatic about the job but knowing that she'd be living in an RV without air conditioning, she made the difficult decision to give up her dog, Sienna, for the summer.

Having Sienna with her parents more than a day's drive away was hard on Shweyk, but she knew that this had been the right decision when summer temperatures crept toward 110 degrees and wildfire smoke burned the lungs. And by staying, she was able to keep saving money. Over the next year, she worked and spent next to nothing on housing. Finally, she saved up enough money to buy land approximately thirty miles south of Bend—with the help of a loan from her mom. Because she didn't have a consistent income history, she'd been denied a traditional loan. Without access to that support, ownership would have been out of reach.

Amira Shweyk uses words like "privileged" to describe her situation today, acutely aware that the help she received is inaccessible to many. And, after fighting so hard to stay in Bend, Shweyk is still fighting. With no water, no electricity, and no septic system on her plot of land, her living situation requires an incredible amount of grit and ingenuity. She's working hard to turn a shed on site into a small house to keep her warm through the punishing winter.

But that's just the physical work. She's also been working to regain her community and face some of the mental health issues that welled up during "a long time of not having [her] basic needs met." As Shweyk put it, "It's not like that was the only thing that was going on in my life. Like, I experienced some major traumas in this whole time that have affected my . . . motivation to seek housing. And it's just like—it seems like there's no margin of error, and there's no margin for the messiness of life if you're looking for housing here. You have to have the money and the motivation and the time all line up together if you want a shot of finding housing."[42]

"The Age of Easy Money"

During COVID, Shweyk was suddenly competing with a wider pool of people who had gained the freedom to work jobs far beyond their geographic bounds. Employees of New York City firms have bought up houses in Bozeman and workers at a Seattle companies have signed leases in Bend. For many, housing costs in their new home pale in comparison to what they paid in the past, even if the price appears astronomical to most locals.

Commentators, economists, and government officials alike have expressed surprise. As author and urban planner M. Nolan Gray explained in an August 2022 article for The Atlantic, "At the onset of the coronavirus pandemic, the shift to remote work was supposed to ease the long-festering housing crisis in 'superstar' metros such as Los Angeles and New York…In reality, two years later, housing costs in those superstar metros are at record highs, while the wave of pandemic-era migrations has helped spread the affordability crisis nationwide."[43]

But none of this should have been surprising; it was foretold by a slate of policies and trends which dated back to the Great Recession. During that time, the Federal Reserve began buying up bonds and doling out massive, nearly interest-free loans to corporations. The goal was to encourage these corporations to spend money, especially encouraging the biggest banks to again loan money. When the Fed signaled that it would taper away from these practices in 2013, the stock market plummeted—an event which would become known as the "taper tantrum"—and the Fed decided to keep interest rates low. Though rates went up small amounts between 2015 and 2019, they still remained close to 2 percent, less than half of what they'd been most years since the late 1970s.

These policies transformed the economic landscape, but not in the way the Fed argued they would. Banks did not loan money to small businesses and prospective homeowners who would make steady payments over a long time. Instead, if they loaned the money at all, banks loaned it to private equity firms and large corporations who would hopefully repay it quickly after making a quick profit.

Between 2009 and 2019, private equity firms bought up assets ranging from homes to hospitals to stores to office buildings. Public companies bought up $6 trillion worth of their own stock, inflating the price for everyone else. Companies, especially tech companies and those which had grown rapidly since the Recession, took on huge amounts of debt in order to grow. If the market ever stopped growing and anyone investing in these companies wished to collect what they were owed, they wouldn't have been able to. There was no rainy-day fund; it was all out on bets. This wasn't an issue as long as the market kept growing and people kept investing, as long as there was nothing unusual that threw the market into disarray. Like a pandemic.

In February 2020, the markets started to flail. With very little money in circulation, the Fed responded by buying trillions in corporate assets and dropping interest rates even lower. When Congress passed the $2.2 trillion CARES Act on March 27, the Fed used its share of the money to buy up corporate debts in rapid succession.

While many companies and individuals went broke, many others were suddenly flush with cash and seeing the writing on the wall. Unemployment rates were rising to levels not seen since the Great Depression. Hospitals and morgues were being pushed beyond capacity. And the stock market was experiencing record highs. As Mohamed El-Arian, the chief economic adviser for insurance behemoth Allianz, said, "When people saw bad news, they said, 'The Fed will have to do more.'"[44]

It did. In the spring of 2020, the Federal Reserve dropped interest rates to nearly zero percent and kept them there for two years. Investments became increasingly speculative, pushing cryptocurrency, tech start-ups, and meme stocks into dangerously bubble-like territory. Housing, meanwhile, was being sold at record numbers at record prices with record percentages of investors. But there was no widespread panic. As the title of a *PBS Frontline* special stated in March 2023, this was "the age of easy money."

• • • • • • •

Banks and investors were not the only ones to benefit from these low interest rates. Millions of people bought homes for the first time, securing an interest rate low enough that the inflated price of a home felt worth it. Many of these people had been granted the flexibility to work from anywhere, entirely independent of a physical office and coworkers. And best of all, independent from the higher cost of living they'd once known.

The situation felt like a dream for these workers. They could live where they wanted and fit their jobs around their lives rather than their lives around their jobs. They could shop online more easily and chat by video with a mental health professional at a reduced cost. They could earn a degree on their own schedule for a fraction of the cost as one on campus. They could spend less time in traffic and more time at home with family and friends.

But these benefits have come at great expense. In addition to the fact that many of the workers most struggling to make ends meet—from bus drivers to servers to construction workers—have no remote option, those who do may also face major changes. Now facing an increasingly global labor pool, workers with resume gaps from bearing a child or taking care of a sick parent lose out. Those unwilling to work under precarious conditions for meager compensation lose out. Hospital administrators begin to ask why they'd pay the salaries of in-person doctors when telehealth doctors can be hired for far less. School boards begin to ask why they'd pay the salaries of in-person professors when their lessons can be recorded and reused.

Employers have a mandate to decrease costs and do not care if that means hiring a person in another state, another country, or a person at all. Once a cheaper way is found to do a job, the current "winners" of this economic competition are spat out as quickly as they saw their lot improve.

The precarity of work shouldn't be surprising. The job market is guided by the same principle that created or doomed entire towns in the boom-and-bust West. This was the same logic that decided the fate of entire nations in the industrial and then postindustrial economy. It is a mandate to accumulate profit, regardless of how it is done. In this environment,

CEOs cutting employees' pay and benefits—or cutting employees altogether—are rewarded with bonuses. Corporations are rewarded with higher stock prices.

As Lawrence Mishel and Josh Bivens wrote for the Economic Policy Institute, "Between 1979 and 2017, the compensation of median workers trailed economywide (net) productivity growth by roughly 43%, leading to rising inequality." In other words, workers have produced far more but accrued little of the benefit. The benefit has instead gone to a tiny segment of the population, what Mishel and Bivens identify as "workers at the top (mostly highly credentialed professionals and corporate managers) and owners of capital."[45]

Workers, of course, have fought back. They've unionized at a series of Starbucks franchises. They've staged a strike at John Deere's Illinois headquarters. They've walked off the job at a string of Amazon warehouses on Black Friday. Rail workers have threatened to strike. Nurses across the country have gone on strike. So have teachers. And journalists. And employees in food service and book publishing and dozens of other industries. A Cornell University study showed that 288 strikes had occurred in the United States in the first nine months of 2022, more than the 260 that occurred in all of 2021.[46] Often, strikes happen through unions, as was the case when more than forty-eight thousand unionized academic workers in California banded together to stage the largest strike of 2022.[47] Others have been wildcat strikes, those that occur without official union support.

What these workers have wanted has varied slightly from better pay to better benefits to safer working conditions. In short, particularly as they watch their company or industry reap mind-boggling profits from their labor, they've demanded fairer compensation. Sometimes, it's worked, with their actions resulting in victories once thought to be impossible. Their lives are tangibly better. Perhaps just as important, they feel something that they haven't in a long time: a sense of agency over their lives.

But these victories are isolated. For every effort that succeeds, several more are crushed. With their own—and often their entire family's—health insurance and retirement benefits bound to their jobs, workers risk severe repercussions for standing up for themselves. Faced with stagnating wages and uncertainty in work, they seek some stability outside of work, starting at home.

This stability will not be found in renting. Expensive and unstable, at the mercy of a landlord's decision whether or not to make repairs or raise monthly costs, renters often find their situation at work replicated at home. They may be successful in pressing for a dollar-per-hour raise—roughly $2,000 more for a year of full-time work—but that will hardly keep pace with inflation in many places. Instead, renters come to see building wealth through homeownership as the only path to some bit of freedom.

And yet, a study by LendingTree in May 2021 revealed that the median costs of homeownership outpaced rental costs in all fifty of the largest metropolitan areas in the United States.[48] This has undoubtedly only worsened since the 24.76 percent rise in national median sale prices between the end of 2019 and end of 2021.[49]

Anyone seeking to buy or rent—seeking to call a place home—must give up an increasing amount of income in order to outbid those who seek to maximize profits from a space. These residents hang family photos on walls and send postcards with their new address. They stock pantries, plant flowers, and paint rooms. All of these have the intended effect, giving them a sense of stability and contentment. The place begins to feel like home.

. . . .

In June 2022, I began subleasing a new room in Flagstaff. It was in a two-bedroom, one-bathroom house that I shared with two roommates. It came with very few frills, was well within earshot of the screech and roar of the freight trains that lumbered across the country, and cost more than I'd ever paid in my life. But it had a yard and a porch. The neighbor from one house next door collected our mail when we were out of town. My roommate brought her groceries when she was recovering from surgery. I felt like I belonged.

The other house beside ours was a short-term rental. It hosted new guests almost every night. Most were quiet enough, pleasant enough. A few were loud and obnoxious. None were neighbors.

In August, just two months after moving in, the rent rose. It wasn't much. Just enough to make me wonder how long I would be able to stay.

· · · · · · ·

The frontier has followed a pattern: Existing communities have been continually marginalized or altogether removed to make room for outsiders. Land has been claimed by doctrine, won by war, dreamed up by policy, and revived by investment. In this way, our past and present has gained an air of inevitability. This has culminated in the present moment, one in which people are made to feel that they can "belong anywhere."

What goes unsaid in all this is that the land being freshly conquered was already someone's home. The so-called war won by White settlers was nothing short of a genocide of Native peoples. The creation of the "American Dream" of homeownership meant a nightmare for those systematically excluded. Government officials whose investment caused an area's revival were preceded by government officials whose disinvestment caused an area's decay. And when travelers and wealthy property owners came to feel that they could belong just about anywhere, existing residents were learning they couldn't afford to belong in their homes.

But we understand our history in the same way that we understand smoke filling confined space. As the smoke pushes people out or pushes them out of sight, others move in. We become habituated to this state. Clean air is such a distant memory that we come to believe this smoke to be our only option. Though we cough and sputter, we continually add fuel to the fire and fan the flames. We lash out at anyone who dares to question whether this smoke and our ailing health may be linked.

Every mineral, every parcel of land, every scrap of space now appears to be for sale to the highest bidder. If we have the money, we are "ready to sell out and take the advantage of the rise in property," as

John Mason Peck said nearly two hundred years ago, "push[ing] far-ther into the interior and becom[ing, ourselves, people] of capital and enterprise in turn."[50]

And yet, there are so many people—there have always been so many people—who have refused this fate. They've seen how the world got this way and know there's something else. Jessi Quizar, an urban studies pro-fessor at the University of Washington, Tacoma, has studied social move-ments and sees understanding how the world got this way as essential. As she put it:

> The world that we have is something that was made. Like, it wasn't—this isn't natural; this isn't inevitable. Whatever we've made was created for purposes by people, and . . . I think there's something about denaturalizing the present that also sort of opens up . . . [a] sense of possibility for other ways of being because we can be like, OK, you know what, even these terrible things that feel totally intransigent [were] created through processes that are intel-ligible. They're graspable. They're human.[51]

For the first time in years, Amira Shweyk has been able to think about what she wants in the long-term. She is thrilled to have a place she can call home, but one of the things really spurring her forward is what she can do for others. From simply offering a place to camp or shower to setting up an outdoor kitchen, she wants her piece of land "to be a place when there's nowhere else to go."

Fittingly, she uses a climbing metaphor to explain her motivation. "It would feel so wrong to have reached this metaphorical summit and then not turn around and help everyone else who's trying to do it with less gear than I have."[52]

French writer and philosopher Albert Camus once wrote, "The only way to deal with an unfree world is to become so unflinchingly free that your very existence is an act of rebellion."[53] There are Navajo, Hopi, Choc-taw, Black, Latino, Asian, and White people finding ways to live this way. They come from every class, have different skills, and are both lifelong and new members of communities scattered throughout the country. They are the dreamers, the doers, the "unflinchingly free." And they remind all of us that another way is possible.

III
where we're going

12

Locals Welcome

"Dog eat dog" offers justification for the cutthroat competition of the market, as if to say that it's natural that one's success or even survival should only be possible through another's demise. But the original phrase says something different entirely. As Roman scholar Marcus Terentius Varro observed in 43 BCE, "Canis caninam non est." In translation, "Dog does not eat dog." Only humans establish systems that require ruthless, relentless, and sometimes deadly competition between each other for the sake of accumulating trinkets and treasures and property.

It doesn't have to be like this. One of my primary takeaways from researching housing has not been simply about short-term rentals or nonprimary homes or even the housing market at all. Rather, it's an understanding that markets and cultures are the result of people making choices within an overarching structure. People, of course, are not entirely free to choose, instead being bound by systems and laws and the pressures of daily life. Expecting them to go outside these bounds ignores the harsh reality of the walls that surround them. But acting as though people are mere data points in some computer program—fulfilling some predestined obligation to maximize their return on investment—refuses the humanity that still serves as the fabric of families, of neighborhoods, and of communities.

The current housing market demands that the value of a person be measured strictly according to the amount of profit they can generate. A home's worth must be measured strictly according to its resale value. This is, transparently, a terrible way to decide who belongs and requires us to build an incredible amount of political will in order to change it. But marshalling this political will first requires overcoming the barriers in our own minds. It requires believing an alternative is possible and committing to it. This alternative must position communities as the bedrock of our species and safe, decent, affordable housing as the core of these communities.

The alternative to our current system starts with a simple premise: housing is for housing people. Accepting this sounds easy if we cast giant, faceless corporations in the role of sitting on properties, extracting large returns on their investments and driving up the local cost of housing. It's easy when we think of massive property management firms evicting families of tenants in order to turn homes into short-term rentals. It's easy to focus on the biggest actors, developing a narrative of villainous developers and greedy landlords generating massive profits at the direct expense of longtime residents. That's sometimes not so far off.

More often, though, nonprimary property owners are not so different in motivation or character, just in means. They're a retired couple who just want a separate place when they visit their grandkids. They're hard-working people with a timeshare property serving as a weekend retreat. They're longtime residents shifting their rental property to short-term in order to better afford rising property taxes. Once we start hearing individual stories, the neat categories we'd made for ourselves of "victim" and "victor" become a little murkier.

It's possible to start to see renters and primary homeowners and non-primary homeowners and vacation property managers and real estate agents and stockbrokers and policymakers as regular people, just trying for a little more security, a little more for their kid's college fund, a little more for an emergency healthcare expense. A little more room to breathe. Their motivations cease to be so different; some just have a little more—occasionally a lot more—money. Before long, we're left not with the righteous anger that stems from viewing radical accumulation alongside crippling debt but with what seems a prudent understanding of the brutality inherent in a world with finite resources. Dog eat dog.

Except that we live in a society in which everything stacks, just as it's been designed.

That's why the homeownership rate for Blacks—cut off from home financing and federal protections for nearly a half-century—has never been within 20 percentage points of that of Whites.[1] That's why the Gini Index, a measure of inequality across time and countries, shows the United States growing steadily more unequal since the 1970s, most recently hovering around fiftieth of more than 160 countries measured. And that's why the COVID-19 pandemic saw the national median home price rise to a record $480,000 at the same time that short-term rentals, second home sales, and investment properties all climbed to new heights.[2] We live in two worlds. They may be separated by forests, by highways, or right next door to each other, but they've never been further apart.

This reality stems from a staggering and systematized transfer of national wealth from one part of the population to another. This is not about a segment of the population having multiple houses but about the fact that this directly diminishes the ability of most other people to afford a roof over their heads. This is not about a smaller segment of the population having immensely more disposable income but about the fact that this disposable income translates directly into the power to set rules, set wages, and set prices. This is about how such a concentration of power maintains itself by draining the majority of us of any sense of agency. And how we take it back.

Tourists Are Not Locals: Addressing Short-Term Rentals

As geographer David Harvey put it, using a phrase oft-attributed to Thomas Jefferson, "There is . . . nothing more unequal than the equal treatment of unequals."[3] We need to acknowledge the differences between those with money to burn and those seeking to carve out a life. We need to elevate the use value of housing as home over the exchange value, wherein housing is reduced to real estate.

The treatment of short-term rentals provides one of the clearest examples of the way in which our society ignores these distinctions. How we address them is an indication of our priorities when it comes to housing. A tourist is, by definition, not a local resident. A hotel is not a home. When we treat these entities virtually the same, we allow the market to decide who deserves access to these spaces. In this setting, preference goes to whatever is more profitable.

This trend was on full display in the small town of Fayetteville, West Virginia. When federal legislation made New River Gorge a national park and preserve on December 27, 2020, Fayetteville cemented its position as a gateway community, what political science professor Rick Kurtz defines as "towns adjacent to and having economic ties to public lands."[4]

Local opinions were mixed. Many pointed to the economic benefits the park designation would bring: the whitewater rafting, the hotels, the restaurants, and all manner of opportunities for money to flow into the community. Others were concerned. They were not simply concerned about their home changing but the possibility that they would have to compete with nonresidents for everything from hunting grounds to housing. Within months, evidence from AirDNA was backing up their fears.

The number of active short-term rentals each quarter, which had never eclipsed 103 at the time of the park's designation jumped up to 162 by the end of 2021. On January 26, 2022, 91 percent of the listed short-term rentals were entire homes.[5] That may not seem like much, but a 57 percent leap and the loss of sixty potential homes in a single year makes a big difference in a town of less than three thousand people.

Another example is the tiny, high-elevation town of Cloudcroft, New Mexico. When I worked at what was then White Sands National Monument in the summer of 2019, I would often escape the 100-degree heat to hike in the far cooler temperatures of the nearby Lincoln National Forest and take in some live music at Cloudcroft's new brewery. I'd frequently have the same server, listen to the same local musicians, and see many of the same faces in the crowd.

Six months later, White Sands became a national park. After a major 2020 drop due to COVID restrictions and uncertainty, the crowds returned in force. And with them came outside investment. White Sands saw visitation climb to 782,469 in 2021, more than 28 percent higher than 2019 totals.[6] By the end of 2021, there were 185 short-term rentals operating in Cloudcroft, with nearly all of them offering entire homes. This was 71 percent higher than the total number present at the end of 2019, pre-park designation.[7]

The reasons tourists came to the seven-hundred-person town hadn't changed much., They still sought outdoor amenities, visited public lands like White Sands, and took in local events like live music at the brewery. It's just that more of them now stayed in former homes that had been converted to short-term rentals.

Examples of the market's bias toward nonresidents are on display everywhere. But so are alternatives. Bozeman reined in short-term rentals by seeking out immense public feedback. The result was a nuanced approach allowing for direct enforcement through a registration system as well as the implementation of a software system to monitor short-term rental activity. All of these are important steps that could be emulated in many places struggling to regulate short-term rentals. As Bozeman official Pat Witton said, they "definitely believe in peer learning" and looked to many cities, including Flagstaff, Austin, Bend, Durango, Bellingham, and Champaign, to determine their own policies.[8]

Another measure Bozeman has undertaken, which is similar to one in St. George, is the encouragement of accessory dwelling units (ADUs). This allowed for increased in-fill, what is generally seen as the third option for city growth, in addition to growing up and growing out. Whether this had the intended effect of creating more long-term housing or simply allowed for more short-term rentals, however, is not certain.[9] St. George and several surrounding cities seem to have embraced a fusion of short-term rentals and hotels, with concentrated resort areas that cause much less impact on existing neighborhoods. Multiple cities used an approach similar to Durango's, which instituted a quota for the number of entire-home short-term rentals allowed in a particular ratio to housing units.

With enforcement, these are potent options for cities seeking to limit short-term rentals. St. George, however, is akin to Flagstaff in having its enforcement ability severely curtailed as the result of a state law. In this context, multiple officials in the area acknowledged a high rate of illegal listings, emphasizing how difficult it would be to actually enforce.[10] The Arizona state law that prevents Flagstaff from directly regulating short-term rentals is quite effective in such a goal, but it does have openings. The city has begun using what little leverage it has to incentivize developers and HOAs to limit short-term rentals.[11]

The National Low Income Housing Coalition has identified many places in the West where residents are bypassing elected officials to call for more restrictions on short-term rentals. In November 2020 alone, voters in the Colorado towns of Leadville, Avon, Ouray, Telluride, and Vail all called for taxes on short-term rentals, with Ouray's 15 percent tax becoming the highest in the state. In addition to restricting short-term rentals and increasing revenue from them, many of the laws require the money to be used toward affordable housing.[12]

Collectively, these measures provide the means of addressing short-term rentals' impacts in some substantial ways. And they could fit on a notecard:

- Tax entire-home, full-time short-term rentals.
- Seek and adhere to public comments, particularly those stemming from the most vulnerable residents.
- Charge fees with annual registration and one-time inspection.
- Enforce regulations through monitoring software and strict fines.

If none of this works, cities need to be ready to clamp down. To do this, they can:

- Allow permanent residents to rent their entire home for thirty days or less each year (enough to allow for four full weeks of vacation).
- Prohibit entire-home, full-time short-term rentals entirely.

Looking Beyond Short-Term Rentals

Tourists and locals are not inherently at odds. Indeed, many residents' livelihoods as well as some of the vibrancy of these towns stems from the steady integration of visitors. As a Polish proverb states, "The guest sees more in an hour than the host in a year." These places are continually infused with outside values, customs, and observations that have the potential to make these places more accepting and more awake to the challenges and promises facing our society more broadly. In a word, visitors have the power to make places reflect.

This has its limits. If visitors play music too loudly or take parking places assigned to neighbors, they are gone the next day. They are much less likely to "drive like your kids live here," as the familiar neighborhood sign says, than those whose kids actually do. Rather than being one factor in informing locals' views of what their city becomes, the situation can very easily become adversarial if officials allow the preferences of tourists to dictate their city's identity. The question of "What type of place do we want to be?" is warped into "What type of place do tourists—especially wealthier ones—want?" In this environment, locals become an afterthought.

Officials in Flagstaff, St. George, and Bozeman seemed to understand this on some level. They acknowledged that entire-home short-term rentals can take potential housing off the market and create some price inflation by offering a more profitable option in housing. These effects were consistently identified as negative.

Yet, these officials overwhelmingly offered reasons why they would not do more. Some officials in St. George, Flagstaff, and many communities like them continually cited state laws forbidding the express regulation of short-term rentals.

Besides, multiple government officials rationalized, these were growing pains of a new technology and new platform. As they understood it, the market would self-correct when no longer profitable, so there was no need to take major action. No need to panic about this particular nuance. Many others still demurred on the overall impact of short-term rentals. While bemoaning the negatives, they also offered positives—that it brought in more tourists, that it allowed homeowners to better afford housing costs—which have not been proven. In fact, for short-term rental hosts who actually live in their home, the proliferation of permanent entire-home rentals limits their earning potential.

When tourists are preferred over locals, the situation becomes untenable—even adversarial—for locals. Signs across the world—from Neighbors, Not Airbnbs in New Orleans to Homes, Not Hotels in Arizona to Berlin Doesn't Love You in the German capital—illustrate that this can lead to local resentment toward tourism. In Barcelona, organizers rallied around the motto Barcelona Is Not For Sale. A prominent housing activist, Ada Colau, wrote an article for the *Guardian* entitled "Mass Tourism Can Kill a City—Just Ask Barcelona's Residents." Less than a year later, Colau was elected mayor.[13]

The relationship between tourists and locals can be contentious when it comes to restaurants and shops, but the situation becomes dire when it comes to locals' needs. The short-term rental market takes something which locals need—housing—and puts it on the market for tourists. And this market has no interest in changing so long as there is profit to be wrung out from the way things are now.

Ultimately, however, many officials said that there were bigger issues ranging from rising land and building costs to university growth to second homeownership to overall growth. In this vein, they fail to see that this is not simply about short-term rentals but rather the link between each of these issues. Namely, that the housing market has become a runaway train.

This runaway train creates challenges for policymakers. Pat Witton saw this in Bozeman, explaining that, "There's some entrepreneur somewhere that moved here because he thinks if we're fifty thousand now, we'll be sixty thousand in two years and they can make money. But most of the residents love Bozeman because of what it is at the moment. They're not wanting to see it grow."[14] At the same time, he noted the many reasons—from low crime to the size of the airport to the proximity of Yellowstone National Park—why it is growing and will continue to grow.

In listing these, Witton joked that he was "wear[ing his] chamber of commerce hat." This is a familiar refrain for places experiencing massive growth. As officials seek out and welcome real estate developers and businesses—"that entrepreneur somewhere"—to grow the local economy, they say to residents that there is no way to stop this growth.

This is reflected on climate change and housing challenges alike. Flagstaff's draft "10-Year Housing Plan" released in October 2021, for example, states, "Because Flagstaff and northern Arizona cannot avoid growth, ensuring that that growth is done in a sustainable way is critical to reducing overall greenhouse gas emissions."[15] Government officials at all levels are always wearing their "chamber of commerce hat" and any policy must first and foremost fit with that perspective.

Having devoted themselves entirely to the growth project, officials' political capital is put toward laying additional track for the runaway train of economic growth. In an effort to ward off a potential crash, they go to great lengths to lure new high-income residents, incentivize new developments, and expand boundaries. Incoming investors and residents are so rapt with the newness and aesthetic beauty of it all that they ignore or altogether fail to see that this is a facade. The shine of the city masks the disinvestment and disdain toward many now-recent and existing residents. Many of those entering and some of those who remain become apologists for growth, too. The train barrels on.

When it comes right down to it, cities and towns need to do whatever it takes to ensure that nonresidents do not compete with residents for housing. This can begin with the simple admission that a second homeowner is not a resident. An investor is not a neighbor. An empty property is not a home. Whereas previous housing prices were already producing parallel economies—one for property owners and one for renters—COVID has laid bare the fact that communities are being hollowed out entirely to make room for outside wealth. Local, state, and federal governments across the country are solely concerned with sustaining this ever-rising market. The only way that they will take action is if residents find a way to force them to.

Dollars and Sense

LEFT TO ITS OWN DEVICES, the housing market functions in the same manner as the cancer cell. It must grow, no matter the cost, an ideology that will eventually kill its host. Once this happens, it will metastasize, or move on, to the next host. In the Old West, this looked like a series of boom towns and ghost towns. In the New West and the service- and knowledge-based economy at work throughout the country, this looks like FOR SALE signs alongside new developments, unhoused people alongside tourists, skyrocketing housing costs alongside a slew of new people settling in.

In this way, the problem of unaffordable housing is pushed out of sight. Sometimes this means into the future, but it usually means to the next neighborhood or city over. This is what geographer David Harvey referred to as the "spatial fix."[1] Housing is unaffordable today—and was yesterday—because we continue to trust that the market will solve our problems.

The market does not identify or pursue solutions unless they are profitable. The unfettered market is a homogenizing force that clears forests to create fields lined by barbed wire. It populates subdivisions with row after row of the exact same house save the address and lawn ornaments. When the profit drops out, the market destroys what it has created, offering a new oasis—a frontier—to disrupt the sea of sameness.

The market then fills that frontier until it ceases to be profitable, circling back around to old frontiers only when they become profitable to re-create. It flips a house after a flood or fire. It offers so-called urban renewal in areas of disinvestment. It turns blank spaces into fresh starts. But these frequently metaphorical and sometimes actual fires and floods are of our own making. The problems they create result from the collusion of the state and industry, the product of policy or lack thereof. As author and activist Derecka Purnell so beautifully articulated in imagining more democratic neighborhoods, "We deserve new kinds of problems."[2]

For now, this insistence on growth at all costs has wreaked havoc on cities. Current and prospective residents are seldom asked to produce their papers like those at the country's southern border. They are seldom searched like those in majority non-White neighborhoods labeled as targeted law enforcement zones. But through rapidly rising housing costs and governmental policy increasingly devoted to maximizing its return on investment, all residents are forced to stand at attention, ready to prove their worth at any time.

Residents are prodded and interrogated, like immigrants facing inspection at Ellis Island. There is no onslaught of questions or demeaning physical exam. Rather, it is all wrapped up in a singular question: *How will you turn a profit?* Unable to provide a satisfactory answer, some are monitored. Others are immediately sent away.

Those able to remain become resistant to any type of growth, many of them fearful of being pushed out by the rapid influx of outside capital. In Bozeman, it becomes common to see bumper stickers reading: "Montana is full." Other places have their own versions. The market does not read bumper stickers.

Deferring to the omniscience of the market has always benefited some at the expense of others. Such a view has produced radical wealth accumulation alongside displacement and arguably made local and global economies even more vulnerable to the boom-and-bust cycle so prevalent in the extractive industries of the West. The solution, then, is also clear, although unpopular with those who most benefit from the current system: close the frontier.

At least, one version of it. The frontier has always operated on two levels. The "opportunity" Turner used as synonym for the West could be understood by some as a means of getting rich and by others as a "safety valve."[3] As economist James Buchanan explained, this safety valve served as an exit option when the walls of society seemed to close in and dramatically limited the potential for interpersonal exploitation.[4]

Our society has offered the means of getting rich to second homeowners and investors—a chance for them to "belong anywhere," as Airbnb would phrase it—at the direct expense of the exit option to long-term residents. The only exit option that remains for these long-term residents is to leave town. But still credit scores and background checks will follow, like a stamp declaring, "You don't deserve a roof over your head." When housing is on the rise everywhere and cities are in competition for high-income residents and visitors, where do those outside these categories go?

• • • • • • •

Too often within our representative democracy we are given a false choice on an issue: should government spend a little money or a lot of money? Answering that question, however, requires answers to two others: *what is being paid for?* and *who is paying?* We are likely to vote against spending a lot of money unless we believe it gets to the root of the problem. In other words, on housing, this money has to flow primarily from the forces making housing unaffordable in the first place to those most struggling to afford it.

There are two general ways of making housing—or anything, for that matter—more affordable: increasing people's income or decreasing the price. Government frequently focuses on the first—raising the minimum wage, subsidizing housing costs for low-income residents—while ignoring what it can do on the second. But attempting to raise individuals' incomes, particularly in fast-growing mountain towns and metropolitan areas, so that they can better afford high-priced housing distorts the issue. Are wages too low or is the true issue that the cost of housing—and of living more generally—is simply too high?

Productivity nationwide has increased dramatically since the 1970s, but wages for the majority of nonmanagerial workers have hardly budged. According to the Economic Policy Institute, net productivity rose 59.7 percent between 1979 and 2019, but worker compensation rose just 15.8 percent during that time. Had they grown at the same rate, "the median worker would be making $9.00 more per hour."[5] This fact and the radical inequality throughout the country seem to justify higher wages, but that is a different policy fight. Without other structural changes, minimum wage hikes or subsidy increases are insufficient for addressing the systemic unaffordability of housing. Without an upward limit on cost-of-living expenses, more income does not equate to enough income.

Moreover, government-induced increases in income are temporary and do not help everyone. Many people, from salaried workers to retirees to those living with a disability and unable to work, are on a fixed income, which is unchanged by minimum wage increases. Similarly, gig workers and those self-employed are unlikely to see many of these gains. For those actively seeking stable work but unable to find it, raising the minimum wage may make this harder as employers opt instead to automate or outsource different aspects of their business. From an environmental standpoint, this may cause more resources to be used as the labor cost of repairing or purchasing items locally grows far higher than the cost of simply replacing or purchasing it from afar.

Higher wages can have other effects, too. A common response to an increase in expenditures, as seen with healthcare coverage, is businesses cutting employees' hours to avoid paying benefits. The cost of doing business gets higher as the minimum wage goes up, usually resulting in higher prices. Perhaps people making more money will be better able to afford those things, but this only makes a difference if they plan to go to these places in the first place. For a tourism town, hospitality industries like restaurants, hotels, and shops were not dependent on local spending to begin with. Locals making more money per hour may simply become better able to afford services they did not need in the first place.

Furthermore, raising the minimum wage only directly affects the wages of those who made less than the new minimum. Some workers may have more ability to argue for a higher wage and some businesses may bring in more money and be able to better compensate employees, but these effects are at the discretion of employers and cannot be assumed. For the many who struggle with housing costs but are financially unaffected by minimum wage increases, any expected inflation in housing cost is actually more harmful.

The other important factor is that many of the places most struggling with unaffordable housing—from Flagstaff to Austin to New York City—have an external demand for housing that far outpaces what a minimum wage or subsidy increase can do for them. Even as they raise the lowest wages astronomically—to fifteen dollars an hour in Flagstaff and New York or twenty dollars an hour for city employees in Austin—these result in annual wages of roughly $31,200 and $41,600. They pale in comparison with the buying power of remote workers, investors, and tourists.

Subsidies provide a more direct example of how infusing money into the market without strings attached affects the price of housing. The 1980s shift toward government vouchers instead of public housing options dramatically reduced the possibility of finding housing outside the private market. Instead, the voucher served as a government promise to foot the remainder of the bill beyond 30 percent of a person's income.

Without conditions attached to overall prices, landlords stand to make more money by raising prices, which some evidence has shown they have done for decades. A 2002 study by economist Scott Susin explained how government policy between the early 1980s and early 1990s shifted away from providing public housing for low-income people toward providing them vouchers to use on the private market. He found that "in the 90 biggest metropolitan areas, vouchers have raised rents by 16 percent on average." As the study concludes, this translated to an overall $8.2 billion rent increase for low-income nonrecipients compared to a $5.8 billion subsidy to low-income recipients.[6]

This means those not receiving government assistance are being disadvantaged by those receiving it. In other words, with government footing the remainder of the bill no matter how high the bill is, the only thing that can put downward pressure on the market is if more units are made available or if people move further out from that area. Or move away entirely.

Subsidies and minimum wage increases can be used to bring down the costs for those most vulnerable, but this is a costly and often shortsighted solution. And nowhere is this clearer than in the way cities treat their unhoused populations.

There are more compassionate and less compassionate responses toward the growing number of people without housing, both of which were on full display when COVID began sweeping the country. Flagstaff, for example, spent approximately $4 million paying for some of its most vulnerable unhoused residents to be temporarily housed in hotels.[7] Las Vegas, meanwhile, was initially subjected to a major outcry for temporarily marking out socially distanced spaces in a parking lot for the unhoused.[8]

The fact that a tourism-driven city like Las Vegas with thousands and thousands of hotel rooms sitting empty sees this as an adequate solution makes clear why "unhoused" may be a more fitting term than "homeless" for this population. "Homeless" implies someone is rootless and personally responsible for their situation. It implies that the individual is deficient. "Unhoused," however, points to someone being removed or kept from housing through more structural means. People who are unhoused are not simply without housing; they are being actively deprived of it. The focus changes from a personal deficit to a societal responsibility, thereby implicating neighbors, churches, organizations, companies, and especially government.

With HUD finding that the number of unhoused people has risen over the last several years—to more than 580,000 in 2020, and even this number almost assuredly an undercount—many government officials are feeling pressure to address the issue.[9] Or, rather, they feel pressure to appease their voter base. Instead of seeking to diminish the causes of houselessness, governments across the country are increasingly seeking to criminalize or marginalize those living without housing in their district. They set policies that prohibit loitering, tents, and panhandling, seeking to remove houselessness from view.

In some cases, cities have invested heavily in addressing houselessness, but how they invest this money matters as much if not more than how much they invest. At first glance, Las Vegas and Flagstaff provide a contrast in priorities. The bigger takeaway, though, may be the similarity in just how little forethought is put into housing policy. Flagstaff's $4 million policy seems to imply compassion and, in a sense, it does. After all, it mattered immensely to these residents whether the city put a small or massive amount of money toward their housing situation. But it was only for a few and only in the short term.

Flagstaff, like other cities, seems to be catching on to this reality. In September 2021, the city of Tempe, Arizona, and Housing Solutions of Northern Arizona, a Flagstaff nonprofit, each purchased forty-plus-room hotels to be used as housing for those in greatest need.[10] This is consistent with efforts elsewhere, the largest of which is California's $600 million Homekey Initiative.

Started as Project Roomkey in order to protect vulnerable unhoused populations from COVID-19, the Homekey Initiative was launched in the fall of 2020 to leverage federal dollars to purchase and rehabilitate vacant properties ranging from single homes to hotels to apartment buildings.[11] These rooms will house people without stable housing, enabling more consistent social services and less costly interventions. According to the California Department of Housing and Community Development, the program has housed more than 8,200 individuals and created 5,911 units at 94 unique sites.[12]

Although critics may be quick to dismiss this housing first model as something which could only work in isolated cities or a state like California, it's been tried and extremely successful in a very different political climate: Utah. The idea of providing housing to the chronically unhoused came to Utah in 2003, after Lloyd Pendleton, then the leader of humanitarian services for the Church of Jesus Christ of Latter-Day Saints, went to a conference in Chicago and listened to a talk from Sam Tsemberis, who'd raised the housing first model in public consciousness. The talk challenged Pendleton's worldview.

"Because I was raised as a cowboy in the west desert," he explained, he could recall seeing people without housing and thinking, "'You lazy bums, get a job, pull yourself up by the bootstraps.'" What really committed him to the housing first model wasn't accepting the existing evidence that says more than half of all people staying primarily in homeless shelters and around 40% of those outside shelters entirely have some type of formal employment during the same year. Neither was it a change in heart, perhaps triggered by the high rate of disability among the unhoused.[13] Rather, what changed Pendleton's mind was the realization—triggered by Tsemberis—that providing housing for people is actually cheaper, saving on tens of thousands of dollars per person in social and emergency services of all kinds. After lobbying for Housing First pilot programs around Salt Lake City, Pendleton became head of Utah's Homeless Task Force.

As of 2015, the number of Utahns estimated to be at least temporarily unhoused remained stubbornly high at roughly 14,000. But this was with heavy increases in the total population. And the number of chronically unhoused people—those who'd been without shelter at least four times in the previous three years or those with disabilities who had been without housing for a year—had been cut by 91 percent.[14]

Homes offer people a stable base and a place to regain their bearings. They offer a place where they can feel safe. Although shelters are often held up as adequate temporary alternatives to more permanent housing solutions, it is standard practice at shelters to have occupants leave the morning after each night's stay, often when the sky is still dark and temperatures still frigid. In these cases, they take all they own back to the street, to the library, to the park, whichever spot they can find that allows them to plan out their day without constant harassment by police and other city authorities. In late afternoon, they can usually return to the shelter, like a hotel with limited vacancy. A hotel in which many fear for their safety and the security of their possessions.

Shelters require people to stand in line and check in. They have inspections and rules implemented by everyone from policymakers to boards to volunteers—everyone except the people who stay there. At their best, shelters are unprepared to provide for the myriad health, social, and security needs of so many. At their worst, they exacerbate these issues. In this way, shelters can never be home.

Although many would say that shelters were never intended to be home, they represent one of many facets of care which has been outsourced from community—friends, family, neighbors, churches, schools, and voluntary associations—to professional services like counselors and case managers. Researcher and activist John McKnight argued in his book *The Careless Society: Community and Its Counterfeits*, "Much of the social welfare system is compensation for the technological society's destruction of social life and its tools. This atomization has degraded or eliminated the forums where community definition and action can be conceived or negotiated." A home is where people can start to regain what McKnight calls "the human necessity to act rather than be acted upon; to be citizen rather than client."[15]

· · · · · · ·

Like most issues, the best way to address unaffordable housing is not simply to grant unlimited resources toward the same market forces that have made fortunes from keeping housing unaffordable. These efforts to buy unused properties and provide an alternative to the profit motive of the market seem to reflect a growing awareness of this fact. But Scott Susin's research illustrated this exact point two decades ago. Furthermore, it is being illustrated right now. Inflation in the consumer price index, or CPI, reached a thirty-nine-year record increase of 7 percent in 2021 based on year-on-year prices. Although this resulted in part from COVID-related staffing shortages and supply chain issues, it was being driven especially by two price increases: used cars and housing.[16]

Perhaps this housing price increase could be understood in the context of reduced supply, but it demonstrates a crucial fact: those who plan to rent or sell property stand to gain from reduced available supply. After all, rental management site Zumper calculated huge leaps in national median rental prices. Between January 2021 and January 2022, one-bedroom rental rates rose by nearly 12 percent and two-bedroom rates rose by more than 14 percent.[17] Not everyone has suffered from inflation, though. The US Bureau of Economic Analysis calculated that posttax profits of non-financial corporations had soared to new heights of $1.73 trillion dollars between July 1 and September 30 (Q3) of 2021, approximately $700 billion higher than prepandemic totals.[18]

In the context of a single industry, the twenty-four largest oil and gas companies made $74 billion in profit during the same quarter, part of $174 billion made during the first nine months of 2021. As of December 2021, gas prices had reached a seven-year high with the average gallon of fuel costing $3.40 compared to $2.10 just one year prior. Kyle Herrig, the president of government watchdog group Accountable.US said in response that "Americans looking for someone to blame for the pain they experience at the pump need look no further than the wealthy oil and gas company executives who choose to line their own pockets rather than lower gas prices."[19]

But the fact that they are able to choose at all is precisely the issue. A March 2022 report from the Department of the Treasury noted that the concentration of the market in relatively few corporations, combined with these corporations' "anti-competitive practices," has held down wages and worker mobility.[20] We have set up a system focused entirely on maximizing profit and yet remain surprised when corporate executives religiously pursue the accumulation of profit. The system is designed for them to do so; shareholders may well ensure that executives who do otherwise are out of a job. When housing is viewed in the same way, it's no wonder why prices are so high for so many.

To arrive at a different place, we need to find different solutions. The reason we have such unaffordable housing—the reason for a host of our problems—is simple: we have entrusted the market to solve it. If we want to change the housing landscape for a year, a generation, or a century from now, we need to change this. And, to do that, we need to care more about where we get the money and where it goes.

. . . .

How unaffordable housing is addressed should vary according to what—or who—is making it unaffordable. There is a reason why so many homes in Flagstaff, St. George, Bozeman, and so many more places across the country are sitting empty and yet not on the market. They exist on an entirely different market not tied to the local labor market. Whether this other market consists of investors, nonprimary homeowners, short-term rentals, or even remote workers, the solution is to price them that way.

Each of these cities has an example of this right within its own boundaries: in-state and out-of-state tuition at public universities. Out-of-state students pay a premium in tuition. This is a national practice justified because these students and their families have not been paying state and local taxes and have not previously been part of these communities like those in-state. Why not apply the same logic to short-term rentals and second homes?

In addition to the short-term rental policies cited from each city, applying a sizable increase to the property taxes of nonprimary homes would disincentivize both their building and purchase. To enforce this, every place struggling with unaffordable housing due to external demand from nonprimary homeowners, investors, and short-term rentals must first know how much of its housing stock is devoted to residential properties not being used as residences. When property values are assessed each year, the property tax on these units should be tied to the overall percentage of all housing units that are devoted to nonprimary home purposes. In other words, if a high percentage of all housing units are being used for purposes other than housing people at least six months of the year, each of these properties should pay a premium on their assessed value in taxes.

A diminished version of this law is already in place in Utah. Such a law would be enormously unpopular among a small subset of the population that treats housing as nothing more than a way to make passive income and enormously popular among the vast majority that treat housing as far more. That is the point. It's not a difficult concept to grasp if we accept that housing is meant for housing people.

Flagstaff can be used to illustrate this. Although Coconino County's primary property tax rate, averaging around 0.5 percent of the home's assessed value, makes it appear to be one of the lowest in Arizona, the county has secondary property taxes that have been added by voter-approved measures over the years to help fund things such as community colleges and emergency funding. These rates are the same for a $400,000 house, whether it is a resident's primary home or whether they bought it solely as an investment property to be rented out as a short-term rental. By raising the primary property rate to 1.0 percent of assessed value for homes used for nonresidential purposes, primary homeowners would be able to continue paying half of this assessed rate, 0.5 percent. This would also be a huge influx of revenue for housing.

Relying on data from the Coconino County Assessor's Office, the October 2021 draft of their ten-year housing plan cites the second-home population as 22 percent of the local housing parcels. The plan states that "it's important to note there are issues with how the data is collected and updated and some unknown percentage of properties are likely misclassified."[21] Interviewees, particularly city officials, consistently articulated a desire for better data. As the second-home number is dependent on how people classify their own properties, it is likely higher. Using that 22 percent as a rough approximation, however, translates to 3,928 parcels being used as second homes.

Using data from the same report, the assessed value of the average nonprimary property is $388,760. If 0.5 percent were added to the property tax rate assessed on each second home, taxing them at a rate of 1.0 percent, this would amount to approximately $1,943.80 per house for each home at this average sale price. Multiplying this by the number of second-home parcels results in $7,635,246.40 for the city. Every year. People can still own a second home and use it as a nonprimary residence; they'll just have to pay an additional amount for the impact on the community.

If this is deemed too small or large, the city can adjust it. To make this transition more gradual for nonprimary homeowners already present, the property tax rate could be raised 0.1 percent, or approximately $388, each year until reaching its designated 1.0 percent of assessed value. If governments have one responsibility to their residents, it has to be to keep the place affordable to people who actually live there. If a place ceases to be affordable, nothing else matters.

Alternatively, the city could address the problem when homes are sold in the first place. Similar to property tax, there is currently no distinction in price between primary and nonprimary uses of properties. Applying a 22 percent surcharge, also known as a transfer or excise tax, could be added in Flagstaff when a home is sold for the purpose of being used as a nonprimary home. This 22 percent surcharge would be added to equate to the total amount of units that nonprimary homes take off the market for potential long-term residents. Using the median sales price of $388,760 and the 3,928 parcels identified as nonprimary homes, this would translate to approximately $336 million in revenue for the city. For the sake of comparison, this would cover the roughly $5 million proposed for the city's 2021–22 Housing and Community Services Fund sixty-seven times over.

The details of this plan are less important than the reasons why this policy, as opposed to many others attempting to address housing, could work. This policy would not be an isolated subsidy or minor tweak; it would be part of a sea change. State laws would need to be changed in order to allow Flagstaff and many other cities the power to enact policies like these. But acknowledging and addressing the impact that nonprimary homes and outside investment has on the overall affordability of housing has the potential to radically improve our entire housing landscape.

Treating housing as real estate has benefited an increasingly small segment of the population and eroded the control millions have over their lives. To this end, action on affordable housing must be large enough to meet the need. Similarly, it must be funded primarily by those forces that make it harder for many people to simply get by. But equally important in all this is how that money is used.

In determining the actions which get funded, we have to look beyond the present moment and imagine an alternative to the current housing landscape. This is no easy feat. The financialization of home at work over the past three decades has ensured that the national housing market—particularly in places of seemingly limitless external demand—has largely moved on from the mission of meeting residents' needs. In this environment, elected officials and governments at all levels have adopted a piecemeal, market-driven approach. The solutions they've employed—from handing out subsidies to nudging the market to build more affordable developments—have not worked and will not work, because they ignore the reason housing is so difficult to afford in the first place.

Rent is too high for locals because the sale price of a home is too high for locals. The price of a home is too high for locals because developers get more money catering to nonlocals. Particularly in the West, empty homes conjure up comparisons with the western frontier by offering land and real estate to outsiders able to pay more. Full-time residents, especially low-income and non-White populations and many who trace their roots in these areas back generations, cannot compete. Government officials become quick to echo the words of Megan Lawson, the economist at Headwaters Economics: "You know, it really is kind of inevitable."[22]

It doesn't have to be. Housing has come to be dominated by investment properties because the market has valued profits above all else. Meanwhile, government has altogether abdicated its role of amplifying the voices of people who actually live there. The fact that many of us have parroted similar sentiments, coming to see this process as inevitable, represents a vexing form of Stockholm syndrome. We come to ascribe competence, even compassion, to the market that imprisons us. History has shown that there has consistently been a need for more affordable housing, which the market has failed to produce because it is not as profitable. The solution is not simply to incentivize the market to build more market-rate and luxury-priced housing. The solution is to provide an actual alternative.

Building a House

The possibilities for this amount of money being directed toward housing are immense. It can help fund alternatives we are already aware of. On the homeownership side, community land trusts (CLTs) are already utilized in Flagstaff, Bozeman, and many other cities across the country. On the rental side, public housing was widespread—and exceedingly popular—until it was defunded upon racial integration in the 1950s. It's also never been tried in a way that makes it sustainable, despite these successful models existing throughout the world.

Under the CLT model, individuals own homes while the city or a nonprofit owns the land. Neighborhood associations could provide other avenues for sustained ownership and maintenance as long as they commit to long-term affordability measures. Particular rules will vary by location, but CLTs are generally restricted to primary homes and potential buyers must be at or beneath the area median income (AMI). Equity from the house is diminished compared to typical homeownership because initial costs are kept under greater control.

As an example, someone might pay $400,000 for a market-rate house versus $350,000 for a CLT. If it is a seller's market when selling the market-rate house, they might earn $100,000 more than the initial price. As the CLT is more consistently tied to inflation, the resale value may be more like $50,000 above the initial price. Since the land on which CLTs stand is ultimately owned by an entity committed to housing affordability, they could be eligible for diminished annual property tax rates. Additionally, with the uncertainty of the traditional market and the increased expense needed in traditional homeownership models to pay off a higher mortgage, CLTs begin to look even more appealing.

CLTs provide both a lower price for those directly living in the place and could create some amount of downward pressure for housing costs more generally. If applying the previous estimates of 3,928 second homes being priced at an average of $388,760, this would result in approximately $7.64 million toward city housing initiatives each year. With this money, the city or a nonprofit or a neighborhood association committed to housing affordability could buy 152 properties to convert to CLTs, cutting the initial price of each by $50,000. That's 152 properties being sold for $50,000 less—or 76 properties being sold for $100,000 less—than the market price each year.

Whether it's the city, a national nonprofit, or a local group running this program does not make much difference. What makes a difference is that this entity is committed to housing affordability and accountable to homeowners in CLTs. The one entity, or nonentity, that has been shown to have no commitment to affordability to locals is the market itself. Allowing the market to regulate affordability when demand has gone global is allowing a fox to guard a henhouse.

On the rental side, this money could fund the purchase or construction of small mixed-income, rent-controlled apartment buildings. In a way, cities across the country already use this model: one of their most common tactics for incentivizing affordable housing is to fast-track permitting for private apartment or condo developers that commit to 10% or 20% of units being at or below the fair market rate. And they still have little difficulty generating large profits.

Normally, developers are only bound to this commitment for a relatively short time period, sometimes with the so-called fair market rate out of reach for many. In mixed-income public housing, a higher percentage of units—but not all units—would be made available at low rates. The goal would not be to maximize profits but to recoup costs. Additionally, an emphasis on multiple uses could help further offset these costs. On-site childcare could help make the space more attractive for those with young kids. So could car-sharing or bike-sharing programs. Furthermore, street-level space could be rented out to businesses such as grocery stores, or local shops. And, just like CLTs, these buildings could be owned and maintained by a nonprofit, city, or neighborhood association.

Every year, Flagstaff could add around 152 homes to its current stock of 47 CLTs and remove $50,000 from the initial price of each property. This could go even further if the state or federal government supported these efforts. It could build or simply purchase multiple apartment buildings, making them mixed-income with rent-controlled housing. Properties would be well-maintained and tenants would pay no more than 30 percent of their monthly income to rent and utilities. These costs would be strictly tied to inflation, limiting the possibility that large increases would price people out.

Or perhaps the policy would have the intended effect of making second homes less palatable, thereby eliminating entire-home short-term rental possibilities and adding long-term residential ones instead.

This will require changes in laws, with some places—like those in Arizona that elevate the rights of individual property owners regardless of residential status—requiring changes at the state level. Some cities may fear that the sudden increase in affordable housing will drive down resale value for residents who recently paid a premium in buying their homes, but there are ways to confront this without preventing any true effort at making housing affordable. Instead of setting aside all funds for CLTs and mixed-income public housing, some revenue could be applied toward reimbursing homeowners who saw their home's resale value dip below what they'd initially paid. Long-term residents who needed to sell their home within five years after the implementation of these affordable housing laws, for instance, could be guaranteed to not lose money.

This backstop is meant to help prevent existing homeowners from feeling their financial interests are threatened by affordable housing. Termed home-equity insurance by Dartmouth College economics professor William A. Fischel, it has been implemented in various forms in the Chicago area dating back to the late 1970s as a method "to discourage panic selling in the face of racial transition."[1]

In many cases, it may not even be needed. Since CLTs, with the limited potential equity, are fundamentally different from homes that have the potential to appreciate—or depreciate—rapidly on these regular markets, it's quite possible they would not hurt the high return on investment on others. There would still be people who would wish to own the land as well as the house built upon it. This law would do nothing to prevent them from doing so. If anything, if it decreased initial prices, it might make that more possible.

The same is true for rent-controlled, mixed-income properties. Often seen in larger cities throughout the country, these are fundamentally different than other rental properties and there will still be a demand for different styles of rentals. But this alternative could provide the safety valve for so many residents who can barely afford rent as it is and might be priced out altogether with a significant increase. Combined, these alternatives in ownership and rent, if enacted and enforced, would immensely improve affordability in cities across the country.

· · · · · · ·

Non-Whites, particularly those of Indigenous and African American ancestry, have been robbed of land and deprived of the land and housing opened to White settlers. This theft has been systemic, ensuring that their descendants inherit debt while White descendants inherited wealth, and has been inflicted by the action and inaction of the federal government. For this reason, federal action is required to truly address the racial aspect of the ongoing commodification of housing.

This does not mean that city and state governments must wait. Any city with large non-White populations just beyond its borders—like the Native reservations bordering Flagstaff and St. George—has great power in addressing racial disparities. Any person who is at least a second-generation resident of the larger region could be granted first priority and reduced standards of financial eligibility to affordable housing options like CLTs and mixed-income housing.

Federal government officials can and should think much more massively. One's residence is a strong indicator of their health, wealth, job prospects, social circle, and overall freedom throughout their life. The racial segregation, relations, and outcomes in this country are a direct result of government land and housing policy, especially at the federal level. There are innovative ways to address the racial gaps that now exist without placing nonrecipients at a disadvantage. They range from waiving property tax fees, with the federal government reimbursing for these amounts, to issuing direct payments. These policies can even take the form of issues far afield from housing such as offering education and child care credits or access to low-interest loans.

The biggest issue with civil rights laws, however, has not been their lack of passage but their lack of enforcement. On paper, the 1968 Fair Housing Act eliminated racial discrimination in housing. The reality is that it was never enforced, with HUD given less than 5 percent of the funding requested by secretary Robert Weaver for the next year.[2] The following secretary, George Romney, adhering to the Fair Housing Act's mandate to "affirmatively further" desegregation in housing, directed "HUD officials to reject applications for water, sewer, and highway projects from cities and states where local policies fostered segregated housing."[3] This policy was immediately quashed. Romney was eventually driven out of his role, the policy never fully implemented under Nixon or any president since.

The federal government frequently withholds funds and services from cities and states that do not comply with federal laws. It should do the same when it comes to cities and states that are not making sincere efforts toward decreasing the racial segregation that exists today. It can start by implementing the Fair Housing Act as it was written, as HUD Secretary George Romney called for fifty years ago.

• • • • • • •

Addressing racial issues means addressing economic ones. After all, as the 1970s and 1980s wore on, the most blatant acts of racial discrimination began to be tolerated less and less. Homeownership and rental opportunities in safe, stable neighborhoods were becoming more legally accessible to non-White residents. But an analysis of 2010 census data by John Logan of Brown University showed that racial discrimination has remained common, with Black residents earning $75,000 a year more likely to live in impoverished areas than White residents earning $40,000.[4] Being Black was akin to an annual $35,000 tax.

No matter a person's annual income, the wealth of their parents or grandparents trickled down through generations. Since prices rose during the thirty-year period in which non-Whites were effectively excluded from homeownership, only Whites were able to accrue this generational wealth. Only Whites can apply this to the purchase of their home. In this context, non-Whites encounter the biggest issue, arguably for decades: stable housing is simply not affordable.

Richard Kahlenberg, a senior fellow at the Century Foundation, has argued that protections against economic discrimination should be added to the Fair Housing Act. Under the original Fair Housing Act, the disparate impact standard allows for a government, organization, or individual to sue if a policy has a discriminatory effect on a protected category, which includes race. Importantly, it does not have to prove intent. Kahlenberg suggests that this disparate impact standard simply be expanded to include class.[5] What this means is that cities and states would not be able to pass exclusionary zoning laws, laws that exclude certain types of buildings or residents, except if related to "'promotion of the public health, safety, and welfare'" of the city.

These were the words of the 1917 Supreme Court ruling in *Buchanan v. Warley* that declared Louisville, Kentucky, could not prohibit a non-White person from moving into a majority-White neighborhood. But the US government has generally refused to implement this policy in relation to zoning laws that exclude people of lower income from moving into an area of higher income. In fact, in 1926, the Supreme Court ruled in *Euclid v. Ambler* that "apartment houses . . . come very near to being nuisances" and therefore could be excluded from areas through zoning. This decision reversed a lower court's ruling that this type of zoning constituted clear class discrimination and is the reason why, within twenty years of the *Buchanan* ruling, the number of cities with zoning ordinances exploded from 8 to 1,246. Almost all of these were focused on restricting smaller lots or multifamily homes.[6]

If residents are actually concerned about their home equity being diminished by changes in their neighborhood, Fischel's idea for home-equity insurance seems well-suited to address these fears.[7] Most of the time, however, these exclusions do nothing to promote "public health, safety and welfare" and are instead focused on creating and preserving wealthier, Whiter enclaves. After watching their residents struggle to afford the growing cost of housing, officials in many cities and states are finally recognizing the role of exclusionary zoning. US Representative Emanuel Cleaver of Missouri recently drafted a bill for an Economic Fair Housing Act to force the federal government to recognize this, too.

· · · · · · ·

When the Homestead Act opened up Native-held land to settlers in 1862, there was a caveat: almost without exception, settlers had to be White. The same was true when the General Allotment Act of 1887 opened up ninety million acres of land held by Native tribes. The theme remained when the FHA underwrote $120 billion in home loans between 1934 and 1962, with just 2 percent going to non-Whites.[8] This history—without even delving into the litany of sundown laws, racial terror incidents, and discriminatory lending practices—does not just belong to people of color. It is our collective history. And the racially segregated landscapes it produced survive and continue to be reproduced today.

Nationally, the 2010 Census recorded Black isolation or segregation at 55 percent.[9] In some northern cities, especially those with large Black populations, this number is a staggering 70 percent. Much of the remaining integration has been shown to be temporary, the result of ongoing neighborhood change.[10] It's tempting, particularly if we feel that we benefit from the current arrangement, to write this off as some intangible preference for in-grouping or dismiss this as a simple difference in where people live. After all, thinking this way requires us to change nothing. It simply requires us to hang on to a delusion.

We realize this is a delusion because, for most of us, our biggest monthly expense and one of the biggest decisions we ever make is where to live. We recognize that where we live determines our ability to breathe clean air, drink clean water, send our kids to good schools, remain gainfully employed, access a wide array of goods and services, and be enmeshed in a strong social community. The commodification of housing does not just price people out of their homes but out of this entire constellation of needs and possibilities. Feeling ourselves locked in an eternal competition, we fear this fate for ourselves. We envy those with more and spurn those with less.

Since all this occurs within the context of our history as a racially unequal society, we continue to be a racially unequal society. By almost every measure related to health, income, wealth, debt, education level, incarceration rates, and mortality rates, people of Western European ancestry fare better than those with ancestry in the Americas, Africa, and much of Asia. This has far less to do with *Guns, Germs, and Steel*, as US geographer and historian Jared Diamond decreed, than it does a system that rewards greed even when it results in suffering, displacement, and death. From its establishment centuries ago, this system continues almost unchecked. If we care about racial justice in this country, we have to confront the issue that undergirds every one of these examples of racial inequality. That issue is housing.

National efforts at making reparations for racism in housing have stalled, but a hopeful blueprint can perhaps be seen in the centuries-old land back movement for Native nations, which has recently gained momentum. There have been isolated victories in which Native nations have been repatriated with tracts of their ancestral land, including the Wiyot Nation in the area of Eureka, California, the Wyandotte Nation near Upper Sandusky, Ohio, and others throughout the country.[11]

In some cases of land being returned to Native nations, such as the InterTribal Sinkyone Wilderness Council in California and the Esselen Nation in Oregon, conservation groups have played major roles. This is a major step toward acknowledging that the original Western frontier was never really empty at all.[12] It also provides a model of acknowledging that the frontiers that came after, whether relating to homeownership in the 1940s, gentrification in the 1990s, or the commodification of housing today, have continually disrupted existing populations and destroyed existing ecosystems.

Recent research uncovered notes that HUD Secretary Romney prepared for a meeting with President Nixon. In them, he states that "equal opportunity for all Americans in education and housing is essential if we are going to keep our nation from being torn apart."[13] We inherit the debts, scars, inheritance, and stories of our direct ancestors. But we also inherit their neighborhoods, their work, their social structure. If we ignore the wretched disparity of the past, reproducing an unequal world, we cannot pretend to be blameless. As author James Baldwin said, "Not everything that is faced can be changed, but nothing can be changed until it is faced."[14]

• • • • • • •

The 2015 film *99 Homes* traces the path of a single father and his family who are evicted from their home and wind up living in a hotel. The young father, having recently lost his construction job and feeling like he's losing any chance of getting his home back, begins working for the same real estate broker who presided over his eviction. Eventually, he earns enough money to get his family back into stable housing and tells his new boss that he wants to buy back his old home rather than another property. The real estate agent immediately tries to steer him in another direction, saying simply, "Don't get emotional about real estate. They're boxes."[15]

But housing is more than that. It's where people find shelter, where they spend their time, and where they lay their heads. It's where people make memories and forge relationships. It's where they start and where they end each day, where they tuck their kids in at night and where they look at their reflection to question who they are. And who they'd like to be.

In describing the power of levers, the Greek mathematician and physicist Archimedes once said, "Give me but one firm spot on which to stand, and I will move the Earth."[16] Housing has the potential to be that spot, the place from which anything is possible.

15

Building a Home

WITHIN AN HOUR, Ethan Hughes had us all questioning our lives. It was 2010, and I was a sophomore in college in the small town of Kirksville, Missouri. Hughes was leading our group around the hundred-acre farm that he lived on with his wife, Sarah Wilcox Hughes, their daughter, Etta, and a half dozen others. They produced fruits, vegetables, grains, meat, dairy, herbs, spices, and timber. They did this year after year, hardly using money at all as they sustained their nine permanent inhabitants and fed any visitors, like the group I went with. They also didn't use petroleum or electricity.[1]

Hughes and the other permanent residents welcomed hundreds, even thousands, of guests each year. They rode their bikes everywhere, including an annual ride to different areas of the country in which they dressed up in homemade superhero outfits and volunteered their energy for community projects along the way. They were living in a way that I'd never seen before, a way that I thought was no longer possible, and they seemed happier and more at peace than most people I interacted with on a daily basis. Appropriately, they called their group the Possibility Alliance.

When several of them rode their bikes north along Highway 63 to speak on campus about the gift economy—an idea as simple as it sounds, giving away surplus that would not be eaten or used—I showed up. I went back to their farm again as part of a class. And I went back once more with the organization that had first led me there, this time organizing the group myself. I was so taken in with the way people at the Possibility Alliance lived that, when I graduated, I considered contacting them about staying and working there for a while. They still had a landline.

I considered this because a part of me felt overwhelmed with the problems of the world. While I felt pulled to do something about these problems, I was also acutely aware that most jobs would have me either furthering these problems or working incredibly hard to play what seemed at that time to be an insignificant part in addressing them. I felt as though I'd written enough papers and studied for enough tests, that I'd spent too much time inside, cut off from something more tangible; at least I would see my impact while working on a farm.

Time passed. I never contacted the Possibility Alliance, a fact that signals that maybe the idea was never all that serious. Five years later, I jumped at the chance to work on a wilderness trails crew in Montana, living for months without cell service, internet, or any roads at all. Maybe the idea was more serious than I let on.

A lot has changed in the ten years since I last went to the Possibility Alliance. Ethan and Sarah have had another child, Isla, and they've moved to a ten-acre farm on the coast of Maine. But, in talking with Ethan Hughes by phone in the summer of 2022, he hadn't seemed to have lost a shred of faith in their original mission of finding another way to live. In fact, they've only added to their mission. As a result of events in the world and conversations with more than fifteen thousand visitors over the years, they've made a point of working with non-White, queer, and impoverished communities across the globe. They've kept a landline.

I never had any illusions that the Possibility Alliance was a model for how all of us would—or should—live. Neither did the families that called the place home. In fact, Hughes emphasized that we need many different ideas, relationships, and solutions.

> *We have these huge sterile shelters for low-income housing. [It's] a beautiful intention, like let's try to solve it. But the reason it's not working is because it's a mass solution, which is actually counter to how nature works. . . . Each relationship creates a coral reef. . . . Any piece of Earth left untouched and unharmed by humans will go through succession till it reaches the most dynamic amount of diversity in life per square foot. That's amazing. The traditional tall grass prairies did that, the rainforests, the coral reefs. And so, how do we imagine that? How do we take our wealth, and think of what can I do with this wealth that creates the most life, the most heal- ing, and the most diversity? Like, those are the questions we should [have] laid down to us in kindergarten.*[2]

All this starts with housing. But housing alone, as Hughes made clear, is not enough. Instead, against the backdrop of a totalizing economic system that forces everyone to compete for housing, for work, for healthcare, for education, for food, and leaves so many without these basic needs or any sense of meaning, Hughes has noticed a strange paradox.

> *When I go to Hurricane Katrina, where everyone lost their homes, I'm in the Ninth Ward, where we're trying to clean up and get rid of the black mold. There's actually more community there, often more community in the unhoused community in Eugene, more commu- nity when I've been in, you know, refugee situations than in upper- class White suburbia.*[3]

The Tragedy of No Commons

Housing offers shelter. Home requires community. That's why there's something intangible lost when neighborhoods see frequent turnover and become hosts to empty spaces. Residents may rarely use public gathering spaces and familiar neighborhood contacts may be fleeting. But even so, they matter.

Less connections with neighbors can lead to more loneliness and social isolation for residents. It can lead to more expenses for child care, dog walking, security systems, increased police presence, home repair, and even the occasional cup of sugar as residents do not know each other. As Jane Jacobs argued in *The Death and Life of Great American Cities*, "Most of it is ostensibly utterly trivial but the sum is not trivial at all."[4]

In a 2019 study, 58 percent of respondents reported "they always or sometimes feel like no one knows them well." Meanwhile, 52% report "sometimes or always feeling alone."[5] Four years later, after the dramatic uptick in remote work, the vitality of neighborhoods matters even more. In some sense, the wide range of connections which Jacobs spoke to arises organically, the result of a wide range of people existing in close proximity. In other words, people interact when their paths cross. But the reason that peoples' paths cross is because society is structured in such a way. Taxes are put toward social and community services such as public schools, spaces, parks, health centers, and transit. This creates what geographer Doreen Massey described as a sort of "thrown-togetherness."[6] Spaces are shared and negotiated, with norms and rules defined by the same people who use them.

The phrase "the tragedy of the commons" has come to be seen as almost irrefutable, implying that every space must be individually owned and operated. People argue that if there were commons—what Hughes described as "spaces where you can go and you don't have to pay to be there"—chaos would reign.[7] Like dog eat dog, no alternative is allowed.

Except that the concept of the tragedy of the commons, popularized in a 1968 article by Garrett Hardin, was disproven by Elinor Ostrom.[8] She won a Nobel Prize in Economic Sciences, the first woman to ever do so, for noting the presence of commons across the world, from ocean waters to airspace to local parks to shared driveways to common spaces within a home. Ostrom explained that the tragedy of the commons wrongfully argued that nobody would care for common space. It was not the case that nobody owned them. Rather, they were owned by everyone who used them.[9]

Hardin even admitted, in so many words, that Ostrom was right, that he should have specified that he had merely been referring to unmanaged commons.[10] And yet, the concept has retained its power over the way in which we've constructed our society. Gradually, then all at once, the commodification of housing dismantles commons. With housing treated as a commodity, cities and neighborhoods become places of isolation rather than places for people to bump into each other. Homes are cut off from businesses, wealthy neighborhoods from poorer ones, and a person's expected lot in life largely predictable by the zip code they're born in.

Rather than putting local money into community services, local government starts to chase outside money. Under the guise of meeting a budget shortfall, government ceases to fund the very services that preserve the fabric of the community. Instead, money is siphoned into luring outside money with new art installations, wider roads, storefront facades, and a host of other features, all of it built under the justification that the newcomers' increased spending and property taxes will filter down to services for all residents.

It doesn't take long for this assumption to be disproven. New year-round and partial-year residents put their money toward charter schools, private pools, country clubs, and security systems. As they build their private utopias, they begin to question where their taxes go. After all, they don't use the myriad community and social services and do not know anyone who does. They increasingly vote, run for office, and organize around their narrow personal interests.

This process transforms a place. Insulated from the problems of their society, new high-income residents and partial-year residents fail to notice or care about the increased housing costs and houselessness that surround them. When they do take note, it is usually because they don't like seeing it, not because they don't like that it's happening. The town's wealthiest residents, whether new or old, cry foul when affordable housing or even simply multiunit housing is proposed to house all the people who build the city's roads, fix its powerlines, and make it run.

This wealthy segment points to parking concerns and congestion and—most important of all—maintaining their property values. After all, they moved there expecting 5 percent gains per year. What is the town for if it can't guarantee that?

When people are forced out entirely, attention is drawn to what replaces them instead of what's lost. What was once a city or town built around finding a place for all the people who make it work—around inclusivity—becomes a country club built around exclusivity. The place's aesthetic takes precedence over its substance. Bob Moorehead observed all this in his aptly named poem "The Paradox of Our Age": "It is a time when there is much in the window, but nothing in the room."[11]

We are so transfixed by what's in the window—the beauty of the town, the spectacle of economic growth—that we fail to consider what's in, or not in, the room. Very soon, in addition to the social and psychological fallout, the displacement of existing residents causes a labor shortage. In this way, believing ourselves independent of other people sounds the death knell for communities.

Similarly, in our narrow focus on growth at all costs and our willingness to ignore the depletion of the natural world, we fail to consider the impacts to our own health and well-being as well as the looming material shortage. The conservationist and author Aldo Leopold once said, "All ethics so far evolved rest upon a single premise; that the individual is a member of a community of interdependent parts."[12] In forgetting this, we have brought ourselves to the brink. Believing our society independent of nature could be the death knell for the species.

"Fall, Fall, Fall" is a slow, melancholic song about the destruction of the environment. Written and performed by the folk band Caamp, one simple, evocative line is repeated throughout: "I want my kids to swim in the creek. Oh, I want my kids to swim in the creek."

In our rush to grow, to accumulate, to seal ourselves off from the natural world, do we have any idea what we're doing?

Do we have any idea what we're losing?

Roots

The fields bore evidence of the most recent snow as I stood looking at an old white farmhouse on the outskirts of a small town in northwest Iowa. My dad grew up there. As did his dad. As did his dad, the son of Irish immigrants. His dad, my great-great-grandpa, likely acquired the land through the Homestead Act of 1862, the landmark bill passed during the Civil War to allow overwhelmingly White settlers to claim land taken, usually violently, from Native peoples like the Iowa tribe, thereby extending US control over the continent. He likely paid to build a house with money from working the rails, one of the principal sources of income for immigrants at the time. That was a forerunner to the house that stands there today, which has held so many past generations of my family.

This is the house that a bank tried to repossess from my great grandparents during the Great Depression, falsely claiming they'd fallen behind on payments when they failed to produce the pink carbon copy of their receipt, perhaps lending support to the idea that there's no end to human greed. It's the house kept in the family by a bank employee who held onto the yellow slip, the only other receipt copy. In doing so, he potentially risked his job in extremely uncertain times to prevent the bank from uprooting a family from its home, perhaps offering evidence to the belief in human decency.

The house was saved again by a stranger driving by who saw a flame billowing up from the roof and banged on the door to alert my unsuspecting ancestors. An ember had escaped the chimney and wedged itself between a crack in the attic. Had that stranger hesitated for a minute, feeling no responsibility to intervene, it's likely the house would have been lost. More evidence of human decency.

That house is where my grandpa stayed to work when times got tough, only to never leave. It's where my dad and his siblings returned even long after they'd moved away. The tiny town of four hundred had not been big enough to keep them. The physical toll and financial uncertainty of farming—of competing against increasingly massive operations receiving increasingly massive subsidies—were enough to make them pursue other lives. But their ties to that place run deep.

That house is where my family gathered in the heavy snows of Iowa winters and sometimes-sweltering heat of summers until my grandma passed away. There's less reason to gather there now. Not to mention the fact that it's harder to gather, with my dad's generation spread throughout the Midwest and mine scattered from Flagstaff to Spain. Each member of his generation left with some degree of choice and found a different community to call home. Each member of mine is searching for the same.

When summer came, the house would be put up for sale. The thought filled me with an ache I couldn't quite articulate, one I knew was about more than just that house. Normally, nostalgia means a longing for places to which we cannot return. But this nostalgia—a sense of grief, or "algia," upon not being able to return home, "nostos"—had become familiar to me, one that found me many places. I noticed it when I did return and felt a sense of loss associated not with a change in sightlines or storefronts or even people but with the knowledge that the place was being sold out from under the feet of its residents. Glenn Albrecht, an environmental philosopher in Australia, would probably call this feeling solastalgia, "a form of homesickness one gets when one is still at 'home.'"[13]

Whatever it's called, I feel this ache for the United States as a whole.

• • • • • • •

Jane Jacobs, the author of *The Death and Life of Great American Cities*, was not the first to realize how millions of mundane, everyday actions combined to create a sense of community. Far from being unique to Jacobs's time (the 1960s) and place (New York City), this elaborate social network was noted by Alexis de Tocqueville in his seminal 1835 text *Democracy in America*. De Tocqueville cited the strong bonds formed within "townships" as the key to the country's ability to hold steady even amid dramatic growth.[14]

This bottom-up social structure existed in sharp contrast to European nations at the time, which maintained stability by concentrating absolute power in monarchies and mighty armies. Like a spoke in a wheel, every community in European society was entirely dependent on its rigid connection to a center. In the United States, a community's ability to function originated from the connections with others. Power was distributed across every neighborhood in every township in every state of the growing nation.

One of the most troubling and incalculable impacts of the rampant commodification of housing, therefore, is on democracy itself. Nonresidents entering the local housing market may pay more in property taxes as a result of their large houses, but they do not contribute in the same way to a community. They do not show up for community meetings, petition for community-minded changes, or vote. They are part of a push to move public money away from roads, parks, and social services and toward the building of private oases. As their ownership of homes disrupts the continuity of neighborhoods, both momentary and intentional interactions become less common. It's not difficult to see how this can affect individuals' motivation or opportunity for civic engagement.

It has become cliché to note how politically divided we are as a country. What is less often noted is just how politically, racially, and socioeconomically similar we tend to be with our neighbors. On the political front, author Bill Bishop and former sociologist Robert G. Cushing calculated that in 1976 barely a third of counties had swung to Gerald Ford or Jimmy Carter by more than 20 percent in final vote tallies. By the 2004 election between George W. Bush and John Kerry, nearly 60 percent of counties were so lopsided. Almost as a rule, cities vote blue and rural areas vote red. Bishop's book was pointedly titled *The Big Sort: Why the Clustering of Like-Minded America is Tearing Us Apart.*[15]

There are likely many reasons for this that have nothing to do with housing. Parties have gerrymandered districts to make electoral maps more advantageous. The amount of news and advertising made to target specific subsections of the population has exploded in recent decades. And, with the sale of data, campaigns and parties become similarly precise in their targeting of those most likely to vote with them, further entrenching whatever polarization already existed.[16]

Consciously or not, people move or are shepherded into areas with people "like them." And, with housing increasingly separated from its core purpose of housing people, it's not simply less likely that we'll have neighbors with different backgrounds or points of view. It's less likely we'll have neighbors at all.

It's true that we are divided as a country. But the uneasy truth is that most people protesting police killings and border crossings, blocking new oil pipelines and storming the US Capitol, have more in common with each other than they do with any of their most esteemed political representatives or the big donors who support them. All the noise we make about unaffordable, unstable housing will be continually drowned out without any limit to the influence of corporate lobbyists or dollars of wealthy elites. All the miles we march for environmental protections will never overcome the distance that's been put between us by political operatives and candidates.

We are left angry, fearful, and divided, with little hope of changing things. We cannot so much as articulate a vision of the world we want, let alone achieve it.

Jessi Quizar, the urban studies professor who has studied social movements, referred to this as a "crisis of imagination." She argued that, no matter how well-funded or well-organized a group is, it needs to "give people something that they're running towards, too." What's attracted her to past organizing efforts is not simply a "frantic preoccupation with the things that are wrong but . . . [where] being around these people makes me feel like there's hope or possibilities other than what's right in front of me."

She mentioned the Black Panthers as an example. Originally called the Black Panther Party for Self-Defense, the group was radical, bold, and—regardless of how people felt about their methods—incredibly effective at advocating for the rights of Black people. And they succeeded in part because, as Quizar stated, "They just were cool."[17]

They didn't sacrifice on their core values. They didn't beg people to show up for an hour or make a few calls. Rather, the Black Panthers invited people to be part of a movement. They invited people to be part of a community.

In fact, out of the litany of actions undertaken by the Black Panthers'—including patrolling the streets with guns—the one that then director of the FBI J. Edgar Hoover deemed "the greatest threat" was their free breakfast program for kids. In 1969, the Black Panthers started serving free breakfast before school in thirteen predominantly Black communities. Nobody else was doing that at the time and teachers immediately noticed the difference in students. People across the country, especially in predominantly White areas, began to scrutinize why the federal government didn't provide breakfast for kids in other impoverished areas. Within six years' time, the federal government was forced to authorize its own nationwide program, a program that today feeds nearly fifteen million kids.[18]

"Beautiful People in a Broken System"

Across the country, places have ceased to be molded by their residents, instead bending to the desires of people with short-term goals. When housing is viewed as a commodity, the only question is what will produce the quickest and highest return on one's investment. Tourists become preferred over residents, second homeowners over primary homeowners, tourists with boats, ATVs, and other so-called toys over tourists without them, large tourist groups over smaller ones, large corporations over smaller ones, the wealthy over the slightly less wealthy, and the list continues.

In our society, the picture of ultimate freedom looks something like a mansion with chauffeurs and servants at beck and call, something found in the exurbs of Wyoming and the gated communities of Florida. In advocating for actions like building more affordable housing or changing the zoning code, we find ourselves entrenched in a culture in which people will stop at nothing to ensure their property value increases astronomically. We are, as Ethan Hughes so eloquently put it, "beautiful people in a broken system. And beautiful people keep trying to make it work, yet we have more poverty and more unhoused people, more species loss, more pollution than ever."[19]

But that doesn't mean we're stuck. Big changes often start from humble beginnings. The program that feeds fifteen million kids daily breakfast started because a relatively small organization, working on behalf of a marginalized people with almost no political representatives who looked like them, articulated a vision for a better world. It started at the breakfast table.

The fight for home starts with imagining a place worth living in. It starts with the basic: needing shelter from the elements. According to the CDC, unhoused people have a life expectancy of only around fifty years of age, decades less than those able to maintain consistent housing. Much of this disparity stems from "a greater risk of infectious and chronic illness, poor mental health, and substance abuse," all factors that have a ripple effect throughout the entire community. In Phoenix, a city that continues to grow quickly and until recently was routinely cited as one of the most affordable cities, as many as five hundred unhoused people died within the first six months of 2022, most from causes that are easily preventable and far less common among those with housing.[20] That is an indictment on our society.

Once we decide to commit ourselves to housing everyone, we can consider the type of housing we need. Safe as well as stable, affordable as well as sanitary. More than that, it needs to be connected to the broader community. This is not simply the right thing to do; it is an acknowledgment that our lives are intertwined.

But, very quickly, we realize that housing alone does not make a home. What good are four walls and a roof overhead if we are constantly threatened by deadly fires, floods, and other disasters? What good is an oceanfront property when the beach is littered with trash? What good is being able to afford housing—even if it's in a neighborhood with good schools, even if it's near a favorite park, even if it is everything we've ever dreamed of—if the surrounding environment is a hellscape? We are part of the surrounding ecosystem.

In reducing everything to a question of short-term profit, we have lost sight of the many costs that escape market valuation. What is the cost of losing faith in the future? What is the cost of being ashamed of your country? What is the cost of feeling like an outsider in your own home? Too much.

A veil has been pulled over our eyes, obscuring any other possibility, but none of this is inevitable. Kids are not born dreaming of endless accumulation and second homes and a higher return on investment. They need food and shelter and the essentials of survival, but beyond that, they are mostly content to swim in the creek. As the twenty-thousand-year-old footsteps found at White Sands make clear, "you take a kid out from anywhere in the world and put a big puddle in front of them and they know what to do."[21]

This is worth fighting for. One of the things that always surprised Ethan Hughes in the early days of the Possibility Alliance was how much people commented on what they were sacrificing by living the way they did. It happened so much that Hughes eventually looked up the dictionary definition of sacrifice and found that one definition is "giving up something of lesser value for something of greater value."

It changed the way Hughes talked about what they were doing.[22] Sacrificing was not suffering; it was living in line with one's values. It was recognizing what was most important. We do not have to live without electricity or petroleum to do this. We exchange a meal out at a chain restaurant to share a barbecue with friends. We pass up a night streaming a movie to see a local play. We forgo a couple unnecessary purchases in order to take several classes that teach us how to make things. In all these cases, we trade a little more time and effort for greater community.

In advocating for affordable housing, it's possible that our property values only rise gradually instead of astronomically. It's possible that there will be fewer second homes and investment properties. We give up our hope for a huge payout down the road in order to better afford housing now, to have neighbors, to be part of something larger than ourselves.

· · · · · · ·

The fight for housing, like the fight for a habitable earth, is a fight for both our collective present and future. For this reason, it must also be a fight for our voices—all of them—to be heard. In our individualistic culture, entangling our lives with others' can feel downright terrifying. But it's the only thing that has ever allowed us to realize better days ahead.

The very fact of trying to collaborate makes people both more willing and more able to do so effectively. As writer and activist George Monbiot, explained, "This seems to be a feature of deliberative, participatory democracy: it works better in practice than it does in theory. Many of the obstacles critics imagine dissolve as people are transformed by the process in which they engage."[23] The tradeoff for listening is being heard. The tradeoff for seeing is being seen. Put another way, as former British diplomat Carne Ross emphasized in his book, *The Leaderless Revolution*, the ends do not simply justify the means. Rather, paraphrasing philosophical writers ranging from Leon Trotsky to Ayn Rand to Aldous Huxley, Ross states that "the means are the ends."[24]

Unaffordable housing. Ecological collapse. The erosion of democracy. The situation facing us can seem insurmountable, requiring such a stubborn and unflappable faith in the promise of a better world that it seems to ignore all evidence to the contrary. Luckily, if America is anything, it is that faith.

It's the faith that led Amira Shweyk to purchase a patch of land in Oregon after struggling for years to find stable housing and the faith that has her opening it up to others who've faced some of the same barriers. It's the faith that led Karen Begay to build a traditional Navajo hogan in Arizona and the faith that has her working with volunteers to build more for unhoused individuals. It's the faith that a broken world is worth mending and the faith to live in a way that leaves no doubt as to why.

This faith stems not from uncritical hope but a deep realization that our lives are bound together. As Begay explained, "[As Native people], we still have that intergenerational trauma. I believe that blood memory is what links us up to our ancestors. . . . And that's also a big part of the reason why I'm doing the housing project that I'm doing is because it's helping me to heal as well as the families that get houses built."

This faith resists writing autopsies for the city or listening to swan songs for the mountain town. It refuses to sing dirges in the dark, wishing there was some way we could have remained in the places we loved. Though we may find our path temporarily impeded, our motivation temporarily lacking, and our values temporarily shaken by the lure of short-term profit, we tend to this faith like a fading ember.

Housing is portrayed as a complicated issue. Wading through rate calculations and industry-specific jargon, balancing trends and local caveats, everything seems to say to all but the most interested and specialized, *You just don't understand.* But the situation we have in front of us is actually quite simple and familiar, as it is akin to the one that has beset this nation since before its birth. As a society, we have enabled and encouraged a system by which people can buy, possess, and enormously profit from the sale of properties that would otherwise be the homes of those who actually belong to the community.

In this environment, the tourist seeking out a famous site, the developer seeking to turn a profit, and the second homeowner buying a weekend retreat are not to blame. Neither are the homeowner who resists low-income housing, the landlord who raises rent at every opportunity, and the politician continually seeking votes. But none of them are invested in the long-term life of a place.

Rather, what sustains a place is people caring immensely about it. These are the people who live in, work in, and *know* that place. They infuse floorboards with memories, brick and mortar with dreams. They know their neighbors. They grapple with a place's flaws. They belong to a place not because it turns a profit but because it's their home.

We have to fight for that or nothing is sacred in this world.

Sticks and Stones: What You Can Do

"Power concedes nothing without a demand. It never did and it never will." [1]

—Frederick Douglass

"Anything—any kind of project—that you're doing right now is worth doing. Right now is the time to be doing something for people."

—Karen Begay

I BEGAN THIS BOOK by noting its origin—a sign in a stranger's yard. Prior to seeing that sign, had I wondered at all about the relationship between the increasing number of entire-home short-term rentals and the increasing difficulty of affording rent, I may well have questioned whether it was worth studying. After all, what if I found a link but then found I could do nothing about it? But because of that sign and the ones like it, the housing stories I've heard from too many people, the articles by curious and stubborn reporters, the tireless work of housing advocates, the thousands of moments in my life in which I've seen people stick their necks out to do what they thought was right, I felt motivated to see if there was a link.

There is. From interviews, collected data, and observations, it is clear that the globalization of housing markets has been actively fostered by government officials, investors, developers, and homeowners who see dollar signs in keeping affordable housing scarce. They care only for their short-term gains, failing to see how this unaffordability is not simply a problem for those who struggle to afford housing; it is undermining the very fabric of their community.

In an article, Conor Dougherty, the author of *Golden Gates: Fighting for Housing in America*, offered caution in how we think about addressing the nationwide housing problem: "One of the most discouraging things about politics is the way people become advocates for policies over outcomes."[2] The precise policies needed to make housing affordable for people in Tallahassee, Florida, or Muscatine, Iowa, or Bend, Oregon, vary as much as the places themselves. As such, they should be determined primarily by the people who live there.

At the same time, while housing has traditionally been understood as a local issue, the affordable housing issues in Flagstaff are linked to those faced in Oklahoma City and even Cape Town, South Africa. Full-time residents the world over need a way out of this buy-to-rent model of housing, a safety valve that does not force them to compete for housing on an untenable scale.

Massive expansion of community land trusts and mixed-income public housing offer two of many possible ways to reverse the calculus that favors short-term wealth accumulation over long-term community stability. But no matter what solutions cities propose, the scale of the problem requires creativity, sufficient political will, and a focus on both the immediate and long-term visions for community. It requires us to look to each other.

Taking Action

It is common for research to conclude with calls for better data and more collaboration, both of which are needed on housing. More consistent and reliable data would go a long way toward crafting more just housing policy. Existing governments and organizations must collaborate to produce more regional and national affordable housing plans. That's the only way to address the fact that the housing market is national—even global—in scope.

This struggle has a long history and no single book can articulate the extent of changes needed. Unaffordable housing is a systemic problem and requires systemic change. But, as developers and investors and government officials use these arguments to excuse their inaction, people everywhere are carving out a life wherever they can. In her time in Detroit, urban studies professor Jessi Quizar saw this firsthand. As she explained,

> *[Home] is where people sort of automatically experiment, and you can see that in Detroit. Why have people done so much stuff, like all these sort of weird, cool experimentations with land and what you can do with abandoned spaces? It's because people were just living next to those spaces.*[3]

Left alone, without hope that the system would work in their favor, they created community gardens and classrooms, parks and tool libraries. They were able to develop new and innovative ways of not just meeting their basic needs but actually thriving.

But this is rare. In everyday life, we exist in an environment of cutthroat competition. We are taught to focus on bettering our own material lives, even if that comes at others' expense. We are taught that this system—which ensures that housing and childcare and healthcare and nutritious food and clean air are at the mercy of those who seek to profit from them—is our only option. We watch as our home becomes unrecognizable. We watch as our local housing markets are transformed into global ones. We watch as governments at all levels quickly forgo their regulatory powers, deferring instead to the market to determine who most deserves housing.

Even if we gain a foothold in some more stable life, we seldom feel empowered to make the choices or build the alliances needed to push back against all this. This starts small, perhaps continuing to shop on Amazon despite objecting to the extreme concentration of wealth. Then it grows. We abhor when people pull strings to climb the social or corporate ladder, but many of us will not hesitate to do so for our own kids. We scrap and claw to afford a house and, if we finally do, we become a vocal opponent of rezoning our neighborhood to allow for the kind of more affordable, multiunit housing we lived in just a few years before. Rather than using our newfound success to truly push back against the system, we begin to resemble what we once so adamantly opposed. We've sold our values to the highest bidder.

But it doesn't have to be this way. Systems change when people force them to change. To make housing home again, we can look first at what we can stop, or avoid, doing. As Henry David Thoreau wrote in his oft-cited essay "Civil Disobedience," "Let your life be a counter-friction to stop the machine. What I have to do is to see, at any rate, that I do not lend myself to the wrong which I condemn."[4] Then, we can move on to how we can actively improve the situation.

This starts with individual actions, choices that we make independently of others' knowledge or permission or support. These stem from a single person and often have small, but visible, impacts. The greatest impacts, however, come about when individuals link their actions together. For this reason, for every individual action that can be undertaken to address unaffordable housing, marked with *I* here, there is an action that can be taken to engage others. These are marked with *We*.

But people play different roles in society. This means they need different roles to play in addressing society's ills, particularly one such as unaffordable housing, which is felt so locally yet subjected to such global economic forces. Everyone has something that they can do.

Tourists

I: Avoid staying in entire-home short-term rentals unless it is the host's primary home. If it is someone's actual home, the host will usually make this known in the ad description and pictures will likely not show pristine, minimalistic space. If that's what you're looking for, consider a hotel.

WE: Talk to people about this issue. A lot of people have never considered the potential impact of short-term rentals or nonprimary homes on housing and neighborhood life. Many are quite receptive to hearing more about it if you admit struggling with it yourself.

I: Be a good guest. Beyond treating the house and any on-site host well, short-term rental neighbors often have no choice in your staying there. Keep noise and trash to a minimum. Be friendly when you see neighbors and, at the very least, avoid taking their parking spaces.

WE: Always be friendly and treat servers, park rangers, staff members, locals, and other guests with respect. When you return home and tell people about your trip or leave a review for places you visit, think about the quality of your interactions more than the quality of the physical space. A sense of belonging comes from people.

I: If you feel the need to stay in an entire-home short-term rental but can't find an entire-home short-term rental that is usually the host's primary residence, be informed about the short-term rental situation in the place you are visiting. Look for relevant articles and check out vacation rental analysis sites like Airdna.co to compare places. Mesa, Arizona, is much larger than nearby Scottsdale, for example, but has a fraction of the entire-home short-term rentals. This means that its housing market is likely not as affected by short-term rentals.

WE: Research local organizations that address community needs and volunteer at one. Buying local is definitely encouraged when you are choosing where to eat, shop, and otherwise tour the area, but giving of your time allows you to step outside the role of consumer for a moment. Your money isn't saving the community and neither will your time, because the community doesn't need a savior. Instead, volunteering for a few hours is a small way of thanking the strangers who've constructed the roads you drive on, cleaned the rooms you rest in, prepared the meals you ate, and altogether built the community that you sought out for your vacation.

Short-Term Rental Hosts

I: Make it clear to guests that you want to preserve a good relationship with neighbors. Give them alternatives for excess trash (e.g., "Additional bin and bags in laundry room."), noise (e.g., "Reduce volume and close all windows after 9 PM."), and parking (e.g., "Additional parking can be found on street near park one block away.") that do not disturb the neighborhood. As the host, your guests are your responsibility.

WE: Publish an op-ed explaining how you ensure your guests do not disrupt the neighborhood. Encourage other hosts to follow similar practices.

I: Do not rent out spaces that are not your primary home.

WE: Push for legislation that puts a tax on nonprimary homes being rented out on a short-term basis. Nonprimary homes available as short-term rentals drive up the cost of housing and generally have a greater impact on neighborhoods. On a personal economic level, they diminish your income potential as a primary-home short-term rental host.

Government Officials

I: Gather accurate data on housing prices and usage. One of the biggest issues I found in my research is that government officials do not often have accurate and updated data relating to housing. This may be from an unwillingness to seek it out for fear that it contradicts other goals, but better policy starts from better information.

WE: Publish this data in an easily accessible and digestible way for residents.

I: Gather the opinions of residents, especially listening to those who tend to be silenced or marginalized. Do not expect them to go to you. Rather, go to them. Whether this is through small meetings in neighborhood parks, social media engagement, or holding a citizens' assembly, it is your responsibility to give people multiple ways of being heard. Lack of engagement, whether a failure to show up at city hall or directly contact officials, does not mean people do not care or that they consent to the policy decisions being promoted. On the contrary, it often means that they feel their opinion will not make a difference.

WE: Whenever possible, let people vote on the issues that affect them. But this does not mean denying a basic human need, like affordable housing, in order to appease the desires of a small, usually wealthy, subset of the population. The town of Woodside, California, in the San Francisco Bay area, for example, pushed back against multiunit affordable housing under the justification that it would disrupt the habitat of mountain lions. This justification is undermined by the fact that Woodside is "a mansion-filled, tech entrepreneur enclave."[5] How many of these residents thought twice about the impact on mountain lions when they initially had their own multi-million-dollar homes built or remodeled?

I: Create local programs that disincentivize empty or nonprimary homes and incentivize homes that house local residents.

WE: Create coalitions with other city, county, state, and federal governments. Be persistent in articulating the costs of too much tourism or too many empty homes, particularly with the chamber of commerce, tourism-related businesses, and nearby public land officials who tend to seek increases in visitation no matter what.

I: The Intergovernmental Panel on Climate Change's 2018 report states that limiting the effects of climate change "would require rapid and far-reaching transitions in energy, land, urban and infrastructure (including transport and buildings), and industrial systems."[6] Housing is a major part of this and allowing potential homes to go unused or used exclusively by nonresidents is the least sustainable thing that government can do on this issue. As a government official, you can offer incentives for people to make more environmentally sustainable decisions when it comes to their homes. A 2021 study published by the Yale Program on Climate Change Communication found that 59 percent of people in the United States say that they are either "Alarmed" or "Concerned" about climate change, the two-highest categories of the six options given.[7] There is an appetite for making positive change on this issue if people do not feel it is too costly.

WE: Make larger changes. Create agreements between cities and state or federal governments that share the cost burden of making the system-wide changes necessary to achieve a more sustainable housing system. Remember that the cost of inaction is growing, as was made clear by the slate of twenty unique billion-dollar disasters in 2021.[8]

I: Just as housing is connected to environmental issues, so, too, is race. As a government official, you can emphasize the connections between these issues and make policies that reflect these connections. While it's important not to focus exclusively on race, all housing policies should acknowledge and seek to alter the continued impact of racist policies.

WE: Think big. Create agreements between cities and state or federal governments that share the cost burden of making the system-wide changes necessary to achieve a more equitable housing system. From education to health to economic opportunity, housing and land disparities are at the core of all racial disparities that exist in our country.

Residents

I: Think about what factors make housing more expensive in your community. Do research. Better yet, go to your local library and ask for resources.

WE: Talk to your neighbors. Make them a cake. Throw a neighborhood barbecue. Sit on your porch. Start a neighborhood newsletter. Walk your dog. Help an elderly neighbor with tasks they cannot easily do. Hire neighborhood kids for tasks you cannot easily do. Put up a swing. Have a yard sale. Ask for recommendations for restaurants, repairs, parks, anything that initiates conversation. The vibrancy of your neighborhood can start with you.

I: If you own your home, rent out a spare room for a below-average rate to a long-term tenant. They'll have an affordable place to live and the extra income will ensure you have a more affordable place, too. You may even enjoy each other's company.

WE: Talk to your elected officials about creating a program to turn your home into a community land trust when you move out. One way that this could operate is by agreeing to a range for how long you plan to remain in your house and a price at which you'd sell it to the city, county, or nonprofit that would operate the CLT. For instance, if you know you'd like to move away when you retire in five years or you know you'd like to downsize when the kids move out in five years, your range could be five to ten years. In exchange for selling your house to the city for a reduced rate, you would not need to pay property taxes for your remaining years.

I: Vote if you are able. In every election, especially the local ones. If you can't, encourage those who can to do so. Pay particular attention to what candidates say about housing.

WE: Get a group together to talk about housing issues in your community. Talk about how you can address them. If you come up with a solution you think would be worthwhile, organize a meeting with city officials to discuss it. If this does not prove helpful, most cities have a process for getting an initiative on the ballot independent of elected officials.

Landlords, Developers, and Investors

If the goal of landlords, developers, and investors is to make the most profitable individual sale possible, I admit that I would be hard-pressed to argue against mega-mansions and luxury-priced condos. But this short-term thinking undermines even their own profits. After all, when people must scrape by to afford the cost of housing, how much do they lose out on in possible renovations and home improvements? How many fewer houses do they sell when the market dips or altogether crashes due to previously inflated prices? Just how profitable is it for them when the last neighborhood they developed refuses their planned development next door?

The list continues. How much do protests or onerous planning processes delay development? How much goodwill is lost with neighbors and community members, affecting them both personally and professionally? How much of the patience of city council? Or, in more familiar terms, how much more money do they spend on labor to meet the heightened cost of living or materials to build larger, higher-end spaces? Or on land to keep up with the runaway housing market? What is lost in the long-term—and perhaps even the short-term—by a narrow focus on maximizing profit on individual sales and casting aside any consideration of the overall effect on the place?

There are ways that they can turn a profit without turning a community against them. There are ways of strengthening a community without selling it to the highest bidder. As an example, studies regarding climate change make clear that communities across the country need to respond aggressively to ecological changes and promote more environmentally friendly living. While this overall means less emissions and less stuff, it also means more solar panels on rooftops, more mixed-use zoning, and more buildings for mixed-income living.

Why not help sponsor a child care center on the ground floor of an apartment building, offering reduced rates to residents? Why not help start a car-sharing service for residents of a high-density building, helping to solve one of the biggest hurdles to high-density building: parking, what one housing policy official referred to as "the tail that wags the dog"?[9]

And, if they truly want to usher in the biggest building boom in generations, the single most effective thing they can do is to vocally support the addition of class as a protected status in the Fair Housing Act. In other words, just as was the case in the early 1900s—when zoning was strictly for the "promotion of the public health, safety, and welfare"—make zoning for purely economic reasons illegal.[10] This would definitively benefit the real estate industry, but it would do a lot more than that. As city planner M. Nolan Grey, the author of *Arbitrary Lines: How Zoning Broke the American City and How to Fix It*, explained, it would also make housing both more affordable and less segregated across the country.[11]

In short, landlords, real estate developers, and investors stand to gain economically when they align their interests with the long-term health of the community rather than replacing what exists—and displacing who exists—for the sake of a quick buck.

Advocates, Activists, and Organizers

Those who work in real estate are inherently focused on individualized, typically short-term benefits. Individuals working as advocates, activists, or organizers, particularly on housing issues, operate on the societal level. It's true that individuals seeking to affect change more broadly must first take care of their own physical, mental, and emotional needs. Phrases like "You can't pour from an empty cup" necessarily reiterate this. Reading and one-on-one conversations about the issue at hand are also important. But, at the end of the day, changemaking is not simply about individual actions; it's about building individual actions into collective action for change.

Protest inherently involves disrupting business as usual and demanding change. Increasingly, this means risking the possibility of a heavy-handed—even outright violent—police response. Organizers are more likely to face arrest, which may mean missing work or losing their job altogether. Furthermore, an arrest threatens to limit organizers' future employment opportunities, saddle them with steep fines that translate into insurmountable debt, and strip them of the right to vote. This begs the question: can a right still be considered a right if it can be taken away for standing too long in a street or sitting too long in a tree or otherwise disrupting the flow of commerce?

In 2021, the Sweden-based thinktank International IDEA (Institute for Democracy and Electoral Assistance) included the United States on its annual list of "backsliding" democracies for the first time. While Alexander Hudson, a coauthor of the report, acknowledged that the US "is a high-performing democracy," he also wrote that "the declines in civil liberties and checks on government indicate that there are serious problems with the fundamentals of democracy."[12]

Hudson noted that the slide began in 2019 but went on to draw particular attention to the "decline in the quality of freedom of association and assembly during the summer of protests in 2020."[13] At the same time that the state of the country requires loud, unrelenting calls for change, economic, military, and political forces have lined up to arrest, assault, and otherwise target protesters and activists.

All this is to say that you're not alone if it feels difficult to affect positive, lasting change in your own neighborhood, let alone more broadly. But, partially for that very reason, it is also a moment of incredible possibility. There's never been a moment in which the problems faced in one community could be linked so directly to those being faced by another, resulting so clearly from decisions made at the state and national level by corporations and politicians alike. There's never been a moment in which communication and funding and people could so easily cut across space, traveling between one locality and another. The challenge is how to take advantage of these circumstances in order to compel change.

When it comes to housing, there are many different ways of uniting personal, seemingly disparate decisions into a movement for better. These will be unique and reflect individual challenges and cultural quirks in the area you live. But generally, nonviolent organizing tactics could be placed within three categories: those of a flea, a fawn, or a force. In other words, organizers can endlessly annoy and obstruct opponents, use the law and public perception to their advantage so that they are beyond reproach, or overwhelm their opposition by the sheer volume of their numbers.

Flea

The flea strategy comes from Robert Taber's 1965 book *War of the Flea*, which describes guerrilla warfare tactics across the world. Rather than engaging directly with a powerful opponent, fleas annoy, disrupt, and otherwise antagonize those most blocking progress. So, instead of risking arrest by blocking a major street outside a developer's office, a rotating collection of car alarms might go off in the parking lot outside for the entirety of the workday. Instead of risking losing jobs through a general strike, workers might simply not work as hard, also known as a slowdown or go-slow strike.

A crucial aspect of being fleas is causing the beast of the opposition to lash out against itself. This could mean helping Airbnb hosts win lawsuits to be seen as employees rather than contractors, as has been debated for Uber and Lyft drivers in California. Or it could mean Scottsdale, Arizona, residents showing the neighboring city of Mesa why changing state law to allow places to regulate short-term rentals could bring more of these guests—and their buying power—to Mesa, if desired.

Fawn

Fawns are helpless baby deer. They use the law to their advantage, making themselves so innocent in the eyes of the law or so amusing in the eyes of the public that they become very difficult to view in a negative light. Cities in Arizona, for example, are extremely limited in their ability to directly regulate short-term rentals. For this reason, some have started demanding an adherence to health and safety codes ranging from cleaning protocols to guest background checks. Many of these have been controversial, but this is also the point. Towns and cities have been stripped of nearly all regulatory authority; they will use what little they have to make a mockery of the state's heavy-handed approach.

Fawns often reveal the brutality or incompetence of their opposition. Such was the case when pro-democracy protesters in both Hong Kong in 2013 and Thailand in 2020 adopted an inflatable yellow duck as their symbol. While it had a practical purpose as a shield against police water cannons and tear gas, it also helped attract international attention to their plight. As Jasmine Chia wrote for the *Thai Enquirer*, "At heart, the appeal of the duck is its innocence. . . . The image of Thai authorities, armed to the teeth with riot gear and shields, facing off against . . . rubber ducks . . . highlights the sheer asymmetry of the battle between protester and state."[14] How could anyone be against a rubber duck?

Force

The force approach is the most difficult to achieve. It is focused on creating a mass movement for change. A force needs numbers and determination to stick with a singular issue, the type of thing that only arises from very dire conditions or decisions that make life extremely difficult for a wide swath of humanity.

The pace and profit motive of the news cycle make this more challenging to achieve. As author and media critic Neil Postman wrote in his 1985 book *Amusing Ourselves to Death*, "There is no murder so brutal, no earthquake so devastating, no political blunder so costly—for that matter, no ball score so tantalizing or weather report so threatening—that it cannot be erased from our minds by a newscaster saying, 'Now . . . this.'"[15]

If this was the case nearly four decades ago, it rings even truer today. Now, with an infinite scroll of advertisements, posts, and moving screens on topics of all kinds, recruiting would-be changemakers to do anything beyond signing a petition seems a herculean task. The flea approach becomes effective when influential individuals are forced to admit that it is in their best interests to address the issue at hand, that failing to do so will result in their business being disrupted or their election being lost. Fleas seek to rewrite the rules, then the culture. Forces for change operate first at the cultural level. They are vocal and visible and, most important, always seeking new converts to their cause. They are not chasing sympathy but solidarity, an understanding of shared destiny. They use this understanding to rewrite the rules.

In this context, it's not surprising that some of the most notable forces for change in our collective memories—from women fighting for suffrage in the early 1900s to Black people fighting for civil rights in the mid-1900s to Native nations and children organizing for climate action now—represent some of the most marginalized people. Change always starts from the people who cannot look away, because it's their life.

No newscaster will erase the memory of a loved one who has been murdered. No commercial break will distract from the earthquake that wiped out one's town. No amount of scrolling will diminish the political blunder that cost someone their livelihood. A movement always starts where it is felt.

• • • • • • •

There was a simple reason that many people camped in New York's Zuccotti Park in September 2011: they had nowhere else to go. They'd been priced out or forced into foreclosure when the housing market crashed. They'd watched as Wall Street banks and insurance companies received hundreds of millions in taxpayer dollars for a crisis Wall Street had caused while taxpayers themselves floundered. The moment was especially distressing for people of color who'd been specifically targeted by these same banks.[16] For many, watching the likes of Citigroup, Bank of America, and Wells Fargo grow as social services shrank was too much to bear.

Since then, much has been written about the impact of what became known as the Occupy Wall Street protest. Advocates have pointed to the Occupy movement spreading to dozens of countries and its efforts at building community beyond traditional market logic as major successes. And yet, on its core issues of housing protection and income inequality, Occupy failed to bring about any fundamental changes. Furthermore, in the ten years since Occupy Wall Street's encampments were raided and dismantled, efforts to address many national problems have splintered between local organizing and national lobbying efforts. When people have taken to the streets or assembled en masse, they seem to be petitioning those in power to listen rather than mobilizing to bring about lasting changes.

Micah White, one of the initiators of Occupy Wall Street, took note of the ineffectiveness of Occupy and other protests in recent years. In his 2016 book *The End of Protest*, he wrote:

> *The only way to fix a broken paradigm is to replace it with a new paradigm. Occupy was a gift to activists across the world who are now searching for the next paradigm of social activism. The event was a wake-up call to break the script of contemporary protest and rethink the principles of achieving social change through collective action. Above all, the lesson of our movement was to embrace the challenge that each generation of revolutionaries has had to overcome: to discover the new form of protest that is effective in the present historical moment.*[17]

I don't pretend to have an answer to this, and I don't think there is one answer. But realizing these answers begins with admitting the lie that has been with us for the entirety of our country's existence. A market centered on concentrating profit is not the best way of ensuring the public good. In fact, it has little interest in the public good at all. The same can be said of government that is in thrall to the concentration of profit.

Shifting societal priorities will not come from appealing to Wall Street. Similarly, it will not come from appealing to elected officials who are more than willing to grow the economy or bring in higher-income individuals and businesses at the expense of current residents. That paradigm for making change is broken and perhaps was broken all along. We need to champion a new one, even many new ones.

The Worlds We Want

We do not simply need a new housing system, but many new housing systems. We need many new worlds. As a group of scientists led by Elinor Ostrom, the political economist who won the Nobel Prize for her work on the commons, wrote, "Institutional diversity may be as important as biological diversity for our long-term survival."[18]

Examples abound of affordable housing advocates winning at the local level. Under pressure from residents, state and municipal governments have started to realize that waiting and hoping for the private sector to build affordable housing is delusional. California has heavily considered a mixed-income public housing bill. Rhode Island has passed one, setting aside $10 million for a pilot mixed-income public housing program. Montgomery County, Maryland, has already started acquiring and building this mixed-income public housing, with a goal of nearly 9,000 new units. Colorado has passed a bill for 3,500 new public housing units to be geared toward median-income households and Hawaii has paved the way for the sale of publicly owned condos with 99-year leases.[19] These governments have shown that they are done waiting on the private sector.

And, when governments have failed to take action, many residents have done so on their own, passing housing measures through ballot initiatives. In addition to the Colorado towns that voted to regulate short-term rentals, the National Low Income Housing Coalition reported that voters in Philadelphia and Albuquerque passed initiatives to increase funds for affordable housing trusts while voters in Denver and Portland, Maine, voted for actions that further protect those without housing. In both Minneapolis and St. Paul, voters approved rent control measures that would seek to put a cap on runaway rent prices.[20]

These actions are huge victories for residents in each of these places, but our fights are connected. Changing the state of housing requires us to think beyond our neighborhood and even our city. As Brian Guyer, the housing director for the "de facto housing authority" in Bozeman, questioned:

> *What is this impact of this rapidly escalating real estate market in this one community? What is the impact on all of the satellite communities . . . and this entire region? . . . As long as you're operating in a silo, all you're really doing when you implement these strategies is passing the buck on to another community to deal with it.*[21]

Treating housing like a commodity has forced us all into the same arena. It's tempting to believe that our state or our city or our house can win this competition. After all, if we are the highest bidder, our house becomes a valuable asset in which we can turn away from others who aren't so lucky. Our retreat from the madness of the world.

And yet, this line of thinking, repeated throughout our country's history, has left us isolated from neighbors, segregated by race, and exhausted by a meaningless pursuit of consumption. We are not islands. As one person loses a house, another loses a neighbor, an employee, a friend. Dog eat dog is no way to live.

Demanding better from the places we live is likely to be met with a familiar refrain: *If you don't like it, why don't you leave?*

But this country is my home. I keep it like a secret. One which I never asked for but to which I find myself bound. The promise of these United States is that there is a place for people of every age, race, creed, and class here. To leave would be to admit that it cannot be what it promised, that this dream has died, and I can't do that.

Seeds of Change

The stalks of corn are at eye level as my family gathers at an old white farmhouse on the outskirts of a small town in northwest Iowa. My dad grew up there. As did his dad. As did his dad, the son of Irish immigrants. The house will soon be sold and this is our chance to say goodbye.

This house remains a link between my family's past and future. My great-grandparents and grandparents are buried in the cemetery within sight of that old farmhouse, that old house that served as the lifeblood of our family for generations, providing a stable base from which they looked out at the changing world.

As I walk through the house, I feel my chest tightening with the knowledge that the house will soon belong to someone else who will repaint the walls and refurnish the rooms. Someone who will form their own memories of this place and for whom it will mean different things.

My thoughts are punctured by my cousins' kids running through the house. Exploring every room. Jumping on the beds. Shrieking as they stumble across each other in hide-and-seek. As we used to do. As I hope someone else's kids will in the future.

I think about these kids running and laughing and growing up here. I look in the bedroom where their parents might teach them to read and comfort them when they wake from a nightmare. These kids would bring home scraped knees and broken hearts. They might bring home the burning anger and self-consciousness that stem from being slighted, targeted, humiliated. Or from being made to feel small, helpless, inferior for something over which they have no control. These experiences would have the potential to harden them, leaving them convinced that the world is an ugly and confusing place.

But then they'd come back to a place where they felt seen and heard and loved. A place where they felt safe. They'd carry this feeling with them no matter what happened, like a key reminding them that they could always come home.

I find my family downstairs talking animatedly in the kitchen. My dad's telling a story from back when he was a kid. My aunt's telling her version. The truth is somewhere in between.

I will remember the house like this, as a place with laughter and love and so many stories. As a place where something was always baking in the oven and someone was always sitting at the piano. Mostly, I'll remember it as one of the first places I ever felt like I belonged.

I know that this is likely the last time we'll all be together here, but the thought no longer fills me with the ache that it once did. We're lucky. We've had the chance to say goodbye to our house on our terms, a chance that millions of people are deprived of every year. A chance that millions of people have never known, and that millions more never will. Unless we change things.

In turning housing into simply another commodity, we've ensured that it is bound up in desperation and uncertainty. That our neighborhoods are hollowed out to make room for tourists and investors. That our communities, like our country, remain segregated and unequal. None of this is inevitable, but changing it requires believing that other worlds are possible.

I believe that. I hear it in the laughter echoing across these gently rolling fields. Like the smell of mulberry pie wafting through the window. Like the sight of faces illuminated by campfire. Like the procession of heights etched into the doorframe. It's a very human type of magic that transforms a mass of sticks and stones into a home. I see this happening to this old house—see it once more becoming a place of stability and identity and possibility—and can't help but smile.

It's not meant to be empty.

Houses are meant for living in.

Acknowledgments

I'VE NEVER FELT MORE INADEQUATE AS A WRITER than in trying to say thank you. In the three years since beginning the research that would ultimately lead to this book, the world has been rocked by the COVID-19 pandemic and I've moved a half-dozen times. All this has only made me more aware of how much I owe to so many people who helped bring this book to life.

First, to all those at the Chicago Review Press who were directly involved in this book. I cannot mention you all by name and will likely never be able to thank most of you in person, but the reach of this book is directly a result of your work. I appreciate you so much for that.

To Preston Pisellini, for wading through endless cover ideas and designing one that so well encapsulates the themes of the book. To Michelle Williams, for finding mistakes and inconsistencies that I overlooked. Your incredible attention to detail kept me humble. To Ben Krapohl, for guiding me through the conclusion of the editing stage and helping to bring all the pieces together. And to Melanie Roth, Rachel

McCumber, Bianca Rodriguez, and Bianca Maldonado, for keeping me sane as I moved from finishing the book to getting it out into the world. Thank you all for your expertise throughout this process. Thanks especially to my editor, Kara Rota. You saw the story when I sometimes didn't, with perfectly placed edits and insights that pushed me to tap into a more narrative, emotive language after so much academic research. You took a chance on a stubborn, relentlessly idealistic first-time author with an overly academic pitch. I really cannot say thank you enough.

To Dr. Jessica Barnes, Dr. Jessi Quizar, and Dr. Brian Petersen. Jessica, for helping me delve into uneven economic landscapes in research and providing reassurance when things felt overwhelming. Jessi, for challenging me to think more critically about race and alternative ways of organizing our communities. Your encouragement to keep thinking about this topic, to keep digging and keep the human element central, helped me through days when it seemed like I was writing into a void. Brian, for your patience and for making me feel like my research could—and should—do more than reinforce the status quo. For challenging me to back up my arguments but, most important, to be willing to change my mind based on the evidence. Your passion for your work has been infectious.

My most heartfelt appreciation to the countless interviewees who gave up their time and offered up insights and expertise, including Karen Begay, Amira Shweyk, Ethan Hughes, David Bustos, Chris Pasterz, Devonna McLaughlin, Adam Shimoni, John Kavanagh, McKenna Marchant, Brian Guyer, Randy Carpenter, Beau Houston, Brumby McLeod, and Megan Lawson. This book is better for your involvement. Though every community is different, writing this book has made it clear that the housing problems in communities across the country are linked. My hope is that this book can help ensure that any attempts to address them are, too.

To JJ Simms, Sarah Stuart-Sikowitz, Will Cannon, Amy Lipschultz, Taylor Sheriff, Katie Guetz, Sarah Smith, Jillian Goulet, Weldon Ryckman, Jo Wheaton, Jess Frank, Kalin Gilman, Thomas Kuefler, Kayla McIntosh, Brooke Randazzo, Colleen Moran, Patrick Firme, Turner Smith, Megan Sanders, John Acker, Kayla Luker, Kat Toomey, Danielle Witt, and so many others, for listening to more about housing—and my writing in general—than you could have possibly wanted to hear. To Ryan Kopatich, Jared McIntosh, and Paul Schneider, for being there through everything—even from a distance—for so many years, and to Caleb Kobilansky, Paul Roman, Ethan Taber, Mark Byrnes, Erica Byerley, and Rosie and Patrick Sweatt. Your friendships have sustained me.

To the many fantastic teachers who have supported my writing and helped inform my thinking on the topics of this book, including Mrs. Wahl, Mrs. Tompkins, Dr. Breault, Dr. Hurst, Dr. Regan, Dr. Barron, Dr. Benevento, Dr. Grimm, and Dr. Stuart. Spanning so many years and so many areas of study, I don't think I could ever articulate just how large of an impact you had.

But my favorite teacher has never changed. Mom, for instilling in me a sense of curiosity about the world and a willingness to speak up for what I know is right. Dad, for teaching me the power in showing up and taking pride in what I do. To both of you, for supporting me on my endlessly meandering path. To my entire immediate family—Kat, Bridget, Steve, Mackenzie, Kevin, and Tim—for putting up with my obsessions and respecting my need to be lost in the woods sometimes. And for always giving me reasons to return.

Finally, to all the neighbors who've given me a sense of what community is. In the moment, fleeting conversations and informal gatherings and simple reciprocity don't seem like much. The reality is, these are the things that give us faith in the world. That give me faith in the world.

Notes

Preface: The Sign

1   Michael Maciag, "Gentrification in America Report," *Governing*, January 23, 2015, https://www.governing.com/archive/gentrification-in-cities-governing-report.html.

Introduction: The Birth of a Unicorn

1   Sarah Childress, "How much did the financial crisis cost?" *PBS Frontline*, May 31, 2012, https://www.pbs.org/wgbh/frontline/article/how-much-did-the-financial-crisis-cost.

2   Rebecca Aydin, "How 3 Guys Turned Renting Air Mattresses in Their Apartment into a $31 Billion Company, Airbnb," *Business Insider*, September 20, 2019, https://www.businessinsider.com/how-airbnb-was-founded-a-visual-history-2016-2.

3   Aydin, "How 3 Guys."

4   Pew Research Center, "Mobile Fact Sheet," pewresearch.org, April 7, 2021, https://www.pewresearch.org/internet/fact-sheet/mobile.

5   Sean Veal and Jonathan Spader, "Nearly a Third of American Households Were Cost-Burdened Last Year," Joint Center for Housing Studies of Harvard University, December 7, 2018, https://www.jchs.harvard.edu/blog/more-than-a-third-of-american-households-were-cost-burdened-last-year/.

6   Leilani Farha, "Report of the Special Rapporteur on Adequate Housing as a Component of the Right to an Adequate Standard of Living, and on the Right to Non-Discrimination in this Context," *A/HRC/34/51* (January 18, 2017), http://unhousingrapp.org/user/pages/04.resources/Thematic-Report-3-The-Financialization-of-Housing.pdf.

7   Manuel B. Aalbers, "The Financialization of Home and the Mortgage Market Crisis," *Competition & Change* 12, no. 2 (June 1, 2008): 148–166, https://doi.org/10.1179/102452908X289802.

8   Ana Hernández Kent and Lowell R. Ricketts, "Has Wealth Inequality in America Changed over Time? Here Are Key Statistics," Federal Reserve Bank of St. Louis, December 2, 2020, https://www.stlouisfed.org/open-vault/2020/december/has-wealth-inequality -changed-over-time-key-statistics.

9   David Roberts, "America Is Facing an Epistemic Crisis," Vox, November 2, 2017, https://www.vox.com/policy-and-politics/2017/11/2/16588964/america-epistemic -crisis.

10 Matthew F. Garnet, Sally C. Curtin, and Deoborah M. Stone, "Suicide Mortality in the United States, 2000–2020," NCHS Data Brief, 433 (March 2022), https://www.cdc.gov/nchs/products/databriefs/db433.htm.

11 Farha, "Report of the Special Rapporteur."

12 DCCA, "Report on the Economic Well-Being of U.S. Households in 2019," Board of Governors of the Federal Reserve System, May 2019, https://www.federalreserve.gov/publications/files/2018-report-economic-well-being -us-households-201905.pdf.

1. Zombie Town, USA

1   "Jerome: Then and Now," Town of Jerome, https://jerome.az.gov/jerome-then-and-now.

2   Alia Beard Rau, "Arizona Forces Cities to Allow Airbnb-Type Rentals," Arizona Republic, May 12, 2016, https://www.azcentral.com/story/news/politics/arizona/2016/05/12/arizona-forces -cities-allow-airbnb-type-rentals/84299858.

3   AirDNA, LLC, Airdna.co. Accessed frequently with dates and specific city searches cited in text.

4   Lorraine Longhi, "Sedona's Housing Woes Threaten Its Sense of Community. Some Blame Vacation Rentals," AZ Central, January 29,2019, updated February 4, 2020, https://www.azcentral.com/story/news/local/arizona/2019/01/29/sedona-faces -housing-shortage-short-term-vaction-rentals-take-over/2342431002/.

5   Veal and Spader, "Nearly a Third."

6   Daniel Guttentag, "Airbnb: Disruptive Innovation and the Rise of an Informal Tourism Accommodation Sector," *Current Issues in Tourism* 18, no. 12 (September 2, 2013): 39, https://doi.org/10.1080/13683500.2013.827159.

7   Miquel-Àngel et al., "Do Short-Term Rental Platforms Affect Housing Markets? Evidence from Airbnb in Barcelona," *MPRA Paper* 96131 (September 23, 2019), https://mpra.ub.uni-muenchen.de/96131/1/MPRA_paper_96131.pdf; David Wachsmuth and Alexander Weisler, "Airbnb and the Rent Gap: Gentrification Through the Sharing Economy," *Environment and Planning A: Economy and Space* 50, no. 6 (June 20, 2018): 1147–1170, https://doi.org/10.1177/0308518X18778038; Dayne Lee, "How Airbnb Short-Term Rentals Exacerbate Los Angeles's Affordable Housing Crisis: Analysis and Policy Recommendations," Harvard Law & Policy

Review 10 (2016): 229–253, https://harvardlpr.com/wp-content/uploads
/sites/20/2016/02/10.1_10_Lee.pdf.

8 David Wyman, Chris Mothorpe, and Brumby McLeod, "Airbnb and Vrbo: The
Impact of Short-Term Tourist Rentals on Residential Property Pricing," *Current
Issues in Tourism* 25, no. 20 (January 29, 2020): 3279–3290,
https://doi.org/10.1080/13683500.2019.1711027.

9 William Riebsame Travis, *New Geographies of the American West: Land Use and the
Changing Patterns of Place* (Washington, DC: Island Press, 2007), 27.

10 Ariel Stulberg, "Airbnb Probably Isn't Driving Rents Up Much, at Least Not Yet,"
FiveThirtyEight, August 24, 2016,
https://fivethirtyeight.com/features/airbnb-probably-isnt-driving-rents-up-much-at
-least-not-yet.

11 Rachel Botsman and Roo Rogers, *What's Mine Is Yours: The Rise of Collaborative
Consumption* (New York: Harper Business, 2010), xi.

12 Murray Cox and Tom Slee, "How Airbnb's Data Hid the Facts in New York City,"
Inside Airbnb, February 10, 2016,
http://insideairbnb.com/reports/how-airbnbs-data-hid-the-facts-in-new-york-city.pdf.

13 Kyle Barron, Edward Kung, and Davide Proserpio, "When Airbnb Listings in a City
Increase, So Do Rent Prices," *Harvard Business Review*, April 17, 2019,
https://hbr.org/2019/04/research-when-airbnb-listings-in-a-city-increase-so-do
-rent-prices.

14 Vidhi Choudhary, "Airbnb's Brian Chesky apologizes for impact on cities, rethinks
future growth," *Forbes*, August 10, 2020,
https://www.forbes.com/sites/vidhichoudhary/2020/08/10/airbnbs-brian-chesky
-apologizes-for-impact-on-cities-rethinks-future-growth.

15 Vrbo, "Vrbo only offers whole vacation homes. So it's always just you and your
people," July 25, 2022,
https://www.youtube.com/watch?v=NjcUm8D0mH0.

16 Scott Shatford, *The Airbnb Expert's Playbook: Secrets to Making Six-Figures as a
Rentalpreneur* (Kindle Scribe, 2014), 5.

17 Shatford, *Airbnb Expert's Playbook*, 7.

18 Brian Fabo, Silvia Hudáčková, and Arthur Nogacz, "Can Airbnb Provide Livable
Incomes to Property Owners? An Analysis on National, Regional and City District
Level," AIAS Working Paper 168 (February 4, 2017): 16,
http://dx.doi.org/10.2139/ssrn.2910272.

19 Jathan Sadowski, "The Internet of Landlords: Digital Platforms and New
Mechanisms of Rentier Capitalism," *Antipode* 52, no. 2 (February 3, 2020): 562–
580, https://doi.org/10.1111/anti.12595; Josh Bivens, "The Economic Costs and
Benefits of Airbnb: No Reason for Local Policymakers to Let Airbnb Bypass Tax or
Regulatory Obligations," *Economic Policy Institute* (January 30, 2019), https://www
.epi.org/files/pdf/157766.pdf; David Wachsmuth et al., "The High Cost of Short-
Term Rentals in New York City," McGill University (January 30, 2048),
https://mcgill.ca/newsroom/files/newsroom/channels/attach/airbnb-report.pdf.

20 Zoe Greenberg, "New York City Looks to Crack Down on Airbnb Amid Housing
Crisis," *New York Times*, July 18, 2018, https://www.nytimes.com/2018/07/18

/nyregion/new-york-city-airbnb-crackdown.html; Amanda Calvo, "Barcelona Fines Homesharing Sites Airbnb and Homeaway," *Reuters*, November 24, 2016, https://www.reuters.com/article/us-spain-airbnb-idUSKBN13J1ZD; Kat Stafford, "Detroit Bans Airbnb Rentals in Some Residential Areas, Angering Hosts," Detroit Free Press, February 8, 2018, https://www.freep.com/story/news/local/michigan/detroit/2018/02/08/detroit-bans-airbnb-rentals-some-residential-areas-angering-hosts/320796002.

21 Julie Bort, "San Francisco Makes Airbnb Legal at Last," *Business Insider*, October 10, 2014, https://www.businessinsider.com/san-francisco-makes-airbnb-legal-at-last-2014-10.

22 Julie Verhage, "Goldman Sachs: More and More People Who Use Airbnb Don't Want to go Back to Hotels," Bloomberg, February 16, 2016, https://www.bloomberg.com/news/articles/2016-02-16/goldman-sachs-more-and-more-people-who-use-airbnb-don-t-want-to-go-back-to-hotels.

23 Chris Adams, "Overtourism Tool Kit," Miles Partnership, December 4, 2018, https://www.milespartnership.com/blog/overtourism-toolkit.

24 Longhi, "Sedona's Housing Woes."

25 Ron Eland, "Sedona Bids Farewell to Clifton," *Sedona Red Rock News*, March 30, 2021, https://www.redrocknews.com/2021/03/30/sedona-bids-farewell-to-clifton.

26 "Best Places to Invest in Vacation Rentals in 2020 + 2021," AirDNA, September 24, 2020, https://www.airdna.co/blog/best-places-to-invest-in-us-vacation-rentals.

27 Jane Jacobs, *The Death and Life of Great American Cities* (New York: Random House, 1961), 56.

2. Going Viral: Short-Term Rentals in Flagstaff

1 Grey Tampa, phone interview, July 21, 2022.

2 William Brune, in-person interview, June 2020.

3 Brune, interview.

4 Lorraine Longhi and Ryan Randazzo, "Arizona Governor Signs Law Regulating Short-Term Rental 'Party Houses'—But Does It Do Enough?" *Arizona Republic*, May 21, 2019, https://www.azcentral.com/story/news/politics/legislature/2019/05/21/arizona-law-crack-down-short-term-rental-party-houses-airbnb-vrbo/3761624002.

5 Airdna.co; US Census Bureau, "Quickfacts," census.gov, https://www.census.gov/quickfacts/US.

6 Internal Revenue Service, "The Restriction of Political Campaign Intervention by Section 501(c)(3) Tax-Exempt Organizations," irs.gov, June 17, 2022, https://www.irs.gov/charities-non-profits/charitable-organizations/the-restriction-of-political-campaign-intervention-by-section-501c3-tax-exempt-organizations.

7 Goldwater Institute, "Out Story," goldwaterinstitute.com, 2022, https://www.goldwaterinstitute.org/about.

8 Jarrett Skorup, "States Should Ban the Bans on Short-Term Rentals," *Hill*, July 31, 2021, https://thehill.com/opinion/finance/565502-states-should-ban-the-bans-on-short-term-rentals.

9   Keli'i Akina, "Short-Term Rental Ban Deserves Short Life," *Grassroot Institute of Hawaii*, October 31, 2022, https://www.grassrootinstitute.org/2022/10/short-term-rental-ban-deserves-short-life.

10 State Policy Network, "Affiliates," https://spn.org/directory.

11 Libertas Institute, "About Libertas," https://libertas.org.

12 Alia Beard Rau, "Arizona Forces Cities to Allow Airbnb-Type Rentals," *Arizona Republic*, May 12, 2016, https://www.azcentral.com/story/news/politics/arizona/2016/05/12/arizona-forces-cities-allow-airbnb-type-rentals/84299858.

13 John Kavanagh, phone interview, August 2020.

14 Adam Shimoni, remote video interview, June 2020.

15 Kavanagh, interview.

16 Shimoni, interview.

17 Jiwon Jung et al., "Social or Financial Goals? Comparative Analysis of User Behaviors in Couchsurfing and Airbnb," paper presentation, proceedings of the 2016 CHI conference extended abstracts on human factors in computing systems, 2857–2863, https://doi.org/10.1145/2851581.2892328.

18 Rau, "Arizona Forces Cities."

19 Doug Ducey, "Executive Order 2016-01: The Governor's Council on the Sharing Economy," Arizona Memory Project, https://azmemory.azlibrary.gov/nodes/view/44916.

20 Chris Pasterz, remote video interview, June 2020.

21 Daniel Guttentag, "What Airbnb Really Does to a Neighbourhood," BBC, August 20, 2018, https://www.bbc.com/news/business-45083954.

22 Pasterz, interview.

23 Brian Guyer, remote video interview, July 2020.

24 McKenna Marchant, remote video interview, September 2020.

25 Kendra Strahan, conference call interview, June 2020.

26 Chart combines information frm housing studies conducted in each city, the 2020 Census, and the American Community Survey.

27 Mark Muro, Robert Maxim, and Jacob Whiton, "The Places a COVID-19 Will Likely Hit Hardest," *Brookings Institute*, March 17, 2020, https://www.brookings.edu/blog/the-avenue/2020/03/17/the-places-a-covid-19-recession-will-likely-hit-hardest.

28 John Feely, phone interview, June 2020.

29 Emily Czachor, "Arizona, Adding as Many New Daily Coronavirus Cases as EU, Reports ICUs Are 89% Full," *Newsweek*, July 2, 2020, https://www.newsweek.com/arizona-adding-many-new-daily-coronavirus-cases-eu-reports-icus-are-89-full-1515007.

30 AirDNA, Airdna.co.

31 AirDNA, Airdna.co; US Census Bureau, "Quickfacts," census.gov, https://www.census.gov/quickfacts/US.

32 Robin Le Page, remote video interview, June 2020.

33 US Census Bureau, "Quarterly Residential Vacancies and Homeownership, Second Quarter 2019," census.gov, https://www.census.gov/housing/hvs/files/currenthvspress.pdf.

34 "AirDNA Market Review: U.S. January 2021," AirDNA, February 9, 2021, https://www.airdna.co/blog/airdna-market-review-us-january-2021.

35 AirDNA, Airdna.co.

36 "Best Places to Invest in Vacation Rentals in 2021 and 2022," AirDNA, February 8, 2022, https://www.airdna.co/blog/best-places-to-invest-in-us-vacation-rentals-2021-2022.

37 Pasterz, interview.

38 US Census Bureau, "Quickfacts."

39 Rau, "Arizona Forces Cities"; "Proposition 207: 1-21-2006; Private Property Rights Protection Act," Arizona Legislature, January 21, 2006, https://www.azleg.gov/2006_Ballot_Proposition_Analyses/final%20I-21-2006%20%20Private%20Property%20Rights%20Protection%20Act.pdf.

40 Brumby McLeod, remote video interview, July 2020.

3. Latchkey Town: Second Homes in St. George

1 US Census Bureau, "Quickfacts."

2 Jessica Guerin, "Wages Aren't Keeping Pace with Home-Price Growth, and It's Putting a Dent in the Housing Market," Housingwire, July 5, 2019, https://www.housingwire.com/articles/49637-wages-arent-keeping-pace-with-home-price-growth-and-its-putting-a-dent-in-the-housing-market.

3 Eric Gallagher, phone interview, July 2020.

4 Office of Policy Development and Research, "St. George, Utah: Comprehensive Housing Market Analysis," US Department of Housing and Urban Development, October 1, 2018, https://www.huduser.gov/portal/publications/pdf/StGeorgeUT-CHMA-18.pdf.

5 Gary Lampton, remote video interview, July 2020.

6 St. George City Code, "Article D. Resort overlay zone," Code Publishing Co., 2019, section update, https://stgeorge.municipal.codes/Code/10-13D.

7 HB 253, Short-term Rental Amendments (2017), https://le.utah.gov/~2017/bills/static/HB0253.html.

8 Lampton, remote video interview.

9 Jared Greene, remote video interview, July 2020.

10 Allen Sanderson, phone interview, July 2020.

11 Airdna.co.

12 Sanderson, interview.

13 Josh Bivens, "The Economic Costs and Benefits of Airbnb: No Reason for Local Policymakers to Let Airbnb Bypass Tax or Regulatory Obligations," *Economic Policy Institute* (January 30, 2019): 2, 11-12, https://www.epi.org/files/pdf/157766.pdf.

14 Verhage, "Goldman Sachs."

15 Pasterz, interview.

16 Gael F. Cooper, "17 Things Millennials Are Killing Off," *MoneyTalksNews*, September 9, 2021, https://www.moneytalksnews.com/slideshows/starter-homes-golf-and-23-other-things-millennials-are-killing-off.

17 Rob Warnock, "Homeownership Rates by Generation: How Do Millennials Stack
    Up?" *Apartment List*, March 17, 2020,
    https://www.apartmentlist.com/research/homeownership-by-generation.
18 Dana Anderson, "Demand for Vacation Homes Soared 84 Percent Year over Year in
    January, Symbolizing Uneven Financial Recovery in the U.S.," Redfin, February 9, 2021,
    https://www.redfin.com/news/second-home-purchases-increase-january-remote
    -work.
19 Dana Anderson, "Work from (Second) Home: Demand for Vacation Homes
    Continue to Soar, Even as Offices Show Signs of Life," Redfin, April 8, 2021, https://
    www.redfin.com/news/second-home-demand-record-high; Cody Nelson, "As a
    'Zoom Boom' Brings the Wealthy to Santa Fe, Locals Are Getting Priced Out,"
    Guardian, January 29, 2021, https://www.theguardian.com/us-news/2021/jan/29
    /santa-fe-new-mexico-zoom-boom-housing.
20 Randy Carpenter, remote video interview, July 2020.
21 Anderson, "Work from (Second) Home."
22 Dana Anderson, "Demand for Second Homes Is More than Double Pre-Pandemic
    Prices," Redfin, May 10, 2021,
    https://www.redfin.com/news/second-home-demand-doubles.
23 Patrick Sisson, "How Vacation Homes Went from Private Escape to Investment
    Opportunities," Curbed, October 2, 2018, https://archive.curbed
    .com/2018/10/2/17925738/property-airbnb-vacation-home-short-term-rental; Paul
    Tostevin, "Spotlight: Second Homes—Global Trends in Ownership and Renting,"
    Savills, September 17, 2018, https://www.savills.co.uk/research
    _articles/229130/264370-0.
24 Richard L. Ragatz and Gabriel M. Gelb, "The Quiet Boom in the Vacation Home
    Market," *California Management Review* 12, no. 3 (April 1970): 57–64,
    https://doi.org/10.2307/41164235.
25 City of Flagstaff, "10-Year Housing Plan," Draft produced by Housing Section, 2021,
    https://www.flagstaff.az.gov/DocumentCenter/View/70585/DRAFT-Flagstaffs-10
    -Year-Housing-Plan-93021-FOR-PUBLIC-COMMENT-MOB-HSS-W10-002.
26 Scott Miller, "Vail Town Council Ponders Tightening Rent-by-Owner Rules," *VailDaily*,
    May 3, 2017,
    https://www.vaildaily.com/news/vail-town-council-ponders-tightening-rent-by
    -owner-rules.
27 Daniel García, "Second-Home Buying and the Housing Boom and Bust," Finance
    and Economics Discussion Series, May 2019, https://doi.org/10.17016/FEDS.2019.029r1.
28 National Association of Realtors, "Second Homes: Recovery Post Financial Crisis,"
    FannieMae, April 7, 2014, https://www.fanniemae.com/media/18811/display.
29 Christine Dugas, "Flagstaff Looks to Second-Home Buyers, Tourists for Recovery,"
    USA Today, February 16, 2009,
    https://abcnews.go.com/Business/story?id=6892885&page=1.
30 Washington County Assessor, https://www.washco.utah.gov/departments/assessor;
    Washington County Assessor, email correspondence, January 2021.
31 American Community Survey, "Occupancy Status," United States Census Bureau,
    2020,

https://data.census.gov/cedsci/table?q=B25002%3A%20OCCUPANCY%20STATUS&g=0100000US,%2404000%2401,%240400000&tid=ACSDT5Y2020.B25002.

32 Greene, interview.

33 Botsman and Rogers, *What's Mine.*

34 "Best Places to Invest in Vacation Rentals in 2020 + 2021," AirDNA, September 24, 2020, https://www.airdna.co/blog/best-places-to-invest-in-us-vacation-rentals.

35 John Cusack, "'The Real Blackwater Scandal: Build a Frontier, You Get Cowboys," Huffington Post, May 8, 2010, updated May 25, 2011, https://www.huffpost.com/entry/the-real-blackwater-scand_b_67741.

36 "Best Places to Invest," AirDNA.

4. Opening the Floodgates: Growth in Bozeman

1 Pat Witton, phone interview, July 2020.

2 Le Page, interview.

3 US Census Bureau, "Quickfacts."

4 Witton, interview.

5 "Fall headcount enrollment history," Montana State University, 2021, https://www.montana.edu/opa/students/enrollment/headhist.html.

6 Witton, interview.

7 Beau Houston, video interview, August 2020.

8 Houston, interview.

9 Witton, interview.

10 Le Page, interview.

11 Witton, interview.

12 Le Page, interview.

13 Le Page, interview.

14 Paul Rosenfeld, in-person interview, July 2020.

15 "Short-term rentals," City of Bozeman, December 1, 2017, https://www.bozeman.net/government/planning/short-term-rentals-str; Rosenfeld, interview.

16 "Accessory dwelling units," City of Bozeman, April 2018, https://www.bozeman.net/Home/ShowDocument?id=8447; Guyer, interview.

17 "Short-term rentals," City of Bozeman; Le Page, interview.

18 Rosenfeld, interview.

19 Le Page, interview.

20 US Census, "Quickfacts"; "Annual Report for Gallatin County," Big Sky Country MLS, January 10, 2021, https://gallatin-public.stats.showingtime.com/docs/ann/x/report?src=map.

21 Wendy Sullivan and Christine Walker, "Bozeman, Montana Community Housing Needs Assessment," WSW Consulting and Navigate, LLC, February 2019, 73, https://www.bozeman.net/home/showdocument?id=8773.

22 NAU College of Business, "2017–2018 Flagstaff visitor study," AZ Office of Tourism and W.A. Franke College of Business, NAU, https://tourism.az.gov/wp-content/uploads/2019/05/Flagstaff-Tourism-Study-2017-2018.pdf.

23 Randy Carpenter, remote video interview, July 2020.
24 Gallagher, interview.
25 Travis, *New Geographies*, 53.
26 Megan Lawson, remote video interview, July 2020.
27 Barron, Kung, and Proserpio, "When Airbnb Listings."
28 Ron Bekkerman et al., "Research: Restricting Airbnb Rentals Reduces Development," *Harvard Business Review*, November 17, 2021, https://hbr.org/2021/11/research-restricting-airbnb-rentals-reduces-development.
29 Witton, interview.
30 Lawson, interview.
31 Estelle Sommeiller and Mark Price, "The New Gilded Age: Income Inequality in the U.S. by State, Metropolitan Area, and County," *Economic Policy Institute*, July 19, 2018, https://www.epi.org/publication/the-new-gilded-age-income-inequality-in-the-u-s-by-state-metropolitan-area-and-county.
32 Travis, *New Geographies*, 132.
33 Travis, *New Geographies*, 44.
34 American Community Survey, "Selected housing characteristics," US Census 2019, https://data.census.gov/cedsci/table?d=ACS 5-Year Estimates Data Profiles&tid=ACSDP5Y2019.DP04.
35 Travis, *New Geographies*, 64.
36 "What Is a Circular Economy?" Environmental Protection Agency, September 29, 2022, https://www.epa.gov/recyclingstrategy/what-circular-economy.
37 Devonna McLaughlin, video interview, June 2020.
38 Lawson, interview.
39 Witton, interview.
40 Sanderson, interview.
41 Travis, *New Geographies*, 22.
42 Lawson, interview.
43 Cusack, "Real Blackwater Scandal."
44 Rachel Grant, in-person interview, June 2020.
45 Lawson, interview.
46 Guyer, interview; Houston, interview.
47 Houston, interview.
48 Guyer, interview.
49 Guyer, interview.
50 Big Sky Country MLS, "Annual Report for Gallatin County."
51 Neil Smith, "Gentrification and the Rent Gap," *Annals of the Association of American Geographers* (September 1987): 21, https://doi.org/10.1111/j.1467-8306.1987.tb00171.x.
52 Guyer, interview.

5. Money Trees

1 National Park Service, "Explorers," NPS.gov, September 21, 2019, https://www.nps.gov/grca/learn/historyculture/explorers.htm.
2 National Park Service, "Explorers."
3 Donald Worster, "New West, True West: Interpreting the Region's History," *Western*

Historical Quarterly 18, no. 2 (April 1987): 145,
https://www.jstor.org/stable/pdf/969580.pdf.

4 Roderick Nash, *Wilderness and the American Mind* (New Haven, CT: Yale University Press, 1973), 24.

5 Nash, 25.

6 Nash, 39.

7 Nash, 87.

8 John Muir, marginal notes found in Muir's copy of *The Prose Works of Ralph Waldo Emerson*, by Ralph Waldo Emerson, Beinecke Rare Book and Manuscript Library, accessed April 25, 2023,
https://vault.sierraclub.org/john_muir_exhibit/writings/favorite_quotations.aspx.

9 Nash, *Wilderness*, 111–112.

10 Nash, 73; Joseph L. Sax, Mountains *Without Handrails: Reflections on the National Parks* (Ann Arbor: University of Michigan Press, 1980), 14.

11 Paul Robbins, *Political Ecology: A Critical Introduction* (New York: Wiley-Blackwell, 2011); Kevin R. Cox, *Making Human Geography* (New York: Guilford Press, 2014).

12 David Gibbs and Rob Krueger, "Containing the Contradictions of Rapid Development? New Economy Spaces and Sustainable Urban Development," in *The Sustainable Development Paradox: Urban Political Economy in the United States and Europe*, ed. Rob Krueger and David Gibbs (New York: Guilford Publications, 2007).

13 Travis, *New Geographies*, 21.

14 Harvey Molotch, "The City as a Growth Machine: Toward a Political Economy of Place," *American Journal of Sociology* 82 (1976): 309–32.

15 Travis, *New Geographies*, 31.

16 Travis, 91.

17 Joel Garreau, *The Nine Nations of North America* (Boston: Houghton, 1981).

18 Travis, *New Geographies*, 25.

19 Travis, 3

20 Richelle Winkler et al., "Social Landscapes of the Inter-Mountain West: A Comparison of 'Old West' and 'New West' Communities," *Rural Sociology* 72, no. 3 (2007): 496, http://citeseerx.ist.psu.edu/viewdoc/download?doi=10.1.1.483.3730.

21 Travis, *New Geographies*, 59.

22 Alex Hern, "Wikipedia Edits Have Massive Impact on Tourism, Say Economists," *Guardian*, September 18, 2020,
https://www.theguardian.com/technology/2020/sep/18/wikipedia-edits-have-massive-impact-on-tourism-say-economists.

23 Jason W. Moore, "Transcending the Metabolic Rift: A Theory of Crises in the Capitalist World-Ecology," *Journal of Peasant Studies* 38, no. 1 (January 13, 2011): 32, https://doi.org/10.1080/03066150.2010.538579; Travis, *New Geographies*.

24 Moore, "Transcending," 3, 22.

25 Richard Peet and Michael Watts, *Liberation Ecologies: Environment, Development, Social Movements* (London: Routledge, London, 2004), 37.

26 Thibaut Abergel, Brian Dean, and John Dulac, "Global Status Report 2017," UN Environment and International Energy Agency (2017),
https://globalabc.org/resources/publications/gabc-global-status-report-2016-towards-zero-emission-efficient-and-resilient.

27 United Nations, "Climate Disasters are Increasingly Interconnected," unfccc.int, September 8, 2021, https://unfccc.int/news/climate-disasters-are-increasingly-interconnected; Chelsea Harvey, "Scientists Can Now Blame Individual Natural Disasters on Climate Change," *Scientific American*, January 2, 2018, https://www.scientificamerican.com/article/scientists-can-now-blame-individual-natural-disasters-on-climate-change.

28 Oxfam, "Profiting from Pain," Oxfam Media Briefing, May 23, 2022, https://www.oxfamamerica.org/explore/research-publications/profiting-from-pain.

29 Moore, "Transcending," 39.

30 Michael Le Page, "Destruction of Nature Is as Big a Threat to Humanity as Climate Change," *New Scientist*, May 6, 2019, https://www.newscientist.com/article/2201697-destruction-of-nature-is-as-big-a-threat-to-humanity-as-climate-change.

31 Krishna Rao et al., "The Fastest Population Growth in the West's Wildland Fringes Is in Ecosystems Most Vulnerable to Wildfires," phys.org, February 8, 2022, https://phys.org/news/2022-02-fastest-population-growth-west-wildland.html.

32 Volker C. Radeloff et al., "Housing Growth in and near United States Protected Areas Limits Their Conservation Value," *Proceedings of the National Academy of Sciences* 107, no. 2 (December 22, 2009): 944, http://doi.org/10.1073/pnas.0911131107.

33 Annette McGivney, "'Everyone Came at Once': America's National Parks Reckon with Record-Smashing Year," *Guardian*, January 1, 2022, https://www.theguardian.com/environment/2022/jan/01/national-parks-us-tourism-crowds-busy.

34 Lori Sonken, "In Search of Reasonable Housing for National Park Service Employees," *National Parks Traveler*, November 2021, https://www.nationalparkstraveler.org/2021/11/search-reasonable-housing-national-park-service-employees.

35 "Airbnb and the National Park Foundation Inspire Travel to Unique US Parks," Airbnb News, August 25, 2020, https://news.airbnb.com/airbnb-and-the-national-park-foundation-inspire-travel-to-unique-us-parks.

36 Nash, *Wilderness*.

37 Simon Kuznets, "National Income, 1929–1932," United States Bureau of Foreign and Domestic Commerce, Presented to 73rd Congress, 2nd Session, January 4, 1934, https://fraser.stlouisfed.org/title/national-income-1929-1932-971; Elizabeth Dickinson, "GDP: A brief history," *Foreign Policy*, January 3, 2011, https://foreignpolicy.com/2011/01/03/gdp-a-brief-history.

38 Jason Hickel, "Is It Time for a Post-Growth Economy?" *Common Dreams*, July 16, 2018, https://www.commondreams.org/views/2018/07/16/it-time-post-growth-economy; "GDP (current US$)," World Bank, 2022, https://data.worldbank.org/indicator/NY.GDP.MKTP.CD.

39 Ian Tiseo, "U.S. Municipal Solid Waste Generation from 1960 to 2018," *Statista*, June 21, 2022, https://www.statista.com/statistics/186256/us-municipal-solid-waste-generation-since-1960.

40 Mathis Wackernagel and Williams Rees, *Our Ecological Footprint: Reducing Human Impact on the Earth* (Gabriola Island, BC: New Society Publishers, 1996).

41 Joseph Mercola, "Kids' Disconnect with Nature Increases Mental Health Disorders," *Defender*, May 17, 2022, https://childrenshealthdefense.org/defender/kids-disconnect-nature-mental-health -disorders.

42 P. E. Moskowitz, *How to Kill a City: Gentrification, Inequality, and the Fight for the Neighborhood* (New York: Bold Type Books, 2017).

43 Nick Visser, "Gulf Spill Settlement Could Save BP Billions in Tax Breaks," *Huffington Post*, April 5, 2016, https://www.huffpost.com/entry/bp-deepwater-horizon -settlement_n_57033e19e4b0daf53af0bcca.

44 Laura Paddison, "How the Rich Are Driving Climate Change," *BBC*, October 27, 2021, https://www.bbc.com/future/article/20211025-climate-how-to-make-the-rich -pay-for-their-carbon-emissions.

45 Tess Riley, "Just 100 Companies Responsible for 71% of Global Emissions, Study Says," *Guardian*, July 10, 2017, https://www.theguardian.com/sustainable-business/2017/jul/10/100-fossil-fuel -companies-investors-responsible-71-global-emissions-cdp-study-climate-change.

46 Niall McCarthy, "Oil and Gas Giants Spend Millions Lobbying to Block Climate Change Policies," *Forbes*, March 25, 2019, https://www.forbes.com/sites/niallmccarthy/2019/03/25/oil-and-gas-giants-spend -millions-lobbying-to-block-climate-change-policies-infographic.

47 Rachel Carson, *The Sense of Wonder* (New York: Harper and Row,1965).

48 Nina Lakhani, "US Hit by 20 Separate Billion-Dollar Climate Disasters in 2021, NOAA Report Says," *Guardian*, January 10, 2022, https://www.theguardian.com/environment/2022/jan/11/us-hit-by-20-separate -billion-dollar-climate-disasters-in-2021-noaa-report-says.

49 Lakhani, "US Hit."

50 Abrahm Lustgarten, "As Colorado River Dries, US Teeters on the Brink of Larger Water Crisis," *Pro Publica*, August 25, 2022, https://www.propublica.org/article/colorado-river-water-shortage-jay-famiglietti.

51 Edward Abbey, *Desert Solitaire: A Season in the Wilderness* (New York: McGraw-Hill, 1968).

52 Thomas Michael Power and Richard Barrett, *Post-Cowboy Economics: Pay and Prosperity in the New American West* (Washington, DC: Island Press, 2001).

53 Gundars Rudzitis, *Wilderness and the Changing American West* (New York: John Wiley, 1996); Gundar Rudzitis, "Amenities Increasingly Draw People to the Rural West," Rural Development Perspectives 14, no. 2 (1999): 13.

54 Travis, *New Geographies*, 29–30.

55 Peet and Watts, *Liberation Ecologies*.

56 Le Page, "Destruction of Nature."

6. Unaffordable Housing

1 Matthew Desmond, *Evicted: Poverty and Profit in the American City* (New York: Penguin, 2016).

2 Sonya Salamon and Katherine MacTavish, *Singlewide: Chasing the American Dream in a Rural Trailer Park* (Ithaca, NY: Cornell University Press, 2017).

3   Jorge Garza, "Gentrification, Neoliberalism, and Place: Displacement and Resistance in Flagstaff," thesis submitted for MA in Sustainable Communities, Northern Arizona University (2018), 107.

4   Garza, 107.

5   Mike Baker, "A Town's Housing Crisis Exposes a 'House of Cards,'" *New York Times*, July 31, 2022, https://www.nytimes.com/2022/07/31/us/sun-valley-workforce-housing.html.

6   Louise Sheiner, "Why Is State and Local Employment Falling Faster than Revenues?" *Brookings Institute*, December 23, 2020, https://www.brookings.edu/blog/up-front/2020/12/23/why-is-state-and-local-employment-falling-faster-than-revenues.

7   Center for Housing and Policy, "Home Ownership Affordability Monitor (HOAM)," Federal Reserve Bank of Atlanta, July 2021, https://www.atlantafed.org/center-for-housing-and-policy/data-and-tools/home-ownership-affordability-monitor.

8   David J. Madden and Peter Marcuse, *In Defense of Housing: The Politics of Crisis* (Brooklyn, NY: Verso Books, 2016).

9   "Daily Trends in Number of Covid-19 Deaths in the United States Reported to CDC," Center for Disease Control, October 15, 2021, https://covid.cdc.gov/covid-data-tracker/#trends_dailydeaths; "Leading Causes of Death," Center for Disease Control, 2019, https://www.cdc.gov/nchs/fastats/leading-causes-of-death.htm.

10   Andrew Witherspoon and Alvin Chang, "Nearly Half of American Workers Don't Earn Enough to Afford a One-Bedroom Rental," *Guardian*, August 12, 2021, https://www.theguardian.com/society/2021/aug/12/housing-renter-affordable-data-map.

11   "How Did Landlords Fare During COVID?" JPMorgan Chase, October 2021, https://www.jpmorganchase.com/institute/research/household-debt/how-did-landlords-fare-during-covid.

12   "Rent Debt in America: Stabilizing Renters Is Key to Equitable Recovery," National Equity Atlas, September 13, 2021, https://nationalequityatlas.org/rent-debt.

13   City of Flagstaff, "10-Year Housing Plan."

14   Anderson, "Demand for Vacation."

15   Katie Gentry, Brian Irvine, and Alison Cook-Davis, "State-Level Legal Barriers to Adopting Affordable Housing Policies in Arizona," Morrison Institute for Public Policy, Arizona State University, November 2021, https://morrisoninstitute.asu.edu/sites/default/files/state-level-legal-barriers-to-adopting-affordable-housing-policies-in-arizona-nov-2021.pdf.

16   National Park Service, "Native Americans and the Homestead Act," nps.gov, 2020, https://www.nps.gov/home/learn/historyculture/native-americans-and-the-homestead-act.htm.

17   Richard Rothstein, *The Color of Law: A Forgotten History of How Our Government Segregated America* (New York: Norton, 2018).

18   Laura Gottesdiener, *A Dream Foreclosed: Black America and the Fight for a Place to Call Home* (New York: Zuccotti Park Press, 2013), 4.

19 Surya Deva and Leilani Farha, Letter from UN Special Rapporteur on Adequate Housing to Blackstone Group, March 22, 2019, https://www.ohchr.org/Documents/Issues/Housing/Financialization/OL_OTH_17_2019.pdf; Surya Deva and Leilani Farha, Letter from UN Special Rapporteur on Adequate Housing to US Government, March 22, 2019, http://wiki.pghrights.mayfirst.org/images/6/65/March_2019_Housing_UN_Rapp_USLetter_Financialization.pdf.

20 James Kleimann, "Blackstone Gets Back into the Single-Family Rental Game," *Housing Wire*, September 1, 2020, https://www.housingwire.com/articles/blackstone-gets-back-into-the-single-family-rental-game; Lauren Aratani, "Blackstone to Buy Company That Rents Out 17,000 Homes in $6 Billion Deal," *Guardian*, June 22, 2021, https://www.theguardian.com/us-news/2021/jun/22/blackstone-6bn-deal-homes.

21 Department of Housing and Urban Development, "Department of Housing and Urban Development (HUD) by Sub-Component for FY 2022," USASpending.com, https://www.usaspending.gov/agency/department-of-housing-and-urban-development?fy=2022.

22 Jonathan Marino, "Blackstone Is Now 'The Largest Owner of Real Estate in the World,'" *Business Insider*, November 15, 2015, https://www.businessinsider.com/blackstone-is-largest-owner-of-real-estate-2015-11.

23 Jonathan Marino, "Here Are the 19 Richest Private Equity Titans in America," *Business Insider*, October 1, 2015, https://www.businessinsider.com/forbes-rich-list-in-private-equity-2015-9#steve-schwarzman-19.

24 *Forbes*, "The Real-Time Billionaires List," forbes.com, https://www.forbes.com/real-time-billionaires/#5b3544e73d78.

25 Lily Katz and Sheharyar Bokhari, "Investor Home Purchases Hit Record, Surpassing Pre-Pandemic Levels," Redfin, July 22, 2021, https://www.redfin.com/news/investor-home-purchases-q2-2021.

26 Rachel M. Cohen, "Democrats Eye New Legislation to Rein in Wall Street Landlords," Vox, December 2, 2022, https://www.vox.com/policy-and-politics/2022/12/2/23485957/housing-banks-corporate-single-family-renters-landlord.

27 Lily Katz, "Investor Home Purchases Rise for First Time in a Year as U.S. Economy Bounces Back," Redfin, May 19, 2021, https://www.redfin.com/news/investor-home-purchases-q1-2021.

28 Anderson, "Demand for Second Homes."

29 Federal Housing Finance Agency, "FHFA Announces Target Increases to Enterprise Pricing Framework," fhfa.gov, January 5, 2022, https://www.fhfa.gov/Media/PublicAffairs/Pages/FHFA-Announces-Targeted-Increases-to-Enterprise-Pricing-Framework.aspx.

30 "New Airbnb Hosts Have Earned $1 Billion During the Pandemic," Airbnb, February 2021, https://news.airbnb.com/wp-content/uploads/sites/4/2021/02/New-Hosts-Earnings-Report-Airbnb.pdf?v2.

31 Marc J. Dunkelman, *The Vanishing Neighbor: The Transformation of American Community* (New York: Norton, 2014), 41.

32 Brune, interview.

33 Census and HUD. (2021a). "Median sales price of houses sold for the United States [MSPUS]," updated October 26, 2021; data from US Census Bureau and US Department of Housing and Urban Development, accessed December 8, 2021, Federal Reserve Economic Data (FRED), Federal Reserve Bank of St. Louis. https://fred.stlouisfed.org/series/MSPUS.

34 Travis, *New Geographies*, 57.

35 Corina Vanek, "Building Boom: Flagstaff Adding Housing Units by the Thousands," *AZ Daily Sun*, October 24, 2016, Updated December 6, 2016. https://azdailysun.com/news/local/building-boom-flagstaff-adding-housing-units-by-the-thousands/article_6637d6f1-5d32-591f-8f41-69b9f64bb0e9.html.

36 US Census, "Quickfacts."

37 Ben Geier, "Hottest Secondary Home Markets in the U.S. – 2021 Edition," SmartAsset, March 2, 2021, https://smartasset.com/mortgage/hottest-secondary-home-markets-2021.

38 Office of Institutional Research and Analysis, "Fact Book 2018–2019," Northern Arizona University, 2019, https://in.nau.edu/wp-content/uploads/sites/129/2019/11/2018_2019FactBook.pdf.

39 Feely, interview.

40 O. M. Kerney, "Workforce Housing Programs and Policies in Three Western United States Amenity Communities," (Master's Thesis, Northern Arizona University, 2007), 119.

41 United Way of Westchester and Putnam, "Day 14: The Effects of Racist Ideology," 21 Day Racial Equity and Social Justice Challenge, https://www.uwwp.org/challenge-day-14.

42 "Real estate glossary," Redfin, https://www.redfin.com/definition/monthsof-supply.

43 Census and HUD, "Monthly Supply of Houses in the United States [MSACSR]," Federal Reserve Bank of St. Louis, November 24, 2021, https://fred.stlouisfed.org/series/MSACSR.

44 Rachel M. Cohen, "Where Are All the Apartments for Families?" Vox, April 23, 2023, https://www.vox.com/policy/2023/4/23/23686130/housing-apartments-family-yimby-nimby-zoning-suburbs.

45 Cohen, "Democrats Eye."

46 Economic and Housing Research Group, "Housing Supply: A Growing Deficit," Freddie Mac, May 2021, http://www.freddiemac.com/fmac-resources/research/pdf/202105-Note-Housing_Supply-08.pdf.

47 Devonna McLaughlin, remote video interview, June 2020.

48 Moore, "Transcending," 27.

49 Grant, interview.

50 Census Bureau, "Characteristics of New Housing," accessed April 27, 2023. https://www.census.gov/construction/chars/current.html.

51 George Lipsitz, *How Racism Takes Place* (Philadelphia: Temple University Press, 2011), 25–70.

52 Heather Vogell, "Rent Going Up? One Company's Algorithm Could Be Why," *ProPublica*, October 15, 2022, https://www.propublica.org/article/yieldstar-rent-increase-realpage-rent.

53 Heather Vogell, "Company That Makes Rent-Setting Software for Apartments Sued for Collusion," *ProPublica*, October 21, 2022, https://www.propublica.org/article/realpage-accused-of-collusion-in-new-lawsuit.

54 *Push*, directed by Fredrik Gertten (WG Films, 2019).

55 Lina Batarags, "China Has at Least 65 Million Empty Homes—Enough to House the Population of France. It Offers a Glimpse into the Country's Massive Housing-Market Problem," *Business Insider*, October 14, 2021, https://www.businessinsider.com/china-empty-homes-real-estate-evergrande -housing-market-problem-2021-10.

7. Blank Space

1 David Bustos, phone interview, May 2022.

2 T. G. Frichner, "Preliminary Study of the Impact on Indigenous Peoples of the International Legal Construct Known as the Doctrine of Discovery," Permanent Forum on Indigenous Issues, Economic and Social Council, United Nations, February 4, 2010, 7, https://doctrineofdiscovery.org/assets/pdfs/DoctrinePrelimStudy2010.pdf.

3 Roxanne Dunbar Ortiz, *An Indigenous Peoples' History of the United States* (Boston: Beacon Press, 2015), 9.

4 Anders Stephanson, *Manifest Destiny: American Expansionism and the Empire of Right* (New York: Hill and Wang, 1995), 19.

5 Francis J. Bremer, *John Winthrop: America's Forgotten Founding Father* (London: Oxford University Press, 2003).

6 Stephanson, *Manifest Destiny*, 11.

7 David Getches et al., *Cases and Materials on Federal Indian Law*, 7th ed. (St. Paul, MN: Westover Academic Press, 2017), 56.

8 John Locke, *Two Treatises of Government* (New York: Cambridge University Press, 1988), 154, digitized version accessed from https://archive.org/details/twotreatisesgov00lockgoog/page/n6/mode/2up.

9 Getches et al., *Cases and Materials*, 57.

10 Stephanson, *Manifest Destiny*, 25.

11 Patrick Wolfe, "Settler Colonialism and the Elimination of the Native," *Journal of Genocide Research* 8, no. 4 (2006): 396, https://www.tandfonline.com/doi/pdf/10.1080/14623520601056240

12 Wolfe, 391.

13 Getches et al., *Cases and Materials*, 35.

14 Getches et al., 37.

15 Getches et al., 3.

16 Getches et al., 96.

17 Andrew Jackson, "Second Annual Message," in *A Compilation of the Messages and Papers of the Presidents* vol II, no. 3, ed. James D. Richardson (Project Gutenberg), https://onlinebooks.library.upenn.edu/webbin/metabook?id=mppresidents.

18 Wolfe, "Settler Colonialism," 395.

19 Alexis de Tocqueville, *Democracy in America*, trans. H. C. Mansfield and D. Winthrop (Chicago: University of Chicago Press, 2000).

20 de Tocqueville, 372–373.

21 de Tocqueville, 65, 227.

22 de Tocqueville, 13.

23 Wolfe, "Settler Colonialism," 395.

24 Getches et al., *Cases and Materials*, 140.

25 Karen Begay, in-person interview, October 2020.

26 Frederick Jackson Turner, "The Significance of the Frontier in American History," in *Rereading Frederick Jackson Turner*, ed. John Mack Faragher (New Haven, CT: Yale University Press, 1994), 31–60.

27 Garreau, *Nine Nations of North America*.

28 Moody's Analytics, "Affordability Rankings: Determining the Most Affordable States," *U.S. News and World Report*, https://www.usnews.com/news/best-states/rankings/opportunity/affordability.

29 Turner, "Significance of the Frontier," 31–60.

30 Veal and Spader, "Nearly a Third."

31 Madden and Marcuse, *In Defense of Housing*; Witherspoon and Chang, "Nearly Half."

32 Madden and Marcuse; Witherspoon and Chang.

33 American Community Survey, "Occupancy Status," United States Census Bureau, https://data.census.gov/cedsci/table?q=B25002.

34 Langston Hughes, "Let America Be America Again," *The Collected Poems of Langston Hughes* (New York: Knopf, 1994).

35 US Census Bureau, "Quickfacts."

36 Census Map, "American Indians and Alaska Natives in the United States," US Census Bureau, 2000, https://media.nationalgeographic.org/assets/photos/678/0c5/6780c5c6-8db6-4d2e -b73b-3b3587958634.jpg.

37 Garza, "Gentrification."

38 Surya Milner, "Bozeman's Sole Multicultural Enclave Faces Evictions Amid a Housing Crisis," *High Country News*, February, 11, 2021. https://www.hcn.org/articles/north-economy-bozemans-sole-multicultural-enclave -faces-evictions-amid-a-housing-crisis.

39 Eduardo Bonilla-Silva, *Racism Without Racists: Color-Blind Racism and the Persistence of Racial Inequality in America*, 5th ed. (Lanham, MD: Rowman and Littlefield, 2018), 24–25.

40 Bonilla-Silva, *Racism Without Racists*, 49.

41 Peter Christensen, Ignacio Sarmiento-Barbieri, and Christopher Timmins, "Racial Discrimination and Housing Outcomes in the United States Rental Market," National Bureau of Economic Research, November 2021, https://www.nber.org/system/files/working_papers/w29516/w29516.pdf.

42 Bonilla-Silva, *Racism Without Racists*, 2.

43 Robbins, *Political Ecology*, 19.

44 George Lipsitz, *How Racism Takes Place* (Philadelphia: Temple University Press, 2011), 25–70; Daniel Aaronson, Daniel Hartley, and Bhash Mazumder, "The Effects of the 1930s HOLC 'Redlining' Maps," Working Paper, No. 2017-12 (revised August 2020), https://www.chicagofed.org/publications/working-papers/2017/wp2017-12; Gregory M. Maney and Margaret Abraham, "Whose Backyard? Boundary Making

in NIMBY Opposition to Immigrant Services," *Social Justice* 35, no. 4 (114): 66–68, https://www.jstor.org/stable/29768515; Dionissi Aliprantis and Daniel R. Carroll, "What Is Behind the Persistence of the Racial Wealth Gap?" *Economic Commentary* (2019-03): 2, https://www.clevelandfed.org/publications/economic-commentary/ec -201903-what-is-behind-the-persistence-of-the-racial-wealth-gap.

45 Lipsitz, *How Racism Takes Place*, 35.

46 Lipsitz.

47 Lipsitz, 245.

48 Farha, "Report of the Special Rapporteur."

49 Madden and Marcuse, *In Defense of Housing.*

50 Gayatri Chakravorty Spivak, "Can the Subaltern Speak?" in *Marxism and the Interpretation of Culture*, eds. Cary Nelson and Lawrence Grossberg (London: Macmillan, 1988)24–28, jan.ucc.nau.edu/~sj6/Spivak%20CanTheSubalternSpeak. pdf.

51 Rothstein, *Color of Law*, 65.

52 Michelle Alexander, *The New Jim Crow: Mass Incarceration in the Age of Colorblindness* (New York: The New Press, 2013).

53 Frederick J. Turner, "The Problem of the West," *Atlantic*, September 1896, https://www.theatlantic.com/magazine/archive/1896/09/the-problem-of-the -west/525699.

54 Sarah Tory, "Where Do Public Lands Factor into the Homelessness Crisis?" *HighCountry News*, October 1, 2021, https://www.hcn.org/issues/53.10/south-public-lands-where-do-public-lands-factor -into-the-homelessness-crisis.

55 Jessica Bruder, *Nomadland: Surviving America in the Twenty-First Century* (New York: Norton, 2017).

56 Turner, "The Problem of the West."

57 Dunkelman, *Vanishing Neighbor*, 32.

58 Robert Nozick. (1974). *Anarchy, State, and Utopia.* New York: Basic Books.

59 Manuel B. Aalbers, "The Financialization of Home and the Mortgage Market Crisis," *Competition & Change* 12, no. 2 (June 1, 2008): 148–166, https://doi.org/10.1179/102452908X289802.

60 Stephanson, *Manifest Destiny*, xiv.

8. Winning the West

1 John Mason Peck, *New Guide for Emigrants to the West* (Boston: Gould, Kendall, and Lincoln, 1837), https://archive.org/details/newguideforemigr00peck.

2 Stephanson, *Manifest Destiny*, 5.

3 Greg Grandin, *The End of the Myth: From the Frontier to the Border Wall in the Mind of America* (New York: Macmillan, 2019), 3.

4 Grandin, 8.

5 Grandin.

6 Gottesdiener, *Dream Foreclosed*, 10.

7 Alexander, *New Jim Crow.*

8 Forrest Stuart, "Race, Space, and the Regulation of Surplus Labor: Policing African-Americans in Los Angeles' Skid Row," *Souls: A Critical Journal of Black Politics,*

Culture, and Society 13, no. 2 (2011): 199–200.

9 Eric Foner, "Reconstruction," *Encyclopedia Britannica,* updated 2022, https://www.britannica.com/event/Reconstruction-United-States-history.

10 Matt Novak, "Oregon Was Founded as a Racist Utopia," *Gizmodo,* January 21, 2015, https://gizmodo.com/oregon-was-founded-as-a-racist-utopia-1539567040.

11 National Park Service, "Native Americans and the Homestead Act," nps.gov, November 29, 2021, https://www.nps.gov/home/learn/historyculture/native-americans-and-the-homestead-act.htm.

12 Ron Chernow, *Grant* (New York: Penguin, 2017).

13 Stephanson, *Manifest Destiny,* 68.

14 Getches et al., *Cases and Materials,* 149.

15 Getches et al., 150.

16 Frichner, "Preliminary Study."

17 Getches et al., *Cases and Materials,* 140.

18 Getches et al., 165.

19 Bonilla-Silva, *Racism Without Racists,* 19.

20 Matthew Desmond, "Where Have All the Rioters Gone?" *Atlantic,* February 2018, https://www.theatlantic.com/magazine/archive/2018/02/matthew-desmond-riots/552542.

21 Rothstein, *Color of Law,* 44.

22 Stephen Meyer, *As Long as They Don't Move Next Door: Segregation and Racial Conflict in American Neighborhoods* (Lanham, Maryland: Rowman and Littlefield, 2000), 23.

23 Rothstein, *Color of Law,* 51.

24 California Newsreel, "The House We Live In," from *Race: The Power of an Illusion,* PBS, 2003, http://newsreel.org/video/RACE-THE-POWER-OF-AN-ILLUSION.

25 Erika Lee, "A Nation of Immigrants and a Gatekeeping Nation: American Immigration Law and Policy," in *A Companion to American Immigration* (Hoboken, NJ: Blackwell, 2006), 12.

26 Rothstein, *Color of Law,* 30.

27 Susan Smith Richardson, "'Black Skin Was a Death Warrant': How the East St Louis Race Massacre Was an Omen for Racial Violence to Come," *Guardian,* December 18, 2021, https://www.theguardian.com/us-news/2021/dec/18/black-skin-was-a-death-warrant-how-the-east-st-louis-race-massacre-was-an-omen-for-racial-violence-to-come; Bayeté Ross Smith, "An Act of Terrorism America Tried To Forget," *Guardian,* May 31, 2021, https://www.theguardian.com/us-news/video/2021/may/31/an-act-of-terrorism-america-tried-to-forget-360-video.

28 National World War I Museum and Memorial, "Red Summer: The Race Riots of 1919," theworldwar.org, 2023, https://www.theworldwar.org/learn/wwi/red-summer.

29 Smith, "Tulsa Race Massacre."

30 Smith.

31 Adrian Horton, "A Fever in the Heartland: How the KKK Gripped the American Midwest in the 20s," *Guardian,* April 11, 2023, https://www.theguardian.com/books/2023/apr/11/kkk-book-american-midwest-fever-in-the-heartland-timothy-egan.

32 Will James, "Seattle Author Timothy Egan on the KKK's Jazz Age Resurgence,"
    KNHX, NPR Network, April 5, 2023,
    https://www.knkx.org/politics/2023-04-05/seattle-author-timothy-egan-on-the
    -kkks-jazz-age-resurgence.
33 Horton, "Fever in the Heartland."
34 National World War I Museum and Memorial, "Red Summer."
35 Meyer, *Don't Move Next Door*, 20.
36 Rothstein, *Color of Law*, 42.
37 Meyer, *Don't Move Next Door*, 7–8.
38 Rothstein, *Color of Law*, 42.
39 Stephanson, *Manifest Destiny*, 27.
40 Meyer, *Don't Move Next Door*, 7.
41 Marie Meloney, ed., "Better Homes in America," *Delineator*, October 1922, 16.
42 Rothstein, *Color of Law*, 61.
43 Rothstein, 61.
44 Rothstein, 63.
45 Manisha Claire, "The Latent Racism of the Better Homes in America Program,"
    JSTOR Daily, February 26, 2020,
    https://daily.jstor.org/the-latent-racism-of-the-better-homes-in-america-program/.
46 Rothstein, *Color of Law*, 52.
47 Rothstein, 63; Michael S. Carliner, "Development of Federal Homeownership
    'Policy,'" *Housing Policy Debate 9*, no. 2 (1998),
    https://citeseerx.ist.psu.edu/viewdoc/download?doi=10.1.1.501.6539.

9. Dreaming the Suburbs

1   Lee, "Nation of Immigrants," 12.
2   Rothstein, *Color of Law*, 63; Emily Badger, "How Redlining's Racist Effects Lasted for
    Decades," *New York Times*, August 24, 2017,
    https://www.nytimes.com/2017/08/24/upshot/how-redlinings-racist-effects-lasted
    -for-decades.html.
3   James Baldwin, "On Being 'White' . . . and Other Lies," in *Black on White: Black
    Writers on What It Means to be White*, ed. David R. Roediger (New York: Shocken
    Books, 1998).
4   California Newsreel, "The House We Live In."
5   George Lipsitz, "The Possessive Investment in Whiteness: Racialized Social
    Democracy and the 'White' Problem in American Studies," American Quarterly 47,
    no. 3 (September 1995): 372.
6   George Lipsitz, How Racism Takes Place (Philadelphia: Temple University, 2011), 26.
7   Frederick Jackson Turner, "The West and American Ideals," *Washington Historical
    Quarterly* 5, no. 4 (October 1914): 254, https://www.jstor.org/stable/40474083.
8   Wolfe, "Settler Colonialism," 396; Stephanson, Manifest Destiny, 26.
9   Lipsitz, Racism Takes Place, 4.
10 Cedric Robinson, *Black Marxism: The Making of the Black Radical Tradition*, 7th ed.
    (New York: Penguin Classics, 2021).
11 Meyer, *Don't Move Next Door*, 65.

12 Meyer, 64.

13 Marshall Berman, *The Politics of Authenticity: Radical Individualism and the Emergence of Modern Society*, 1st ed. (Brooklyn: Verso Books, 1970), 55.

14 Josh Sides, "Straight into Compton: American Dreams, Urban Nightmares, and the Metamorphosis of a Black Suburb," *American Quarterly* 56, no. 3 (September 2004): 586, https://www.jstor.org/stable/40068235.

15 Robinson, *Black Marxism*.

16 Lipsitz, *Racism Takes Place*, 13.

17 David M. P. Freund, *Colored Property: State Policy and White Racial Politics in Suburban America* (Chicago: University of Chicago Press, 2007), 1–44.

18 Arnold R. Hirsch, *Making the Second Ghetto: Race and Housing in Chicago, 1940–1960*, 2nd ed. (Chicago: University of Chicago Press, 2021), 299; Meyer, *Don't Move Next Door*, 6.

19 Lipsitz, *Racism Takes Place*, 61.

20 Pete Daniel, *Dispossession: Discrimination Against African American Farmers in the Age of Civil Rights* (Chapel Hill: University of North Carolina Press, 2013).

21 Sides, "Straight into Compton," 588.

22 Freund, *Colored Property*, 8.

23 Rothstein, *Color of Law*, 12.

24 Rothstein, 13.

25 Rothstein, 65.

26 Rothstein, 21.

27 Rothstein, 23.

28 Rothstein, 31.

29 Meyer, *Don't Move Next Door*, 159–61.

30 Getches et al., *Cases and Materials*, 3.

31 Meyer, *Don't Move Next Door*, 116.

32 Fair Housing Center of Greater Boston, "1937: Housing Act (Wagner-Steagall Act)," accessed April 29, 2023, https://www.bostonfairhousing.org/timeline/1937-Housing-Act.html.

33 Federal Works Agency, "United States Housing Act of 1937, As Amended," United States Housing Authority, accessed April 29, 2023, https://archive.org/details/Housingact1937/page/n7/mode/2up.

34 Meyer, *Don't Move Next Door*, 142; Rothstein, *Color of Law*, 19.

35 Meyer, 143.

36 Rothstein, *Color of Law*, 32.

37 Meyer, *Don't Move Next Door*, 143; P. E. Moskowitz, *How to Kill a City: Gentrification, Inequality, and the Fight for the Neighborhood* (New York: Bold Type Books, 2018).

38 Getches et al., *Cases and Materials*, 230.

39 Meyer, *Don't Move Next Door*, 129.

40 John Collier, *Annual Report of the Secretary of the Interior for the Fiscal Year Ended June 30, 1938*, History Matters (website), American Social History Productions, http://historymatters.gmu.edu/d/5058.

41 Rothstein, *Color of Law*; California Newsreel, "House We Live In."

42 Meyer, *Don't Move Next Door*, 214–215.

43 Nikole Hannah-Jones, "Living Apart: How the Government Betrayed a Landmark Civil Rights Law," *ProPublica*, updated June 25, 2015, https://www.propublica.org/article/living-apart-how-the-government-betrayed-a-landmark-civil-rights-law.

44 Lipsitz, *Racism Takes Place*, 5.

45 Greg Grandin, "What Was the Confederate Flag Doing in Cuba, Vietnam, and Iraq?" *Nation*, July 7, 2015, https://www.thenation.com/article/archive/what-was-the-confederate-flag-doing-in-cuba-vietnam-and-iraq/.

46 Calvin Coolidge, "A Nation of Homeowners," *Delineator*, October 1922, 16.

10. Reviving the City

1 Divya Subramanian, "Ruth Glass: Beyond 'Gentrification,'" *New York Review*, January 20, 2020, https://www.nybooks.com/online/2020/01/20/ruth-glass-beyond-gentrification/?lp_txn_id=1450601.

2 Paolo Tolfo, "Go On Play with the Words, the Effect Is the Same: How Gentrification and Liveability Feature in Public Discourses of Neighbourhood Change" (master's thesis, University of Waterloo, 2019), 25, http://hdl.handle.net/10012/15162.

3 Moskowitz, *Kill a City*, 28.

4 Neil Smith, "Gentrification and the Rent Gap," *Annals of the Association of American Geographers* (September 1987): 21, https://doi.org/10.1111/j.1467-8306.1987.tb00171.x.

5 Moskowitz, *Kill a City*, 23.

6 Subramanian, "Ruth Glass."

7 Elvin Wyly, "Gentrification on the Planetary Urban Frontier: The Evolution of Turner's Noösphere," *Urban Studies* 52, no. 14 (October 6, 2015): 2519, https://journals.sagepub.com/doi/pdf/10.1177/0042098015601362; Neil Smith, *The New Urban Frontier: Gentrification and the Revanchist City* (New York: Routledge, 1996); C. Patrick Heidkamp and Susan Lucas, "Finding the Gentrification Frontier Using Census Data: The Case of Portland, Maine," *Urban Geography* 27, no. 2 (May 16, 2013): 101–125, https://doi.org/10.2747/0272-3638.27.2.101.

8 Phil Hubbard, "Hipsters on Our High Streets: Consuming the Gentrification Frontier," *Sociological Research Online*, 21, no. 3 (August 31, 2016): 106–111, https://doi.org/10.5153/sro.3962; William M. Denevan, "The Pristine Myth: The Landscape of the Americas in 1492," *Annals of the Association of American Geographers* 82, no. 3 (September 1992): 369–385, https://www.jstor.org/stable/2563351.

9 Jessi Quizar, "Land of Opportunity: Anti-Black and Settler Logics in the Gentrification of Detroit," American Indian Culture and Research Journal 43, no. 2. (2019): 116, https://doi.org/10.17953/aicrj.43.2.

10 Wolfe, "Settler Colonialism."

11 David Ley, "Liberal Ideology and the Postindustrial City," *Annals of the Association of American Geographers* 70, no. 2 (June 1980): 254, https://www.jstor.org/stable/2562952.

12 Cusack, "Real Blackwater Scandal."

13 Moskowitz, *Kill a City*, 9.

14 Moskowitz, 40.

15 Moskowitz, 35.

16 *I Am Not Your Negro*, directed by Raoul Peck (2016, Magnolia Pictures).

17 Rothstein, *Color of Law*, 35.

18 Rothstein, 40.

19 Rothstein, 36.

20 Richard Schaffer and Neil Smith, "The Gentrification of Harlem?" *Annals of the Association of American Geographers* 76, no. 3 (September 1986): 362, http://www.jstor.org/stable/2562585.

21 George L. Kelling and James Q. Wilson, "Broken Windows," *Atlantic*, March 1982, https://www.theatlantic.com/magazine/archive/1982/03/broken-windows/304465.

22 Xochitl Gonzalez, "Why Do Rich People Love Quiet?" *Atlantic*, August 1, 2022, https://www.theatlantic.com/magazine/archive/2022/09/let-brooklyn-be -loud/670600.

23 Smith, *New Urban Frontier*.

24 Cusack, "Real Blackwater Scandal"; Denevan, "Pristine Myth."

25 Wolfe, "Settler Colonialism"; Stephanson, *Manifest Destiny*.

26 Getches, *Cases and Materials*, 156; Locke, "Two Treatises," 154.

27 Robbins, *Political Ecology*.

28 Cusack, "Real Blackwater Scandal."

29 Moore, "Transcending."

30 Travis, *New Geographies*, 27.

31 Travis, 27, 32.

32 Travis, 53.

33 Rachel M. Cohen, "How the Largest Known Homeless Encampment in Minneapolis History Came to Be," *Appeal*, July 15, 2020, https://theappeal.org/minneapolis-homelessness-crisis-powderhorn-park -encampment.

34 Cohen.

35 Cohen.

36 Zhao, *Nomadland*.

37 Bruce Meyer et al., "Learning About Homelessness Using Linked Survey and Administrative Data," Becker Friedman Institute for Economics, University of Chicago, June 1, 2021, https://bfi.uchicago.edu/working-paper/learning-about-homelessness-using-linked -survey-and-administrative-data/.

38 Jeremy Kohler, "St. Louis Can Banish People from Entire Neighborhoods. Police Can Arrest Them If They Come Back," *ProPublica*, December 1, 2022, https://www.propublica.org/article/st-louis-can-banish-people-from-entire -neighborhoods.

11. "Belong[ing] Anywhere"

1 Bill Clinton, "1993 Dedication Remarks by President Clinton," John F. Kennedy Presidential Library and Museum, October 29, 1993, https://www.jfklibrary.org/about-us/about-the-jfk-library/history/1993-dedication-remarks-by-president-clinton.

2 Turner, "Problem of the West."

3 Grandin, *End of the Myth*, 240.

4 Manuel B. Aalbers, "The Financialization of Home and the Mortgage Market Crisis," *Competition & Change* 12, no. 2 (June 1, 2008): 148–166, https://doi.org/10.1179/102452908X289802.

5 Gottesdiener, *Dream Foreclosed*, 7.

6 Amira Shweyk, remote video interview, August 2022.

7 *Push*, Gertten.

8 *Push*, Gertten.

9 Farha, Letter . . . to Blackstone Group; Farha, Letter . . . to US Government.

10 Farha, Letter . . . to US Government.

11 David Harvey, "The 'New' Imperialism: Accumulation by Dispossession," *Socialist Register* 40 (2004): 74, https://socialistregister.com/index.php/srv/article/view/5811.

12 Rothstein, *Color of Law*; Lipsitz, *Racism Takes Place*.

13 National Low Income Housing Coalition, "NLIHC Releases The Gap: A Shortage of Affordable Homes," nlihc.org, April 25, 2022, https://nlihc.org/resource/nlihc-releases-gap-shortage-affordable-homes.

14 Harvey, "'New' Imperialism."

15 Chris Paris, "Re-Positioning Second Homes Within Housing Studies: Household Investment, Gentrification, Multiple Residence, Mobility And Hyper-Consumption," *Housing, Theory and Society* 26, no. 4 (October 8, 2008): 292–310, https://doi.org/10.1080/14036090802300392.

16 HR 1424, "Emergency economic stabilization act of 2008," House of Representatives, October 3, 2008, https://www.congress.gov/bill/110th-congress/house-bill/1424/text.

17 Michael Lewis, *The Big Short: Inside the Doomsday Machine* (New York: Norton, 2010), 210.

18 Harvey, "'New' Imperialism," 80.

19 Michael Mitchell et al., "State Higher Education Funding Cuts Have Pushed Costs to Students, Worsened Inequality," Center on Budget and Policy Priorities, October 24, 2019, https://www.cbpp.org/sites/default/files/atoms/files/10-24-19sfp.pdf.

20 Naomi Klein, *The Shock Doctrine: The Rise of Disaster Capitalism* (New York: Allen Lane, 2007).

21 Klein, 242.

22 Jason W. Moore, "Transcending the Metabolic Rift: A Theory of Crises in the Capitalist World-Ecology," *Journal of Peasant Studies* 38, no. 1 (January 13, 2011): 21, https://doi.org/10.1080/03066150.2010.538579.

23 Robbins, *Political Ecology*.

24 NAU Factbook, "State General Fund Appropriations History," *Factbook*, 2020–2021, 12, https://in.nau.edu/wp-content/uploads/sites/129/2021/10/I_20-21-Finances.pdf.

25 Allie Wilkins, "Students Are Not the Problem with Housing: They're the Scapegoat," *Lumberjack*, March 14, 2017, http://www.jackcentral.org/opinion/students-are-not-the-problem-with-housing -they-re-the/article_6e120794-03ac-11e7-9762-3379d53c4811.html.

26 Annie Lowrey, "NIMBYism Reaches Its Apotheosis," *Atlantic*, February 22, 2022, https://www.theatlantic.com/ideas/archive/2022/02/uc-berkeley-university -enrollment-nimby/622927.

27 Jordan T. Camp, "Blues Geographies and the Security Turn: Interpreting the Housing Crisis in Los Angeles," *American Quarterly*, 64, no. 3 (September 2012): 668, https:// www.jstor.org/stable/23273538; Raquel Rolnik, "Report of the Special Rapporteur on Adequate Housing as a Component of the Right to an Adequate Standard of Living, and on the Right to Non-Discrimination in This Context," Geneva: Human Rights Council, February 12, 2010, 8, https://drpop.org/wp-content/uploads/2010/04/UN -Rapporteur-report-Rolnik.pdf.

28 Farha, Letter . . . to US Government.

29 Farha, Letter . . . to US Government.

30 US Census Bureau, "Quarterly residential vacancies and homeownership, second quarter 2019," Census 2019, https://www.census.gov/housing/hvs/files /currenthvspress.pdf.

31 Veal and Spader, "Nearly a Third."

32 Veal and Spader, "Nearly a Third."

33 US Census Bureau, "American Housing Survey," census.gov, https://www.census.gov/programs-surveys/ahs.html.

34 Rothstein, *Color of Law*.

35 Lipsitz, *Racism Takes Place*, 32.

36 Rothstein, *Color of Law*.

37 Lipsitz, *Racism Takes Place*, 48.

38 Fraklin Leonard (@franklinleonard), "When you're accustomed to privilege, equality feels like oppression. (It's not.)," Twitter, October 10, 2015, 11:35 AM, https://twitter.com/franklinleonard/status/652885246220734464.

39 Othering and Belonging Institute, "What the 2020 Census Reveals About Segregation," University of California, Berkeley, October 11, 2021, https://belonging.berkeley.edu/what-2020-census-reveals-about-segregation.

40 Gottesdiener, *Dream Foreclosed*, 4.

41 Sadowski, "Internet of Landlords."

42 Shweyk, interview.

43 M. Nolan Gray, "How California Exported Its Worst Problem to Texas," *Atlantic*, August 10, 2022, https://www.theatlantic.com/ideas/archive/2022/08/housing-crisis-affordability -covid-everywhere-problem/671077/.

44 James Jacoby, "The Age of Easy Money," *PBS Frontline*, March 14, 2023, https://www.pbs.org/wgbh/frontline/documentary/age-of-easy-money/.

45 Lawrence Mishel and Josh Bivens, "Identifying the Policy Levers Generating Wage Suppression and Wage Inequality," *Economic Policy Institute*, May 13, 2021, https://www.epi.org/unequalpower/publications/wage-suppression-inequality.

46 Sharon Zhang, "Workers Have Held More Strikes So Far in 2022 than in All of 2021, Data Finds," *Truthout*, October 3, 2022, https://truthout.org/articles/workers-have-held-more-strikes-so-far-in-2022-than -in-all-of-2021-data-finds.

47 Grace Toohey, Summer Lin, and Gabriel San Román, "UC Officials Call for Mediator as Strike by 48,000 Academic Workers Causes Systemwide Disruptions," *Los Angeles Times*, November 14, 2022, https://www.latimes.com/california/story/2022-11-14/university-of-california -strike-academic-workers-graduate-students.

48 Tendayi Kapfidze, "LendingTree Compares Renting and Owning a Home in the 50 Largest Metropolitan Areas in the U.S.," LendingTree, May 19, 2021.

49 FRED Economic Data, "Median Sales Price of Houses Sold for the United States [MSPUS]," fed.stlouisfed.org, Retrieved December 8, 2021, https://fred.stlouisfed.org/series/MSPUS.

50 Peck, *New Guide*.

51 Quizar, interview.

52 Shweyk, interview.

53 Albert Camus, *The Rebel: An Essay on Man in Revolt*, trans. Anthony Bower (New York: Knopf, 1954).

12. Locals Welcome

1   US Census Bureau, "Quarterly Residential Vacancies and Homeownership, Second Quarter 2019," Release Number: CB23-08, January 31, 2023, https://www.census.gov/housing/hvs/files/currenthvspress.pdf; US Census Bureau, "Historical Census of Housing Tables: Homeownership," census.gov, 2000, https:// www.census.gov/data/tables/time-series/dec/coh-owner.html.

2   FRED Economic Data, "Median Sales Price"; Katz and Bokhari, "Investor Home Purchases," retrieved April 25, 2023.

3   David Harvey, "Debates and Developments: The Right to the City," *International Journal of Urban and Regional Research* 27, no. 4 (December 2003): 940, abahlali.org/files/Harvey_right_to_the_city_0.pdf.

4   Rick S. Kurtz, "Public Lands Policy and Economic Trends in Gateway Communities," *Review of Policy Research* 27, no. 1 (2010): 77, http://citeseerx.ist.psu.edu/viewdoc/download?doi=10.1.1.822.3604.

5   AirDNA, AirDNA.co.

6   NPS Stats, "White Sands NP," irma.nps.gov, https://irma.nps.gov/STATS/SSRSReports/Park%20Specific%20Reports/Annual%20 Park%20Recreation%20Visitation%20(1904%20-%20Last%20Calendar%20 Year)?Park=WHSA.

7   AirDNA, Airdna.co.

8   Witton, interview.

9   Guyer, interview.

10 Greene, interview.

11 Grant, interview.

12 National Low-Income Housing Coalition, "Voters Approve Affordable Housing, Homelessness, And Minimum Wage Measures in 2021 Local Elections," nlihc.org, November 21, 2021, https://nlihc.org/resource/voters-approve-affordable-housing-homelessness-and-minimum-wage-measures-2021-local.

13 Johannes Novy and Claire Colomb, "Urban Tourism and Its Discontents: An Introduction," in *Protest and Resistance in the Tourist City*, ed. Claire Colomb and Johannes Novy (New York: Routledge, 2017), 1–3.

14 Witton, interview.

15 City of Flagstaff, "10-Year Housing Plan."

13. Dollars and Sense

1 David Harvey, *Spaces of Capital: Towards a Critical Geography* (Edinburgh, Scotland: Edinburgh University Press, 2001).

2 Derecka Purnell, *Becoming Abolitionists: Police, Protests, and the Pursuit of Freedom* (New York: Astra Publishing House, 2021).

3 Turner, "Significance of the Frontier."

4 Grandin, *End of the Myth.*

5 Lawrence Mishel, "Growing Inequalities, Reflecting Growing Employer Power, Have Generated a Productivity-Pay Gap Since 1979," *Economic Policy Institute*, September 2, 2021, https://www.epi.org/blog/growing-inequalities-reflecting-growing-employer-power-have-generated-a-productivity-pay-gap-since-1979-productivity-has-grown-3-5-times-as-much-as-pay-for-the-typical-worker.

6 Scott Susin, "Rent Vouchers and the Price of Low-Income Housing," *Journal of Public Economics* 83, no. 1 (January 2002): 109, https://doi.org/10.1016/S0047-2727(01)00081-0.

7 Bree Burkitt, "'Investing in Our Community': Route 66 Hotel to Become Emergency Housing," *AZ Daily Sun*, April 9, 2022, https://azdailysun.com/news/local/investing-in-our-community-route-66-hotel-to-become-emergency-housing/article_58077d8c-bd7e-53eb-a657-d8d77b30cf19.html.

8 Adam Jeffery, "Photos: In Las Vegas, a Parking Lot Hosts Homeless People During Coronavirus Outbreak," CNBC, April 15, 2020, https://www.cnbc.com/2020/04/15/photos-las-vegas-parking-lot-hosts-homeless-people-during-coronavirus.html.

9 Meghan Henry et al., "The 2020 Annual Homeless Assessment Report (AHAR) to Congress," Department of Housing and Urban Development, January 2021, https://www.huduser.gov/portal/sites/default/files/pdf/2020-AHAR-Part-1.pdf.

10 Vaughan Jones, "Hotels in Tempe and Flagstaff Purchased to Repurposed for Homeless Assistance," KJZZ, September 19, 2021, https://kjzz.org/content/1717873/hotels-tempe-and-flagstaff-purchased-be-repurposed-homeless-assistance.

11 Jacqueline Garcia, "Newsom Allocates $600 Million for Permanent Housing for Homeless," Cal Matters, October 2, 2020, https://calmatters.org/housing/2020/10/newsom-permanent-housing-homeless.

12 California Department of Housing and Community Development "Bringing California Home," ca.gov, https://www.hcd.ca.gov/grants-and-funding/homekey.

13 Meyer et al., "Learning About Homelessness."

14 Kelly McEvers, "Utah Reduced Chronic Homelessness by 91 Percent; Here's How," NPR, December 10, 2015, https://www.npr.org/2015/12/10/459100751/utah-reduced-chronic-homelessness -by-91-percent-heres-how.

15 John McKnight, *The Careless Society: Community and Its Counterfeits* (New York: Basic Books).

16 Reade Pickert, "U.S. Inflation Hits 39-Year High of 7%, Sets Stage for Fed Hike," *Bloomberg*, January 12, 2022, https://www.bloomberg.com/news/articles/2022-01-12/inflation-in-u-s-registers -biggest-annual-gain-since-1982.

17 Jeff Andrews, "Zumper National Rent Report," Zumper, January 27, 2022, https://www.zumper.com/blog/zumper-2021-annual-rent-report/.

18 FRED Economic Data, "Nonfinancial Corporate Business: Profits After Tax (without IVA and CCadj)," fred.stlouisfed.org, December 22, 2021, https://fred.stlouisfed.org/series/NFCPATAX.

19 Oliver Milman, "Exclusive: Oil Companies' Profits Soared to $174bn This Year as U.S. Gas Prices Rose," *Guardian*, December 6, 2021, https://www.theguardian.com/business/2021/dec/06/oil-companies-profits-exxon -chevron-shell-exclusive.

20 "The State of Labor Market Competition," US Department of Treasury, March 7, 2022, https://home.treasury.gov/system/files/136/State-of-Labor-Market -Competition-2022.pdf.

21 City of Flagstaff, "10-Year Housing Plan."

22 Megan Lawson, remote video interview, July 2020.

14. Building a House

1 William A. Fischel, "An Economic History of Zoning and a Cure for Its Exclusionary Effects," *Urban Studies* 41, no. 2 (February 2004): 335, https://www.jstor.org/stable/43100684.

2 Meyer, *Don't Move Next Door*, 214–215.

3 Hannah-Jones, "Living Apart."

4 Hannah-Jones, "Living Apart."

5 Jerusalem Demsas, "Could a 54-Year-Old Civil Rights Law Be Revived?" Vox, January 17, 2022, https://www.vox.com/22883459/martin-luther-king-jr-fair-housing-act-housing -crisis.

6 Fischel, "Economic History."

7 Fischel.

8 California Newsreel, "House We Live In."

9 Bonilla-Silva, *Racism Without Racists*, 24–25.

10 Bonilla-Silva, 24–25.

11 Harmeet Kaur, "Indigenous People Across the U.S. Want Their Land Back—and the

Movement Is Gaining Momentum," *CNN*, November 26, 2020, https://www.cnn.com/2020/11/25/us/indigenous-people-reclaiming-their-lands -trnd/index.html.

12 Dani Anguiano, "Native American Tribes Reclaim California Redwood Land for Preservation," *Guardian*, January 25, 2022, https://www.theguardian.com/us-news/2022/jan/25/native-american-tribes -california-redwood-preservation.

13 Hannah-Jones, "Living Apart."

14 *I Am Not Your Negro*, Peck.

15 *99 Homes*, directed by Ramin Bahrani (Broad Green Pictures, 2014).

16 *The Oxford Dictionary of Quotations*, 2nd ed. (London: Oxford University Press, 1953), 14.

15. Building a Home

1 Billy Baker, "They Quit Petroleum, Electricity, and Money—and Found Happiness," *Boston Globe*, June 22, 2019, https://www.bostonglobe.com/metro/2019/06/22/they-quit-petroleum-electricity -and-money-and-found-happiness/gbU91CTDP0vT1VqzdpbW1M/story.html.

2 Ethan Hughes, phone interview, August 2022.

3 Hughes, interview.

4 Jacobs, *Death and Life*, 56.

5 Ipsos, "Loneliness and the Workplace: 2020 U.S. Report," conducted on behalf of Cigna, https://www.cigna.com/static/www-cigna-com/docs/about-us/newsroom/studies -and-reports/combatting-loneliness/cigna-2020-loneliness-report.pdf.

6 Doreen Massey, *For Space* (Newbury Park, CA: Sage Publications, 2005), 154.

7 Hughes, interview.

8 Garrett Hardin, "The Tragedy of the Commons," *Science* 162 (December 13, 1968): 1243–8, https://math.uchicago.edu/~shmuel/Modeling/Hardin,%20Tragedy%20of%20 the%20Commons.pdf.

9 Elinor Ostrom, *Governing the Commons: The Evolution of Institutions for Collective Action* (Cambridge, England: Cambridge University Press, 1990).

10 Garrett Hardin, "Extension of the Tragedy of the Commons," Garrett Hardin Society, June 10, 2003, https://www.garretthardinsociety.org/articles/art_extension_tragedy_commons.html.

11 Bob Moorehead, *Words Aptly Spoken* (Kirkland, WA: Overlake Christian Press, 1995), 197–198.

12 Aldo Leopold, *Aldo Leopold: A Sand County Almanac and Other Writings on Conservation and Ecology*, ed. Curt Meine (Boone, IA: Library of America, 2013), 391.

13 Glenn Albrecht et al., "Solastalgia: The Distress Caused by Environmental Change," *Australasian Psychiatry* 15 Suppl. 1, no. 1 (February 2007), https://doi.org/10.1080/10398560701701288.

14 de Tocqueville, *Democracy*.

15 Bill Bishop, *The Big Sort: Why the Clustering of Like-Minded America is Tearing Us Apart* (New York: Houghton Mifflin, 2008).

16 Dunkelman, *Vanishing Neighbor*, 38.

17 Quizar, interview.

18 Erin Blakemore, "How the Black Panthers' Breakfast Program Both Inspired and Threatened the Government," History.com, January 29, 2021, https://www.history.com/news/free-school-breakfast-black-panther-party.

19 Hughes, interview.

20 Nina Lahkani, "As Many as 500 Homeless People Died in Phoenix Area in First Half of 2022," *Guardian*, July 21, 2022, https://www.theguardian.com/us-news/2022/jul/21/homeless-deaths-phoenix-arizona-maricopa-county.

21 Bustos, interview.

22 Hughes, interview.

23 George Monbiot, "Feeling the Urge to Take Back Control from Power-Mad Governments? Here's an Idea," *Guardian*, July 13, 2022, https://www.theguardian.com/commentisfree/2022/jul/13/take-back-control-governments.

24 Carne Ross, *The Leaderless Revolution: How Ordinary People Will Take Power and Change Politics in the 21st Century* (London: Simon and Schuster, 2011).

16. Sticks and Stones: What You Can Do

1 Lawrence W. Reed, "A Hero of Black History in America: 9 Powerful Quotes from Frederick Douglass," FEE Stories, February 23, 2020, https://fee.org/articles/a-hero-of-black-history-in-america-9-powerful-quotes-from-frederick-douglass.

2 Conor Dougherty, "America's Housing Crisis: A Reading List," *Literary Hub*, February 19, 2020, https://lithub.com/americas-housing-crisis-a-reading-list.

3 Quizar, interview.

4 Henry David Thoreau, "Civil Disobedience," in *Walden and Civil Disobedience*, ed. P. Lauter (Boston: Houghton Mifflin, 2000), 25.

5 Maanvi Singh, "Wealthy California town Cites Mountain Lion Habitat to Deny Affordable Housing," *Guardian*, February 5, 2022, https://www.theguardian.com/us-news/2022/feb/05/california-woodside-mountain-lions-development.

6 IPCC, "Summary for Policymakers," in *Global Warming of 1.5°C. An IPCC Special Report on the impacts of global warming of 1.5°C above pre-industrial levels and related global greenhouse gas emission pathways, in the context of strengthening the global response to the threat of climate change, sustainable development, and efforts to eradicate poverty*, ed. V. Masson-Delmotte et al. (Cambridge, UK: Cambridge University Press, 2018), https://doi.org/10.1017.

7 Maya Yang, "Six in 10 Americans 'Alarmed' or 'Concerned' About Climate Change," *Guardian*, January 13, 2022, https://www.theguardian.com/environment/2022/jan/13/record-number-americans-alarmed-about-climate-crisis.

8 Lakhani, "US Hit."

9 Guyer, interview.

10 Demsas, "54-Year-Old Civil Rights Law."

11 M. Nolan Gray, "Cancel Zoning," *Atlantic*, June 21, 2022,
https://www.theatlantic.com/ideas/archive/2022/06/zoning-housing-affordability
-nimby-parking-houston/661289.

12 Agence France-Presse in Stockholm, "US added to List of 'Backsliding' Democracies
for First Time," *Guardian*, November 22, 2021,
https://www.theguardian.com/us-news/2021/nov/22/us-list-backsliding
-democracies-civil-liberties-international.

13 Agence France-Presse, "US Added."

14 Jasmine Chia, "How the Rubber Duck Became a Thai Protest Symbol," *Thai Enquirer*,
November 19, 2020,
https://www.thaienquirer.com/20903/how-the-rubber-duck-became-a-thai-protest
-symbol.

15 Neil Postman, *Amusing Ourselves to Death: Public Discourse in the Age of Show
Business* (New York: Penguin, 1985).

16 Taylor Gordon, "8 Major American Banks That Got Caught Discriminating Against
Black People," *Atlanta Black Star*, March 3, 2015,
https://atlantablackstar.com/2015/03/03/8-major-american-banks-that-got-caught
-discriminating-against-black-people/2.

17 Micah White, *The End of Protest: A New Playbook for Revolution* (New York: Knopf,
2016), 4.

18 Elinor Ostrom et al., "Revisiting the Commons: Local Lessons, Global Challenges,"
Science 284, no. 5412 (April 9, 1999): 278–282,
https://www.science.org/doi/full/10.1126/science.284.5412.278.

19 Rachel M. Cohen. (2022). "How State Governments are Reimagining American
Public Housing," Vox, August 4, 2022.
https://www.vox.com/policy-and-politics/23278643/affordable-public-housing
-inflation-renters-home.

20 National Low-Income Housing Coalition, "Voters Approve"; National Low-Income
Housing Coalition, "Housing Is Built with Ballots: Key 2018 Ballot Measures Across
the Country," hlihc.org, November 7, 2018,
https://nlihc.org/sites/default/files/Housing-Ballots_Initiatives.pdf.

21 Guyer, interview.

Index

Index